Romans: A Concise Commentary

By Marianne Manley

Romans: A Concise Commentary

All scripture references are taken from the King James Bible. The Simple Bible Timeline by Les Feldick, the Simple Timeline by Alex Kurz, the Three Time Periods and Five Dispensations Article and Bible Timeline by Richard Jordan, and Paul's Ministry Timeline by Sam Gerhardt are used by permission. Permission is granted to copy and use all contents of this book.

Acknowledgement

To God be the glory for helping me write this book! I am grateful for the support of my dear husband Chuck and my children during this time. I would like to thank Marla Dent for sharing her brilliant Romans Study with me which I highly recommend to everyone if and when she publishes it. Eric Neumann has also written an excellent commentary on Romans which I read. I am blessed that Pastor Richard Jordan contributed his article and his timeline – find them in the Appendix. I want to thank Sam Gerhardt, Les Feldick, and Alex Kurz for letting me print their timelines, and LeighAnn Mycko for her memes. We all want to share what God is saying so we all end up saying the same thing. My students Maureen Parker and Patty Carlson helped with the proofreading. I am very grateful to Tiffany Hanson for her help with the formatting and putting the book up on CreateSpace. Finally, I am thankful to Aaron Howay for the cover photo.

A Note from the Author *See the <u>Right Division Bible Timeline</u> (page 149). This book is divided into the 16 chapters found in Romans. After some introductory notes (where some of the commentary is also posted) the entire chapter is printed with the commentary within brackets in the text. This is done to keep the commentary concise and information easy to find.

I recommend the Scofield Study Bible III in the King James Version. It is wise to get a leather cover for it that holds a pen and zips. I mark up my Bible. I underline, circle important facts (I color some of them), make notes, and write in cross references so that I have them next time I read that passage.

This is an intermediate level book. I also recommend reading my book *God's Secret A Primer with Pictures for How to Rightly Divide the Word of Truth* before this commentary. It is an overview of the Bible in 100 pages available on Amazon in paperback or on Kindle and covers the basics of right division.

Table of Contents

The Three Most Important Things
First, be saved by believing the gospel, ". . . how that Christ died for our sins according to the scriptures; And that he was buried, and that he rose again the third day according to the scriptures" (1 Cor. 15:3b, 4).

After we believe, the **second** most important thing is to know **which Bible** is the true perfect word of God. Once we have done the research into the textual issue and are convinced that God has preserved His word in the King James Bible then the last little part remains to put our faith in that. By faith based on facts we become King James Bible believers.

Third, we must learn how to **rightly divide the truth** by applying 2 Timothy 2:15 and recognizing the division God makes in His word between mystery and prophecy.

Time Management

The best illustration of time management that I have ever heard goes like this: Think of time as a large clear glass jar. First put in as many big rocks as you can, followed by gravel (little rocks); follow this by pouring sand into the spaces, and then finally add as much water as possible. What is the point? Not that we should try to do as much as we possibly can, but that we should be sure to get our big rocks in first. What are the big rocks in your life? Prayer and daily Bible study.

We need to be able to prioritize. Knowing our priorities helps us structure our time. We must redeem the time. History is a record of what man has done with the time God has given him. Let us use our time wisely.

George Muller said that the first time through the Bible is like toasted bread, the second time like toast with butter, and the third time like toast with butter and jam. Reading the Bible just becomes more interesting, exciting and delightful every time we do it, until we just cannot get enough. It is so fascinating to put the pieces of the puzzle together.

So cultivate a love for God's word and you will fall in love with its Author. Be diligent to read it first thing in the morning after a time of prayer. I use a reading list from helpersofyourjoy.com that goes through the Bible in a year and Paul's letters 16 times a year. But beginners can start by reading a chapter of Romans a day till they have read Romans through five times. Then read the rest of Paul's letters, Romans to Philemon. After that read the whole Bible from a Pauline perspective.

Preface

"In the beginning God created the <u>heaven</u> and the <u>earth</u>" (Genesis 1:1). God made two realms. But beginning with the second sentence God starts talking about the earth and continues focusing on His plans for the earth until Acts 9. Christ returns from heaven one year after His crucifixion, death, burial, resurrection, and ascension to dramatically saves Saul (Paul) of Tarsus on the road to Damascus making him His minister.

Paul is "the apostle of the Gentiles" (Romans 11:13) and he was the first person into the body of Christ. "This is a faithful saying, and worthy of all acceptation, that Christ Jesus came into the world to save sinners; of whom I am chief. Howbeit for this cause I obtained mercy, that **in me first** Jesus Christ might shew forth all longsuffering, for **a pattern** to them which should hereafter believe on him to life everlasting (1 Timothy 1:16). He is our pattern. After the stoning of Stephen (the blasphemy of the Holy Ghost by the religious leaders of Israel) God was poised ready to pour out His wrath, but postponed that plan. God revealed to Paul that He had begun a new "dispensation of grace" (Ephesians 3:2) and was forming a new agency, the body of Christ to inhabit the heaven (2 Corinthians 5:1).

God had kept His reclaiming of heaven a secret from Satan in order to catch him in his own craftiness. Because if Satan had known this secret he would not have allowed Christ to be crucified. "But we speak the wisdom of God in a mystery, even the hidden wisdom, which God ordained before the world unto our glory: Which none of the princes of this world knew: for had they known it, they would not have crucified the Lord of glory" (1 Corinthians 2:7, 8).

God's design for our edification today is the progressive teaching set forth in Romans to Philemon. In Romans we discover the fundamental doctrine of who God has made us "in Christ" and how we now have Christ's life in us (Romans 8:2). Because we died with Christ when we believed, we can present our bodies to him and "walk in newness of life" (Romans 6:4). At salvation we receive Christ's imputed righteousness. By faith alone in what He has done, we are saved, justified, sanctified, treated as adult sons, and have been made joint-heirs with Christ.

The key to understanding the Bible is ". . . rightly dividing the word of truth" (2 Timothy 2:15). Rightly dividing means separating between mystery (the books written by Paul) and prophecy (the rest of the Bible).

Introduction

How can sinful man stand before holy God and live with Him forever? The book of Romans is about the righteousness of God and answers this question.

God loves righteousness and justice. "For the word of the LORD is right; and all his works are done in truth. He loveth righteousness and judgment: the earth is full of the goodness of the LORD" (Psalms 33:4, 5). Understanding Romans is essential to our Christian life and having something of value to show at the judgment seat of Christ.

God talks about His righteousness throughout the Bible. The theme of Romans is that the gospel of Christ reveals "the righteousness of God." In Romans Paul tells us how God solved the sin problem. The righteousness of Christ is needed in order to come before the holy God. We learn how a sinner can be justified, be "conformed to the image of his Son" (Romans 8:29), and bring glory to God. We will also understand that we are living during the time of Israel's national blindness and how we can live a life of service to God.

Romans is the "Manual" of foundational truths for equipping the saints to function and live stable, productive lives. As we will find out, God is now offering the whole world grace and peace when it deserves wrath. God is giving every person (both Jew and Gentile) equal access to Him by faith. Because of Christ's accomplishment at the cross anyone who believes the gospel can be saved.

God's dealings with the nation of Israel who stumbled (at the cross of Christ), fell (at the stoning of Stephen), and diminished (during the Acts period) have been postponed until after the Rapture. But in the meantime individual Jews can be saved by believing the same gospel as the Gentiles and becoming members of the body of Christ. God will resume His dealing with Israel as a nation after the Rapture.

Romans is the first book we need to read and understand before we can understand the rest of the Bible. We cannot proceed to advanced doctrine without first mastering the basics of the fundamental doctrine of Romans.

Paul wrote: Galatians in Acts 16 from Antioch, 1 Thessalonians from Athens in Acts 18 and 2 Thessalonians from Corinth about a month later. He wrote 1 Corinthians from Ephesus in Acts 19 and 2 Corinthians from Macedonia about a year later. Then he wrote Romans from Corinth in Acts 20:3.

Romans is the last book written by Paul during the Acts period before the end of the diminishing of Israel was complete in Acts 28. During the diminishing Paul went to the Jew first to inform them of the dispensational change that God had brought about and to tell them that they can be saved by joining the Gentiles. Needless to say, this news did not go over well with most Jews who had been told by God through Moses ye "shall not be reckoned among the nations" (Numbers 23:9) and "For thou art an holy people unto the LORD thy God: the LORD thy God hath chosen thee to be a special people unto himself, above all people that are upon the face of the earth" (Deuteronomy 7:6).

Although Romans is the sixth letter that Paul (God's spokesman) wrote it is the first in the canon of scripture (the order in the Bible) because the books follow the pattern given in 2 Timothy 3:16. "All scripture is given by inspiration of God, and is profitable for <u>doctrine</u>, for <u>reproof</u>, for <u>correction</u>, for <u>instruction in righteousness</u>."

The books of the Bible follow a divine order. Romans is the foundational doctrine of the Christian faith. Corinthians is a book reproof (telling believers what is wrong) and Galatians is correction (helping believers get back on the right track). God expects us to have read and understood Romans before we read Ephesians which is further doctrinal and practical knowledge that builds upon that foundation. Philippians and Colossians build on Ephesians and is advanced knowledge on how to live our lives. The pastoral epistles to Timothy and Titus contain practical information for the local church which God has designed to be "the pillar and ground of the truth" (1 Timothy 3:15).

The letters to the Thessalonians are "instruction in righteousness" to make us mature in our conduct as believers. Finally, in Philemon the servant returns to his master with the request "receive him as myself" (Philemon 17). This is a picture of us in the body of Christ when this dispensation of grace ends and we are "caught up . . . to meet the Lord in the air" (1 Thessalonians 4:17).

Hebrews through Revelation are the books of the Bible that describe God's resumed dealings with Israel. These books tell those believers how they can navigate through the seven-year Tribulation known as "Jacob's trouble" (Jeremiah 30:7), and His plans and purpose for them on the earth. God places these books after Paul's thirteen epistles to indicate that they will apply after the Rapture.

Romans Outline

Written by Paul from Corinth (Acts 20:2, 3) on his third journey c. AD 58.

Theme: The gospel of Christ reveals "the righteousness of God" (1:16, 17, 3:22)

Key verses: "For I am not ashamed of the gospel of Christ: for it is the power of God unto salvation to every one that believeth; to the Jew first, and also to the Greek. For therein is the righteousness of God revealed from faith to faith: as it is written, The just shall live by faith" (Rom. 1:16, 17)

Purpose: To establish saints in the faith (Rom. 1:11, 6:17, 16:25)
Salutation (1:1-7)
Purpose for writing the letter (1:8-17)

I Sin – (Righteousness needed)
A. Gentiles under sin (1:18-32)
B. Jews under sin (2:1-3:8)
C. Whole world under sin (3:9-20)

II Salvation (Righteousness imputed)
A. Justification explained (3:21-31)
B. Imputation – The Case of Abraham (4)
C. Result of justification (5)

III Sanctification (Righteousness performed)
A. Our new position in Christ (6)
B. Our new problem in the flesh (7)
C. Our new power in the Spirit (8)

IV What About Israel? (Righteousness Rejected)
A. Election and Rejection of Israel (9)
B. Present Salvation Opportunity for Individual Jews to believe (10)
C. Has God Cast Away His People? (11)

V Serving God Out of Gratitude (Righteousness practiced)
A. How do we live a life of service to God? (12)
B. Living with government (13)
C. Consideration for the weaker brother (14)

VI Conclusion
A. Paul's Ministry to the Gentiles (15)
B. Christ was a minister to the Jews with Gentiles in mind (15:8-12)
C. Paul talks of his apostleship and the ministry God sent him to do (15:13-33)
D. Friends, house churches, and benediction concerning the revelation of the mystery (16:1-27)

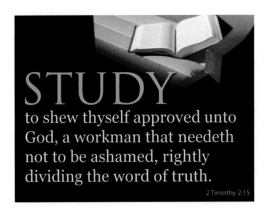

The Key Verse in the Bible:

The only verse in the Bible that tells us how to study the Bible is <u>2 Tim. 2:15</u>: "<u>Study</u> to shew thyself approved unto God, a workman that needeth not to be ashamed, <u>RIGHTLY DIVIDING THE WORD OF TRUTH</u>."

Mandate: Study.

Motive: to shew thyself approved to God, a workman that needeth not to be ashamed (at the judgment seat of Christ).

Method: Rightly dividing the word of truth (making the divisions that God makes in His word).

Second Timothy which contains this instruction was the last book of the Bible to be written (Col. 1:25, 26).

Four divisions in Romans:
1-5 Justification
6-8 Sanctification
9-11 What about Israel?
12-16 Practical application

1-5 Justification – How God solved the sin problem
6-8 Sanctification – God has provided a way that we can live above sin now
9-11 What about Israel? The nation of Israel has been temporarily blinded until the Gentile opportunity to be saved ends. After that, God will be done forming the body of Christ to live in heaven and will again focus on Israel.
12-16 Practical application – How to offer our bodies a living sacrifice for Christ to live through and manifest Himself to the world.

Sam Gerhardt's excellent Timeline of Paul's Ministry

TIMELINE OF PAUL'S MINISTRY

33(AD)	 Death Burial Resurrection	Progression Thru Book of Acts, and other references as noted	
34	Steven is Stoned	7	8:14 Last of John in Acts
35	1) Saul is Saved	9	
38	2) 3yrs in Damascas & Arabia	9:20-25 Gal 1:16-18 (4:25)	
38	3) 1st visit to Jerusalem (Stayed 15 days)	9:26-29 22:17-21 Gal 1:18-19	W/Barnabas, Peter, & James
42	4yrs in Tarsus, then to Antioch	Acts 9:30, Gal 1:21, Acts 11:25-26	
43	2nd Visit to Jerusalem	11:30 - 12:25	12:17 First mention of James in Acts
44	1st Journey begins: Saul is now Paul	13:1 – 14:28 13:9	13:46 Turn to Gentiles
45	4) Paul stoned in Lystra*	14:19, 2Cor 12:1-7	
46	Return to Antioch	14:26-28	
52	5) 3rd visit to Jerusalem w/James, Peter, and John Antioch	15, Gal 2:1	15:7-11 Peter's Last words in Acts, 15:14 Peter last mentioned, 15:35 Peter's visit of Gal2:11-13, Gal 2:9 Paul mentions John one time.
52	6) 2nd Journey begins	15:36 - 18:22	15:39 Last of Barnabas in Acts, 18:6 Turn to Gentiles
54	7) 4th visit to Jerusalem, / Return to Antioch / 3rd Journey begins	18:23 – 21:17, 18:1-18, Gal 1:6-9, 1Thes 1:1, 3:1-8, 2Thes 1:1, Acts 20:31, 1Cor 4:17, 1Cor 8-9	2nd Journey Epistles, AD54: Galatians, 1st&2nd Thessalonians from Corinth. 3rd Journey Epistles, AD59: 1st Corithians, from Ephesus.
60	5th visit to Jerusalem * w/James & Elders	Acts 21:15	21:18 Last mention of James in Acts. 2nd Corinthians AD60 from Philippi, Romans AD60 from Corinth. Acts 20:1-2
60-62	8) Paul taken Prisoner	Acts 21:31 23:11 24:27	Tesitifies to the Multitudes, Sanhedrin, Felix (2yrs in Caesarea), Festus, Appeals to Caesar and Agrippa
62	Paul sent to Rome – Held for 2yrs	27:1-28:16, 28:28	Salvation sent to Gentiles:They will hear it
62-64	2yrs in Rome: writes 1st Imprisonment Epistles from Rome	Acts 28:30-31	1st Imprisonment Epistles from Rome: Ephesians, Colossians, Philemon (Laodicea), Philippians
64	The End of ACTS / 4th Journey begins	End of Acts Romans 15:29 - Titus 1:5 - Titus 3:12 - 2 Timothy 4:20 - Philemon :22 - 1 Timothy 1:3 - Philippians 2:23-24 - 2 Timothy 4:13-18	4th Journey Epistles written 64-66: 1st Timothy, Titus
66-67	Paul is Imprisoned	2Tim 1:8, 2Tim 2:8-9	2nd Imprisonment Epistle written: 2nd Timothy
68	Paul is Beheaded		

7 years

3 years

2 years

14yrs between 1st & 3rd visits to Jerusalem

4 years

2 years

6 years

Paul's Revelations: Rom 16:25-27, Eph 3:1-12

1) Acts 9,22,26
2) Gal 1:16-17
3) Acts 22:17-21
4) Acts 14:19 (2Cor 12:1-7)
5) Gal 2:1-2 (Acts 15)
6) Acts 16:9-10
7) Acts 18:9-10
8) Acts 23:11

All of Paul's letters were Inspired by revelation

1st Journey: Seleucia, Salamis, Paphos, *Perga, Antioch (Pisidea), Iconium, Lystra, Derbe, *Atlalia (Acts 13:1 – 14:28)
Accompanied by Barnabas

2nd Journey: Tarsus, Derbe, Lystra, Iconium, Antioch (Pisidea)/ Troas, Neopolis, Philippi, Amphipolis, Appollonia, Thessalonica, Berea, Athens, #Corinth, Cenchrea, Ephesus, Caesarea, Jerusalem (Acts 15:36 – 18:22)
Accompanied by Silas #Paul spent 1.5yrs in Corinth **(Acts 18:11)**

3rd Journey: Tarsus, Derbe, Lystra, Iconium, Antioch (Pisidea), #Ephesus, *Troas, Neopolis, Philippi, Thessalonica, Berea, #Corinth, *Assos, Mitylene, Trogillium, Miletus, Patara, Tyre, Ptolemis, Caesarea, Jerusalem (Acts 18:23-21:17)
Accompanied by Timothy #Paul stayed in Ephesus for 3yrs, and 3mos in Corinth **(Acts 20:3, 31)**

4th Journey: (Spain), Crete, Nicopolis, (Corinth), Miletus, Laodicea, Ephesus, Philippi, Troas
(Rom 15:29, Tit 1:5, Tit 3:12, 2Tim 4:20, Phm 22, 1Tim 1:3, Phil 2:23-24, 2Tim 4:13-18)

1 Timothy 2:3-4 KJV
[3] For this is good and acceptable
in the sight of God our Saviour;
[4] Who will have all men to be saved,
and to come unto the knowledge of the truth.

BIBLE BELIEVER'S COWBOY CHURCH
NEWPORT TN

Service 10am Sunday   Pastor Sam Gerhardt

Matthew AD37, Hebrews AD34-42, James AD45, 1Peter AD45-52, Mark AD57-63, Luke AD63, Acts AD63-64, 2Peter AD64, John & 1,2,3 John AD65, Jude AD66, Revelation AD66

Romans Chapter 1 – Gentiles under sin
1-7 Salutation
8-17 Purpose for writing the letter
18-32 Righteousness needed

Sin in Romans refers to the sin nature.
Sins means the wrong things a person does because of the sin nature.
Sin is missing the <u>mark</u> of God's high standard for eternal life given in His law.

In chapter 1, Paul warns the Gentiles (and then the Jews in chapter 2) about the wrath of God so they can do something about it. Like a brilliant prosecuting attorney Paul unfolds the predicament mankind is in. His arguments are foolproof as he builds his case first against the Gentiles and then against the Jews. The verdict – is that all people are guilty and worthy of eternal damnation in the Lake of Fire. Therefore, having everyone's full attention, everyone will listen to Paul when he delivers God's remedy to their problem with the words "But now . . . (Rom. 3:21).

Paul's purpose is to "impart unto you some spiritual gift [further revelation from the Lord Jesus Christ], to the end that ye may be established" (1:11).

Paul writes Romans to the believers in Rome at a time when he was ministering **to the Jew first, and also to the Greek (Gentiles).** This letter appeals to both the Jew and the Gentile believers. He mentions his ministry of the **"gospel of God" in the first sentence. The "gospel of God" appears 7 times in the King James Bible. Six times in Paul's writings and once in Peter's (1 Peter 4:17). The "gospel of God" is the good news of the coming Redeemer.**

So did Peter preach the same gospel as Paul? The "gospel of God" is the basic prophesied information of the Redeemer, who would redeem all that was lost in Adam. Adam plunged the world into sin (knowing good and evil), death (physical separation from God and spiritual death) and corruption of creation. Adam and his bride Eve were to be co-regents and reign over the earth (Gen. 1:28). Because Adam and Eve forfeited their dominion of the earth, Satan gained it by default. (In the future, the Lord Jesus Christ will reign over the earth and the 12 will rule with Him and so will the rest of His Bride, the nation Israel.) The body of Christ is the one new man (Eph. 2:15) we have a union with Christ who is our Head. Occasionally Paul will use a husband and wife analogy related to the Church and Christ but he never calls us the "Bride" and he never says that we will live in an earthly kingdom.

Both Peter and Paul preached the "gospel of God" because the Lord Jesus Christ is the prophesied Redeemer (Gen. 3:15) for both groups. But Peter emphasized the "gospel of the kingdom" and Paul the "gospel of Christ." Peter said that Christ was the Redeemer (1 Peter 1:18, 19) and King of the Jews to sit on the throne in the coming kingdom on earth and Paul preached the "gospel of Christ" (because when Christ died He paid for all sins past, present and future and then He rose). Paul said that today Gentiles can be saved apart from the law and apart from going through Israel and become part of the body of Christ. The destiny for the body of Christ is the heavenly places (Eph. 2:6; 2 Cor. 5:1).

So what is the difference between Paul's gospel and Peter's? Paul said Christ died for **OUR SINS** (the Gentiles). Paul never said that the body of Christ would live in a kingdom on earth but in heavenly places. Gospel means "good news." There is more than one gospel in the Bible but there is only one that saves today, Paul's. **Part of Paul sharing the "gospel of God" is the revelation of the sweeping redemptive salvation that Christ accomplished.** God gave Paul the "mystery of Christ" which in part is the full revelation of all that Christ accomplished on the cross. Christ provided the "remission (forgiveness) of sins" (Rom. 3:25) for the earthly kingdom believers. At present, God justifies us because God has "at this time declared his righteousness . . . on him which believeth in Jesus" (Rom. 3:26). Paul explains that it has always been by faith that a person is saved in any dispensation. God hates unbelief. **Unbelief in Paul's gospel, not our sins, is what sends a person to hell today.** While we were yet sinners Christ died for us. As sinners, we qualify to be saved. **All we have to do is believe (1 Cor. 15:3, 4). We do not have to clean ourselves up.** Just come as we are. Only believe! God made it simple for us to be saved on purpose, because if He had made it hard, no one would be saved.

When we study Rom. Ch. 3, we will examine the broad redemptive work that Christ accomplished at Calvary in more detail. After His death, Christ went to "the heart of the earth" (Matt. 12:40) also called "paradise" (Luke 23:43) and took the saved in the compartment known as "Abraham's bosom" (Luke 16:22) to heaven (2 Cor. 12:4; Heb. 12:23) because He had redeemed them with His blood. In the future, when the kingdom of heaven comes to earth (Deut. 11:21) paradise will be with the kingdom on earth believers (Rev. 2:7).

Why does Paul say he goes to the "Jew first, and also to the Greek"?
The first 8 chapters of the book of Acts records the "stumbling" and "fall" of Israel. Then in Acts 9, the Lord Jesus Christ returns from heaven and saves Saul of Tarsus (Paul). Christ commissions Paul to be a brand new apostle and to preach a

new message. The incredible news is that **God is holding back the day of wrath!** He is suspending Israel's program and bringing in a new dispensation of grace. Therefore, the Lord's day of wrath is still future and so is the establishment of His earthly kingdom.

After God raised up Paul, He informed His 12 apostles in Jerusalem of His change in program in Acts 15 and Galatians chapter 2. The rest of the book of Acts describes the "diminishing" of Israel as **God makes sure that those Jews that lived outside of Israel knew that God had changed the program after the nation rejected the Father, the Son, and the Holy Ghost.** This is why Paul visits the synagogues first at that time. **By doing this God left the Jews without excuse, and also provoked them to jealousy by His new program to the Gentiles.** But God in His mercy gave them a new opportunity to be saved through faith in Paul's gospel. This is why Paul goes to the "Jew first, and also to the Greek" until the end of Acts 28. This is still the pattern during the writing of the book of Romans since it was written in Acts 20:3.

How, when and where did God give up the Gentiles?

After the flood, "God blessed Noah and his sons, and said unto them, Be fruitful, and multiply, and replenish (spread out) the earth" (Gen. 9:1). But within just a few generations, people again became wicked, disobeyed God, refused to spread out, made their own religion, and a **tower to heaven**. They did not believe nor obey God. "And the whole earth was of one language, and of one speech . . . they found a plain in the land of Shinar . . . they said one to another, Go to, let us make brick, and burn them throughly . . . Go to, let us build us a CITY and a TOWER, whose top may reach <u>unto heaven</u>; and let us <u>make us a name, lest we be scattered abroad upon the face of the whole earth</u>" (Gen. 11:1-4).

The Tower of Babel is where the LORD <u>God gave the Gentiles up, hoping to return and to save them later.</u> Paul by revelation of Jesus Christ explains this in Romans chapter 1:18-32. "Because that<u>, when they knew God, they glorified him not as God, neither were thankful; but became vain in their imaginations, and their foolish heart was darkened</u>" (Rom. 1:21). The downward stages of their unbelief:

Romans 1:24 . . . God also gave them up to uncleanness . . .
Romans 1:26 . . . God gave them up unto vile affections . . .
Romans 1:28 . . . God gave them over to a reprobate mind . . .

Because the people wanted to be "like gods" and make their own one world religion and government at the Tower of Babel, God confused their languages,

making the people divide into nations. God rejected them because they had first rebelled against His word and Him. They wanted to be their own authority and to take credit for being the most powerful and wise when that is who God is. **In the future Christ will set up His righteous one world religion and government.** "Gentiles" means nations. "Therefore is the name of it called Babel; because the LORD did there <u>confound the language of all the earth</u>: and from thence did the LORD scatter them abroad upon the face of all the earth" (Gen. 11:9). God did not send another flood. About 175 years later, God decided to form His own nation from Abram (Abraham).

<u>Gentiles were under sin since the Tower of Babel</u>. "Wherefore remember, that ye being in TIME PAST Gentiles . . . having NO HOPE, and WITHOUT GOD in the world. **But now** in Christ Jesus . . ." (Eph. 2:11-13a). The ungodly and unrighteous acts mentioned at the Tower of Babel are still continue in the unbelievers of today, but now all mankind has a chance to be saved apart from His nation of Israel.

1:16 <u>Salvation</u> is an encompassing word that includes: grace, justification, imputation, propitiation, redemption, forgiveness, sanctification, and glorification. Salvation is in three tenses. One, the Christian has been saved from the penalty of sin. Second, he is being saved from the power of sin. Third, he will be saved from the presence of sin at the Rapture.

Salvation is by grace through faith in what Christ has done, not something we did. It is a gift, not something we worked for so that no one can boast (Rom. 3:21-28, 4:5, 23-25, 6:23; 1 Cor. 15:3, 4; Eph. 2:8, 9). But after we are saved we can work to serve the Lord with Christ living through us (Eph. 2:10).

Romans 1:1 Paul [all his 13 letters begin with Paul, c/w James 1:1, notice that the period does not come until after verse 7 and that a new paragraph begins then, every word and comma is important in the KJV], a servant of Jesus Christ, called to be an apostle [Gal. 1:1, 11, 12; Eph. 3:1-6 How did Paul get his message? Did the 12 or anyone else know about the mystery before Paul?], separated unto the **gospel of God** [Paul was separated in Antioch Acts 13:2, the gospel of God is the gospel of the promised coming Redeemer (Gen. 3:15), a far reaching gospel that relates to all mankind], **2** (Which he had promised afore by his **prophets** in the **holy scriptures** [the coming Redeemer was prophesied elsewhere Psa. 22, Psa. 89:20-37; Isa. 9:6, 7, 53],) **3 Concerning his Son Jesus Christ our Lord [God]**, which was made of the **seed of David** according to the flesh [He is Man and the Son of God; Isa. 7:14; Matt. 1:23) would be a Jewish man of the seed of David (1 Chron. 17:11-14; Matt. 1:1 *notice the Davidic and Abrahamic covenants).

Because Jesus was the Son of David according to the flesh, He was the God-Man who could Redeem us by dying in our place. His royal lineage also entitles Him to rule Israel's earthly kingdom (**Luke 1:31-33**). Paul the due time testifier will explain the significance of all that Christ accomplished for mankind at Calvary. This is one of the reasons Romans is such an important book]; **4** And declared to be the Son of God [The Father declared the Lord Jesus Christ to be the Son of God when He resurrected Him because He had the power over death. "This day have I begotten thee" (Acts 13:33, Psa. 2:7; Heb. 1:5, 5:5, Eph. 1:20)] with power, according to the spirit of holiness [Christ lived a perfect life so the justice of God's holiness demanded that He could not stay dead, death could not hold Him see Psa. 16:10; Acts 2:24], by the **resurrection from the dead** [His resurrection proved His power to overcome sin, Satan, and death, that His blood payment for our sins was accepted, 1 Cor. 15:20]: **5** By whom we have received **grace** and **apostleship** [God showed grace to Paul, a blasphemer, making him His minister 15:16], for obedience to the **faith among all nations** [that all nations would believe. Was this true in Mark 10:24? c/w 1 Tim. 2:6], for his name [the Lord Jesus Christ]: **6** Among whom are ye also the called of Jesus Christ [called by His gospel 2 Thess. 2:14]: **7** To all that be in Rome, **beloved of God [**God calls us the same as He did His Son in Matt. 3:17], called *to be* **saints** [After believing we are no longer called sinners but saints, not because of anything we did, but only because of what Christ did for us. We are now set apart for God's possession and service.]: **Grace to you and peace from God our Father, and the Lord Jesus Christ** [God offers grace and peace today because Christ has **PAID IN FULL** for all sins so God is not imputing sins today. "To wit, that God was in Christ, reconciling the world unto himself, not imputing their trespasses unto them; and hath committed unto us the word of reconciliation" (2 Cor. 5:19). Furthermore, God is holding back His wrath (Jacob's trouble) until after this time that He is dispensing grace and offering salvation to anyone who will believe what Christ has done for him. God is offering grace and peace to believers (5:1)].

8 ¶ First, I thank my God through Jesus Christ for you all, **that your faith is spoken of throughout the whole world** [when Paul prays he thanks God of the fame of their faith, he wants what God wants, for the body of Christ to thrive and succeed]. **9** For God is my witness, whom I serve with my spirit in the gospel of his Son [our spirit is in our mind (Eph. 4:23)], that without ceasing I make mention of you always in **my prayers** [God knows Paul prays for them]; **10** Making request, if by any means now at length I might have a prosperous journey by the will of God **to come unto you** [Paul asked God to allow him to come and see them]. **11** For I **long to see you**, that I may **impart** unto you some **spiritual gift**, to the end ye may be **established** [you can hear the excitement in Paul's words that

15

he can't wait to share what Christ has revealed to him so that they can be solid in the faith. **Paul's purpose is to "impart unto you some spiritual gift, to the end that ye may be established" See Rom. 16:25**]; **12** That is, that I may be comforted together with you by the **mutual faith both of you and me** [Paul wants to enjoy their fellowship in their mutual faith because Christ lives in all believers working through them]. **13** Now I would not have you ignorant, brethren, that oftentimes I purposed to come unto you, (**but was let hitherto,**) [Paul was hindered, not by Satan but because he was so busy with ministry opportunities that there may be some fruit among the Gentiles, 15:19-23] that I might have some **fruit** [that they may win some souls and help the weaker believers just like Paul was] among you also, even as among other Gentiles. **14 I am debtor both** to the **Greeks**, and to the **Barbarians**; both to the **wise**, and to the **unwise** [Paul owes a debt to all unsaved people to have a chance to hear the gospel so that they may be saved. Likewise we should do what we can when we can]. **15** So, as much as in me is, I am **ready to preach the gospel to you that are at Rome also**. [Paul shares all that he has learned and is willing to share with those at Rome. Next Paul will follow a logical sequence of explanation. Notice how Paul makes use of the word "for" (which explains why the previous statement is correct) while "because" (is similar indicating the cause and its effect] **16 For** I am **not ashamed of the gospel of Christ**: **for** it is the **power of God unto salvation to every one that believeth** [Paul knows that hearing and believing the gospel of what Christ has done has the power for God to translate them out of Adam and into Christ (Col. 1:13). See 1 Cor. 1:18 about God's power. Every time a person is saved God does a miracle, the Gospel of Christ works and Paul knew that.]; to the **Jew first**, and **also to the Greek** [In the past, Jesus was sent to Israel only (15:22-24), but Gentiles could be blessed at that time by blessings Israel (Gen. 12:3). After Jesus ascended to heaven salvation was still sent only to the Jews (Acts 2:5, 10, 14, 3:12, 25, **26**, 11:19) not until Jesus saved Paul did salvation go to the Gentiles (Acts 26:16-18; Rom. 10:12, 13). Paul went to the Jew first and then to the Greek until the end of Acts, then preached to Gentiles after that. God wanted the Jews that lived outside of Israel to hear that He had changed the program from Peter to Paul so that they would be without excuse and have a chance to be saved. Salvation **is an encompassing word that includes: grace, justification, imputation, propitiation, redemption, forgiveness, sanctification, and glorification. Salvation is in three tenses. One, the Christian has been saved from the penalty of sin. Second, he is being saved from the power of sin. Third, he will be saved from the presence of sin at the Rapture. A person who studies the Bible rightly divided is also saved from false doctrine.**] **17 For** therein is the **righteousness of God revealed** from **faith to faith** [God's righteousness is revealed from Christ's faith to our faith. Two faiths are necessary for God's righteousness to come upon man. We place our

faith in CHRIST'S faith.]: as it is written, The just shall live by **faith** [This is a quote from Hab. 2:4, which actually says "the just shall live by <u>his</u> faith." We are justified by the faith of Christ (Gal. 2:16) There is only one cloak for our sin His faith. We live (walk) by His perfect faith, as He lives in us. "I am crucified with Christ: nevertheless I live; yet not I, but Christ liveth in me: and the life which I now live in the flesh I live by the faith **of** the Son of God, who loved me, and gave himself for me" (Gal.2:20).].

18 ¶ For the **<u>wrath of God is revealed from heaven against all ungodliness and unrighteousness of men</u>**, who **hold the truth in unrighteousness** [Did not believe. Just like God's righteousness is revealed so is His wrath revealed on all those who reject truth which God has showed them. God's righteousness demands His justice. Man knew the truth but rejected it. Paul will now explain how Gentiles ended up "without God in the world" (Eph. 2:11, 12). God's righteousness was offended at the Tower of Babel (Gen. 11) so God gave the Gentiles up and men are in need of God's righteousness. The ungodly and unrighteous acts mentioned at the Tower of Babel are still continue in the unbelievers of today. **It is not evolution, but devolution because man has become like a beast. Paul warns the Gentiles (and then the Jews in chapter 2) about the wrath of God so they can do something about it. Like a brilliant prosecuting attorney Paul unfolds the predicament mankind is in so that they will listen to him when he delivers God's remedy to them with "But now . . . (Rom. 3:21)]; 19 Because** that which may be known of God is manifest in them [the knowledge of God is "inside" the Gentiles]; for God hath shewed it unto them [God showed them who He is by two means creation and conscience (external and internal evidence of God)]. **20 For** the invisible things of him from the creation [in the beginning God created the heaven and the earth (Gen. 1:1)] of the world are **clearly seen** [all around us], being understood by the things that are made [creatures know that God made these things], even his eternal power **[God's eternal character and His infinite everlasting Almightiness power is everywhere in the DNA, blood, the sun, water, plants, our eyes and so forth] and Godhead [trinity]**; so that they are without excuse [People are without excuse because: "The heavens declare the glory of God; and the firmament sheweth his handiwork" (Psalm 19:1, see Psa. 97:6)]: **21 Because** that, when they knew God [they knew who God was], they glorified him not as God, neither were thankful [they did not give God the credit, the glory He deserved, and they were not grateful for all that He did]; but became vain in their imaginations [Not only man's Greek and Roman philosophy, but intellectual thoughts, and theories are "vain" which means empty or useless. Man believes that because he can imagine things in his mind that he can create, and is god. The theory of evolution, that something can evolve out of nothing with a big bang is an example of this. Sadly, "scientists" like Carl Sagan and Richard Dawkins know better now.], and their foolish heart was **darkened** [their heart have no light, Eph. 4:17-19]. **22** Professing themselves to be wise, they became **fools** [Pride is man's problem and it leads him to be a fool, Psa. 10:4, 14:1] Previously the Gentiles were ignorant but now they are warned and should change their minds (repent) and believe God); Acts 17:29-31], **23** And changed the glory of the **uncorruptible God** into an image made like to **corruptible [mortal] man**, and to birds, and fourfooted beasts, and creeping things [idolized man and other created things like beasts, notice the de-evolution from man to creeping things]. **24** Wherefore <u>**God also gave them up to uncleanness**</u> through the **lusts** of their own hearts, to dishonour their own **bodies** between themselves [Jer. 17:9. Notice the downward spiral of idolatry. **An idol is a man-made god.** Man creates a god in his mind that he can feel comfortable with so he can feel superior. Paul is describing a man-made religious system when they should be worshipping the true and living God who made them. At the Tower of Babel, the people disobeyed God's word. They made an evil one world religion and government apart from faith in God, and said they were able to reach heaven, that they were God's. **Idolatry is spiritual adultery. Therefore, God gave them over to physical sexual adultery**]:

25 Who **changed the truth of God into a lie** [Satan's lie program 'ye shall be as gods, knowing good and evil" (Gen. 3:5), worshipped man. The same lie that Satan believed that he could be "like the most High" (Isa. 14:14) as God "possessor of heaven and earth" (Gen. 14:22)]**, and worshipped and served the creature [changing this truth results in idolatry.] more than the Creator, who is blessed for ever. Amen. 26** For this cause <u>**God gave them up unto vile affections [emotions of the soul]**</u>: for even their women did change the natural use into that which is against nature [notice that homosexuality is against nature]: **27** And likewise also the men, leaving the natural use of the woman, burned in their lust one toward another; men with men working that which is **unseemly** [homosexuality], and receiving in themselves that recompence of their error which was meet [got their just reward]. **28** And even as **they did not like to retain God in their knowledge [today also many do not want to read the Bible and know God]**, <u>**God gave them over to a reprobate mind [The mind is the spirit of man (Eph. 4:23). So God gave them up body-soul- and spirit (See the opposite order which is true for saved people in 1 Thess. 5:23. Their hearts and minds were hardened. "Reprobate" means not passing the test, discredited. No one without God's imputed righteousness can pass the test to stand before Holy God. God let the Gentiles go at the Tower of Babel hoping to save them later through the nation He would create through Abraham. Unbelievers today are also the enemies of God.**</u>], to do those things which are not convenient [they did and still do disgusting vile things and Paul gives a list of some of them here]; **29 Being filled with all unrighteousness**, fornication, wickedness, covetousness, maliciousness; full of envy, murder, debate, deceit, malignity; whisperers, **30** Backbiters, haters of God, despiteful [insolent], proud [pride is the same as Satan had], boasters, inventors of evil things, disobedient to parents [hating those that love and care for them most], **31** Without understanding, covenantbreakers [they brake their contracts and promises], without natural affection [no real care for others], implacable [relentless], unmerciful: **32 Who knowing the judgment of God** [Job. 32:8. They know that God is going to judge but disregard that truth. God has given man free will and does not force them to believe.], that **they which commit such things are worthy of death, not only do the same, but have pleasure in them that do them. [These reprobates are the mobs of the past and unbelievers of the present].** *Les Feldick's Timeline (with approximate dates):

Simple Bible Timeline

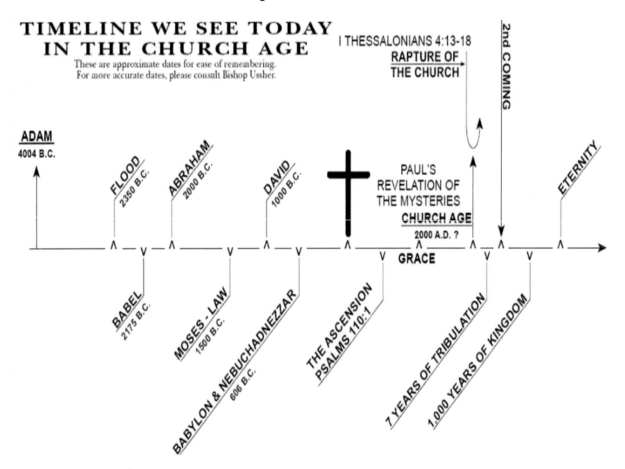

Romans Chapter 2 – Jews under sin

2:1-29 Paul says the Jews are under sin naming them in 2:17.

There are several times when God will judge mankind. Three of these judgements are: the judgement seat of Christ (1 Cor. 3:8-15, 4:5; 2 Cor. 5:10) when the body of Christ will be judged for their service; the judgement of the nations at Christ return to earth (Matt. 25:31, 32; Rev. 20:7-10) which continues until the after the final Gentile rebellion after Satan is released at the end of Christ's first 1,000-year reign; and then the Great White Throne (GWT) judgment of the lost (Rev. 20:11-15).

2:1-16 Paul addresses those who think they will be accepted by God because of their human good (which he explains in Romans 7:18 is not good). Paul says that the things that the self-righteous people judge others about are the things that they themselves do. **Believers are to judge doctrine** (truth, teaching) **and behavior** that is bad (John 7:24; Phil. 1:9; 2 Tim. 3:1-5), **but we are not to judge** other **people** because God will do that (Matt. 7:1-5; Rom. 14:10-13; Duet. 32:4).

In Romans, Paul refers to two kinds of people Jews and Gentiles (1:16). First, the Gentiles are without excuse (1:18-32). Then from 2:1 to 3:9 Paul begins to talk to the Jews who think they are superior to the Gentiles, and shows them that they are also without excuse. He masterfully produces each piece of evidence as he builds God's case against them. This news comes as a gigantic shock to the privileged Jews! He asks them, do you not know that God is going to judge you? Then in the rest of the chapter, Paul proceeds to point out the divine principles of judgement that prove that the self-righteous Jews are equally condemned with the Gentiles. From 3:10-19 Paul proves that the whole world is guilty and under sin.

8 Principles by which God will judge mankind
1. God will judge "according to truth" (2)
2. There are degrees of punishment "hardness and impenitent heart treasurest [storing] up unto thyself wrath against the day of wrath" (5) wrath accumulates more as people hardens themselves against the truth about them (Isa. 30:1 says "add sin to sin." Matt. 23:14 shown that the false religious leaders have "greater damnation." Matt. 11:24 says it will be more tolerable for some than other in the day of judgement.
3. God will judge by the same standard, "render to every man according to his deeds [works]" (6)

4. "For there is no respect of persons with God" (11) "Shall not the **judge of all the earth do right**?" (Gen. 18:25).

5. According to the light or truth available to a person, for example if he did not have the law he will not be judged by it (Luke 12:47, 48; Matt. 11:21-24). "For as many as have sinned without law shall also perish without law: and as many as have sinned in the law shall be judged by the law" (12).

6. "In that day [at the GWT] God shall judge the secrets of men . . ." (16). God will judge the secrets of men's hearts (their motives, not just their actions). God sees and knows everything even our thoughts. "Neither is there any creature that is not manifest in his sight: but all things are naked and opened unto the eyes of him with whom we have to do" (Heb. 4:13).

7. God will judge "by Jesus Christ" (16). "For the Father judgeth no man, but hath committed all judgment unto the Son: That all men should honour the Son, even as they honour the Father . . . And shall come forth; they that have done good, unto the resurrection of life; and they that have done evil, unto the resurrection of damnation" (John 5:22, 23a, 29). The first time Jesus came to earth, He came to save the world, but the next time He will come to **judge.**

8. The Lord Jesus Christ will judge "according to my gospel" (16) Paul's gospel.

Paul warns people who think they will be accepted because of their human good saying they will be judged according to truth (2:2), their deeds (2:6), and "my gospel" (2:16). The truth is the resurrection of the Son of God. Paul calls the gospel Christ gave him "my gospel" to differentiate it from the gospel of the kingdom preached by the twelve. Paul preached the good news of Christ crucified and risen again for our sins (the gospel of Christ) and wants the Jews to know that they need to listen to him in order to be saved now. People will be judged by Paul's gospel. God will reveal the secrets of men, their heart motives, to show that evil unbelievers are worthy of eternal damnation because they did not accept to provision God freely gave them – the sacrifice of His own dear Son. God has warned people before in several places in the Bible (Eccl. 12:14; John 5:29).

God has been good and kind to everyone. He has patiently waited for His people to trust and obey Him. His goodness was supposed to lead them to repentance (a change of mind about who God is) instead they hardened their hearts and stored up wrath for the day of wrath (the Great White Throne Judgment, Rev. 20:11-15). If a person believes what Christ has done, he is judged by Christ's works; but if a person does not believe in Christ he is judged by his own works.

The Jews thought that God would show them favor because they were born Jews. They were proud thinking that the Gentiles were inferior to them and getting what they deserved. People are basically the same. Someone once said "We hate our own faults, especially when we see them in others." When we point the finger at someone there is three fingers point back at us.

We can be patient, kind, and godly examples to our family too, and our hearts break when they reject God and His word. Their deceitful hearts think that somehow they will get into heaven (Jer. 17:9).

The Jews and sinners today think that somehow God is going to let them into heaven while they worship their human reason, pamper their bodies so they can live a year longer, google their televisions, computer, and cell phones without cracking open their Bibles. They care nothing about knowing God or His word, or even the requirements for eternal life. They ignore God's Book which can give them faith (Rom. 10:17). The Bible has the word of eternal life. They are more concerned about everything else and are throwing away their chance of eternal life. They have heard that God is love, but forget that He is also just. People today are like the Jews saying to themselves, "I am better than most so I don't need a Saviour." If people are seeking for the fountain of eternal life it is in God's word.

Repentance (2:4) simply **means to change our mind**. It does not mean to be sorry for what we have done or to stop sinning. It is impossible for a sinner to stop sinning. That is why we come to God by faith in His gospel just as the imperfect sinners that we are. We cannot clean ourselves up until after we are saved and have Christ in us. God doesn't force people to have faith but wants them to.

Men will be judged according to the knowledge of God which they possess. The Jews will be judged more severely because they had the Law and did not keep it. The same will happen to sinners who hear God's word today, but still will not believe. The more they know and reject the greater the punishment in the day of judgement (**2:5** and **16**). Somehow people know this and that is why they do not want to hear truth.

2:17-19 The Jews were instructed in the law and rested in it, boasting about their favored position to God. They thought of themselves as a guide to the blind (Gentiles), a light to those in darkness, instructor of the foolish and a teacher of babes. The Jews had a form of knowledge and of the truth of the law, but they missed the **purpose** of it since they thought they could keep it. But they themselves did not obey the Law. The result was that they brought dishonor to God so that His name was blasphemed among the Gentiles (2 Sam. 12:14; Isa. 52:5; Ezek. 36:21, 22). God's purpose for Israel was that they were to be His nation of priests (Ex.

19:5, 6) to teach His word to the other nations (Isa. 2:1-4). The nation will fulfil its purpose in the future and be a light to the Gentiles (Isa. 60:1-3 ***Notice this will be at Israel rise, not their fall (Rom. 11:11**, 62:1, 2; Matt. 5:14). **Similarly, today, many "Christians" depend on their religion to save them, but have no knowledge of or faith in the word of God.** The Jews had the benefit of God's written law but many did not believe God. <u>**Thanks to the revelation of the Lord Jesus Christ given to Paul the members of the body of Christ now have their own word of God and can "approve things that are excellent" (Phil. 1:10).**</u>

2:25-29 Paul says that the Jews circumcision is worthless if they break the law (Gal. 5:3). If the uncircumcised Gentiles keep the law by following their conscience they will do better in God's judgement than the physical Jew. The circumcised Jew without faith is seen as uncircumcised by God. Their religion was an outward ceremony not an inward reality. God requires a spiritual circumcision of the heart not just one in the flesh. The Jews knew that they were to be a light to the Gentiles. A true Jew is one who by faith has inwardly changed his heart and mind and trusted God, not one who merely keeps the letter of the law in the flesh. This is the Jew that will receive praise, not from men, but from God.

By the time we finish chapter 2, Paul has masterfully proved that both Jews and Gentiles are under sin. As we will find out in the next chapter the whole world is guilty and worthy of God's wrath. But, as we will learn **the gospel of Christ reveals the righteousness of God**. This good news has the power, <u>"To open their eyes, and to turn them from darkness to light, and from the power of Satan unto God [those "in Adam" are under the power of Satan], that they may receive forgiveness of sins, and inheritance among them which are sanctified by faith that is in me"</u> (Acts 26:18).

Romans 2:1 Therefore thou art **inexcusable**, O man, whosoever thou art that **judgest**: for wherein thou judgest another, thou condemnest thyself; for thou that judgest doest the **same things** [Paul addresses those who think they will be accepted by God because of their human good. Paul says that the things that the self-righteous people judge others about are the things that they themselves do.] **2** But we are sure that **the judgment of God is according to truth** [God will judge fairly knowing all things] against them which commit such things. **3** And thinkest thou this, O man, that judgest them which do such things, and doest the same, that thou shalt **escape the judgment of God?** [Adam found out that the wages of even <u>one</u> sin is death (Gen. 2:17; Rom. 6:23; James 2:10)] **4** Or despisest thou the riches of his **goodness** [God's grace, Him giving what is not deserved] and **forbearance [God restraining Himself by** holding back His judgment] and **longsuffering**

[patient enduring 2 Peter 3:9, 15]; not knowing that the goodness of God leadeth thee to repentance? [Repentance simply means to change our mind. It does not mean to be sorry for what we have done or to stop sinning. That is impossible, because a sinner is unable to stop sinning. That is why we come to God by faith in His gospel just as the imperfect sinners that we are. We cannot clean ourselves up until after we are saved and have Christ in us. God doesn't force people to have faith but wants them to] **5 But after thy hardness [stubborn] and impenitent [not feeling shame or guilt for actions, unwilling to believe] heart treasurest up [storing and adding up, accumulating] unto thyself wrath against the day of wrath [2 Thess. 1:9, 2:12; Rev. 20:9] and revelation of the righteous judgment of God at the Great White Throne Judgment (GWT) (Rev. 20:11-15)]; 6 Who will render to every man according to his deeds** [all people will be judged by God according to what they have done]: **7** To them who by patient continuance in well doing seek for glory and honour and immortality, **eternal life** [those who seek and find God and put their faith in what He says. The problem is that only Christ lived a perfect life we cannot because we are born with the sin nature (Jer. 13:23; Rom. 8:3a, b)]: **8** But unto them that are contentious, and **do not obey the truth**, but obey unrighteousness, indignation and **wrath** [unbelievers will get wrath], **9** Tribulation and anguish, upon every soul of man that doeth evil, of the Jew first, and also of the Gentile [Paul warns against unbelief. The Jews will be judged in the tribulation, and then the Gentiles at His Second coming] **10** But **glory, honour**, and **peace**, to every man that worketh good, to the Jew first, and also to the Gentile [with Christ's righteousness believers can do good works]: **11** For there is **no respect of persons with God** [God will judge everyone by the same standard]. **12** For as many as have sinned **without law shall also perish without law**: and as many as **have sinned in the law** shall be **judged by the law** [according to the light or truth available to a person, for example if he did not have the law he will not be judged by it (Luke 12:47, 48 and Matt. 11:21-24). Sin has the same effect on a person with or without the law. Sin produces death (Rom. 5:12-14). Next is a parenthesis from v. 13-15]; **13** (For not the hearers of the law are just before God, but the doers of the law shall be justified [Just knowing right from wrong does not justify anyone]. **14** For when the Gentiles, which have not the law, do by nature the things contained in the law, these, having not the law, are a law unto themselves: **15** Which shew the work of the law written in their hearts, their conscience also bearing witness, and their thoughts the mean while accusing or else excusing one another;) [Everyone has a conscience, God's law written on their hearts, that is why 1:18-20 is about the guilt of the whole world. God's wrath against the ungodly and unrighteous who deny God's power and deity that God has revealed both "in them" (1:19) and in His "creation" (1:20)] **16 In the day** when **God shall judge the secrets of men by Jesus Christ according to my gospel** [At the GWT, God will judge the secrets of men's hearts (their motives) not just their actions. God sees and knows everything even our thoughts. God will judge by Jesus Christ "by Jesus Christ." "For the Father judgeth no man, but hath committed all judgment unto the Son: That all men should honour the Son, even as they honour the Father . . . And shall come forth; they that have done good, unto the resurrection of life; and they that have done evil, unto the resurrection of damnation" (John 5:22, 23a, 29). The first time Jesus came to earth, He came to save the world, but the next time He will come to **judge.** The Lord Jesus Christ will judge "according to my gospel" Paul's gospel].

17 ¶ Behold, thou art **called** a Jew ["called" does not mean that they are true Jews in their heart], and **restest in the law** [The Jew's religion set Israel apart from all other nations (Deut. 4:5-8). They thought that their religious works could save them. They should not think that just because they were given the law that that makes them any better. They became self-righteous thinking they could keep the law (9:31, 32). **Similarly, today, many "Christians" depend on their religion to save them, but have no knowledge of or faith in the word of God.**], and **makest thy boast of God** [the Jews were proud and puffed up because God had given them His law], **18** And **knowest his will** [but having the law made the Jews more accountable to God because they knew His will], and approvest the things that are more excellent, **being instructed out of the law [The Jews had the benefit of God's excellent law but many did not believe God. <u>Thanks to the revelation of the Lord Jesus Christ given to Paul the members of the body of Christ now have their own word of God and can "approve things that are excellent" (Phil. 1:9)</u>]; 19** And art confident that thou thyself art a guide of the blind, a light of them which are in darkness [God's purpose for Israel was that they were to be His nation of priests (Ex. 19:5, 6) to teach His word to the other nations (Isa. 2:1-4). The nation will fulfil its purpose in the future and be a light to the Gentiles (Isa. 60:1-3 ***Notice this will be at Israel rise, not their fall (Rom. 11:11;** Isa. 62:1, 2; Matt. 5:14)], **20** An **instructor of the foolish**, a **teacher of babes**, which hast the **form of knowledge** and of the **truth in the law** [Heb. 4:2, Rom. 8:3a, b, the Jews didn't know that without God's Spirit in them by faith and the understanding of His times they were not qualified to teach yet. They will be qualified after they have received their glorified bodies and the New Covenant in the 1,000-year Kingdom of Christ. At that time, they will have the right heart to serve the Lord out of gratitude and care for others]. **21** Thou therefore which **teachest** another, **teachest thou not thyself**? thou that preachest a man should not steal, dost thou **steal**? [because they do not have Christ's Spirit yet they still have the sin nature with its evil thoughts and intents] **22** Thou that sayest a man should not commit **adultery**, dost thou commit adultery? thou that abhorrest idols, dost thou commit **sacrilege**? [Sadly the

Jews were notorious for idolatry (Isa. 65:2, 3)] **23** Thou that makest thy boast of the law, **through breaking the law dishonourest thou God? 24 For the name of God is blasphemed [spoken badly of] among the Gentiles through you,** as it is written [Ezek. 36:21, 22]. **25** For **circumcision** verily profiteth, if thou keep the law [God gave circumcision to the nation of Israel as a **token of the covenant** He made with Abraham after Abraham had a son by his own effort in the flesh (Gen. 17:11), not the son of promise which was a miracle since at that time both Abraham and Sarah were unable to conceive. Things done in the flesh are not approved by God, but the things done by faith are. Circumcision means death to the flesh, and alive unto God]: but if thou be a breaker of the **law**, thy circumcision is made uncircumcision [worthless]. **26** Therefore if the uncircumcision keep the righteousness of the law, shall not his uncircumcision be counted for circumcision? [God values and approves of righteousness (Psa. 33:4, 5) and therefore the Gentile who does them is approved to God] **27** And shall not uncircumcision which is by nature [who naturally do what is right because the law on their hearts], if it fulfil the law, judge thee, who by the letter and circumcision dost transgress the law? [Those Gentiles are righteous in God's sight] **28** For he is not a Jew, which is one **outwardly**; neither is that circumcision, which is outward in the flesh [notice Paul's modest, concise, and clear language]: **29** But he is a Jew, which is one **inwardly**; and circumcision is that **of the heart**, in the **spirit [Circumcision represents the heart and spirit that God desires in them (Deut. 10:12-14, 30:5,6; Ezek. 36:26-28)]**, and not in the letter [His law and Spirit will be in their hearts and they will not need to follow what is written because they will know it]; whose **praise is not of men,** but **of God [**today God considers the nation of Israel spiritually uncircumcised like the Gentiles because of their unbelief. In the kingdom, the Jews will love and serve God and God will love and serve them].

It is interesting to compare Israel's future circumcision with the circumcision we have today. "For <u>we are the circumcision</u>, **which worship God** <u>in the spirit</u>, and rejoice in Christ Jesus, and have **no confidence in the flesh**" (Phil. 3:3). "In whom also ye are circumcised **with the circumcision made without hands**, in putting off the **body of the sins of the flesh by the circumcision of Christ**" (Col. 2:11). We are crucified with Him and dead to sin. We are all one in Christ. The outward body does not matter; being part of a new creature in Christ is all that matters. "Where there is neither Greek nor Jew, **circumcision nor uncircumcision**, Barbarian, Scythian, bond nor free: but Christ is all, and in all" (Col. 3:11).

<u>**Man is a triune being, spirit, soul, and body**</u>. "And the very God of peace sanctify you **wholly**; and I pray God your whole <u>**spirit**</u> and <u>**soul**</u> and <u>**body**</u> be preserved blameless unto the coming of our Lord Jesus Christ" (1 Thess. 5:23).

The **spirit** is the mind (Eph. 4:23). In an unsaved person, has a spirit but it is dead to the things of God and cannot understand anything about Him. At salvation, the person's spirit is quickened (made alive) to God (1 Cor. 2:11, 12). God's Spirit joins with the saved person's spirit and helps them to understand His word.

The **soul** is the unique component of who we really are (our core being or eternal personality). It has a heart and mouth. It is the part of us that has faith.

The **body** is the physical vehicle that caries the soul and spirit. The body is made up of flesh, bones, and blood. Sin and the flesh nature dwell in the body.

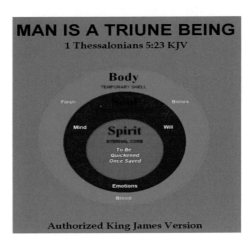

Two Operating Systems: Law vs. Grace

Law	Grace
Applies to the past and future	Applies to the present
People get what they deserve	People get undeserved kindness
Works on the outward man, the flesh	Works on the inward man, the spirit
Physical blessings	Spiritual blessings
Physical curses	No curses
Future on earth	Future in heaven
Given to Israel only	Jews are the same as Gentiles
Fear motivates obedience	Gratitude and love motivates obedience
Focuses on human failures	Focuses on Christ's victory
God commands people like children	God beseeches people as free adults
Bondage	Liberty

Read on – Gentiles under sin (1) Jews under sin (2) Solution to the sin problem (3) Totally forgiven (4) In Christ, not Adam (5) How to live above sin (6-8) Living at the time of Gentile opportunity for salvation, but Israel's national blindness will end at the Rapture (9-11) Practical Christian living serving God and others (12-16).

Romans Chapter 3 – Justification Explained

3:1-20 The Bad News (which really began in 1:18): The whole world is under sin and worthy of God's wrath. No human has kept His law perfectly.

3:21-31 The Good News: Justification by faith. <u>But now</u> (that began in **Acts 9**) the righteousness of God is revealed by Christ's faith and perfect keeping of the law not our works. Read 9:30-33 to see why Israel missed this righteousness.

In chapter 2 we learned that the Jews are under sin. Their religion could not save them, neither could physical circumcision and having the law. They became legalistic following the letter of the law (tithing mint) and not the spirit of it (loving God and others).

Are you ready for judgement day? Paul said, "**<u>In the day when God shall judge the secrets of men by Jesus Christ according to my gospel</u>" (Rom. 2:16).** At the Great White Throne judgment of the lost, Christ will ask "did you believe the provision I made for you since you could not keep the law (<u>the standard for eternal life</u>)?" The soul will stand before Him suspended in mid-air and having not met the standard will be cast into the Lake of Fire. Would it not be horrible to hear them say "I thought I was believing the right gospel, or I just believed what my pastor and Bible teacher said, I never checked the Bible. Or, I had no idea that Satan had counterfeit Bibles because I never did the research. Or, I could not rightly divide the Bible because I was not using the King James Bible." I am not saying that a person has to know how to "rightly divide" to be saved. <u>I am simply pointing out that if we want people to be saved today we must preach the right gospel.</u> I sang:
Years I spent in vanity and pride,
caring not my Lord was crucified,
knowing not it was for me He died on Calvary.
(At Calvary by William Newell)

In 3:10-20, Paul will proceed to show the precarious predicament of mankind. Left to ourselves we do not seek after God or care about Him because of our evil hearts. <u>We should never forget where we were so that we can humbly save others. Salvation is not because of anything we have done, but what our Lord Jesus Christ has done.</u> We are "justified by the faith of Christ" (Gal. 2:16). **Many people do not fear** God's judgment. Unsaved people are Satan's children of disobedience. "Wherein in **time past** [before salvation] ye walked according to the course of this world, according to the prince of the power of the air, the spirit that now worketh in the **children of disobedience**" (Eph. 2:2). They are <u>helpless</u> to improve themselves because they lack any respect or knowledge of God. **They refuse to read or listen to the Bible so they cut themselves off from the words of eternal life.** If God didn't show us grace and patiently use the gospel in His word to seek us, we would all be helplessly lost for eternity. No one would be saved or have eternal life.

Many people do not rightly divide the word of truth (2 Tim. 2:15) so they do not know which gospel saves today. They do not know that the "gospel of the kingdom" preached by John the Baptist, Christ in His earthly kingdom, and Peter and the 11 cannot save anyone today. **The gospel of our salvation is not found in John 3:16-18, 20:31, nor Matt. 16:15, 16, because if you read those verses you see that it is talking about believing that Jesus is the name of Israel's Messiah the Son of God.** Notice that the disciples did not understand about His death, burial, and resurrection for sins in Luke 18:31-34.

But what about Peter after Jesus rose, what did he preach in Acts 2:22, 23, 36? Did Peter preach the good news of Christ death as payment for our sins and resurrection for our justification? No! He preached the cross as bad news, and repent and be baptized just like John the Baptist and Jesus had done. The gospel that has the power to save today is the **gospel of Christ which was not revealed until Paul** (Acts 13:39; 1 Cor. 15:1-4). Because it was a secret "hid in God" (Eph. 3:9) until it was due time for God to reveal it (1 Tim. 2:6). Because if Satan had known he would not have "crucified the Lord of glory" (1 Cor. 2:8).

Peter taught that ". . . which God hath **spoken by the mouth of all his holy prophets** since the world began." **(**Acts 3:21). Now notice the opposite.

Paul preached "the revelation of the **mystery**, which was **kept secret since the world began . . .**" (Rom. 16:25). **Things that are different are not the same.** We must be able to make the divisions in the Bible that God makes, between prophecy and mystery. Law and grace never mix.

Paul uses some terms which need to be defined and understood:
Justification – To reckon or legally declare righteous. We are justified in God's sight through the merits of Christ, by his imputed righteousness put to our account. We have been "made the righteousness of God in him [Christ]" (2 Cor. 5:21). Christ's resurrection proved that His full payment for our sins was accepted "raised again for our justification" (Rom. 4:25). Justification is a free gift.

Sin – missing the mark of God's high standard for eternal life given in His law.

Freely – We did nothing to earn it. (Salvation is as a gift.)

Forbearance – Self-restraint while patiently waiting for payment of a debt.

Remission – forgiveness, to pass over or overlook a debt.

Propitiation – fully satisfying sacrifice. One which is sufficient to satisfy justice and allow for reconciliation. The same Greek word for propitiation is translated "mercy seat" in Heb. 9:5. The mercy seat sat on top of the arc which contained the law that the people had broken. Once a year the High Priest put blood on it to cover his and the people's sins (Ex. 25:21, 22; Lev. 16:15). The tabernacle and mercy seat on earth were a replica of the one in heaven. **Christ kept God's law perfectly so God was satisfied (Isa. 53:11)**. After His resurrection Christ entered into the most holy place in heaven and sprinkled His blood there having obtained eternal redemption for all (Heb. 9:11, 12, 22-28).

Redemption – Repurchased by payment of a price. A ransom paid to free a person. The "redemption that is in Christ Jesus" refers to the ransom God paid to get us back from Satan. Man was God's creation, but came under Satan's ownership when Adam and Eve sinned. We have been "bought with a price" so we can serve God (1 Cor. 6:20; Titus 2:14). We are redeemed from Satan, sin and its penalties, and death by the payment of Christ blood (Eph. 1:7; 1 Peter 1:18, 19).

3:21-31 We are justified freely by His grace through faith in the redemption that is in Christ Jesus. Freely! God spared not His own Son but by His grace and love He delivered Him up for us all because there was no other way to save us from sin, Satan, and death. Christ experienced the Second Death for us so we did not have to. We are not saved by anything that we have done; but by grace alone, through faith in Christ ALONE. Because Christ perfectly kept the law, had perfect righteousness, and the perfect faith to pay for our sin, God is able to give us His righteousness. With Christ's righteousness God can accepted us. Now we sing:
Jesus paid it all, All to Him I owe;
Sin had left a crimson stain,
He washed it white as snow.
(Jesus Paid It All by Elvina M. Hall)

The requirements for Christ our Kinsman-Redeemer are given in Lev. 25:47-55, the book of Ruth and elsewhere in the Old Testament. The redeemer had to be (1) near kin (2) able to pay the full price (3) willing. Christ met all three requirements He became a man (John 1:14; Phil. 2:8; Heb. 2:14-17). He was able,

Christ had to be God because no man can redeem another (Psa. 49:7; Col. 1:15, 2:9; Heb. 1:8) and sinless (Eph. 1:7;1 Peter 1:18, 19, **2:22**). Christ did not inherit sin like other men, this is why His virgin birth was important (Luke 1:30-35). If He had one sin of His own He could not have died for ours. He was willing (Luke 22:42; John 10:18; Eph. 5:25; Heb. 12:2).

To what extent did Christ save us? Christ met every requirement of the law in our place. Jesus Christ bore our sins in His own body on the cross (1 Peter 2:24). "For he hath made him to be sin for us, who knew no sin; that we might be made the righteousness of God in him" (2 Cor. 5:21). But He also sacrificed His soul "being made a curse for us" (Gal. 3:13). He made "his soul an offering for sin . . . and shall be **satisfied**: by his knowledge shall my righteous servant **justify many**; for **he shall bear their iniquities** . . . he hath poured out **his soul unto death**" (Isa. 53:10-12). While on earth the Lord warned His people about this dreadful place: "Where the worm dieth not, and the fire is not quenched" (Mark 9:43-48).

In the dark hours while Jesus was nailed to the cross, the Father poured out His wrath on His Son's soul for our sins. He became a worm in our place. **"But I** *am* **a worm**, and no man; a reproach of men, and despised of the people" (Psa. 22:6).

I used to wonder why people called Christ's death "vicarious" because He really died while we just identify with His death. But then I finally realized that this was His soul-death that He experienced on our behalf when He became a "worm" in our stead. In the garden Jesus prayed to the Father, "let not the pit shut her mouth upon me" (Psa. 69:15). Satisfied, the Father raised Him. "The waters compassed me about, even to the **soul** . . . I went down to the bottoms of the mountains; the earth with her bars was about me for ever: yet hast **thou brought up my life from corruption**, O LORD my God . . . Salvation is of the LORD" (Jonah 2:5-9).

The sign of Jonah is about more than three days in the heart of the earth (Matt. 12:40). Christ went to the extreme measure of tasting death for all mankind, "that he . . . should taste death for every man" (Heb. 2:9). He experienced the destruction of His soul into a "worm" in the Lake of Fire, "the second death" (Rev. 20:14, 15) so we will never have to. Thank You, LORD! After He knew that everything was accomplished He dismissed His Spirit and died physically.

Our Savior did not take any short cuts in saving us but went to the extreme. Why? Because we are extremely sinful, and yet, His love for us is beyond degree. At the cross He purchased us from Satan, sin, and the second death with His own blood. The **"law of faith"** (27) looks to what He did for us, not us. He saved us to the "uttermost" (Heb. 7:25). Hallelujah! That is the kind of Savior we need and have.

Romans 3:1 What advantage then hath the Jew? or what profit is there of circumcision [What good was it to be a Jew if they are under sin just like the Gentiles]? **2** Much every way: chiefly, because that unto them were committed the **oracles of God** [God's written word as well as their conscience, while Gentiles only had the conscience. Therefore, the Jews had an extra way to know that they were sinners in need of a Saviour.]. **3** For what if some did not believe? shall their unbelief make the **faith of God without effect?** [Some believed, God will judge each person individually. **God had faith** that the Mosaic system would cause Jews to believe. In Luke 18:10-14, the Publican was honest with himself, not the Pharisee who supposedly kept the law.] **4** God forbid: yea, let God be **true**, but every man a liar [Because every person's sin is only against God, the unbelief of the Jews as a whole, cannot affect those Jews who trusted in God to save them. If every man disagrees with God's word, then who is a **liar**? The only way man can have eternal life is if God is true to His word to save his soul and give him that life. Next Paul shows some foolish arguments mortals (liars) have against God]; as it is written, That thou mightest be justified in thy sayings, and mightest overcome when **thou art judged** [Psa. 51:4 David confesses his adultery with Bathsheba and murder of her husband. David admits his guilt and puts up no defense so that God may be just in His judgement. David says that his sin is only against God and that God is not unjust in forgiving him. David put his faith in God as the only one who could save Him. God is justified in saying David is forgiven and will overcome the argument that He is not just. **Acknowledging our guilt before God shows that we realize our need for a Saviour**]. **5** But if our unrighteousness commend the righteousness of God, what shall we say? Is God unrighteous who taketh vengeance? (I speak as a man) [Here is some men's crazy arguments: since my sin reveals God's righteousness should He not be grateful and not punish me for it?] **6** God forbid: for then how shall God judge the world? [God's justice demands that He judge the wrong things people do] **7** For if the **truth** of God hath more abounded through my **lie** unto his glory; why yet am I also judged as a sinner? [Human reasoning likes to think that the end justifies the means, that sin is excusable if God can use it for His good. But God would not be just if He excused sin and did not judge it]. **8** And not rather, (as we be slanderously reported, and as some affirm that we say,) **Let us do evil, that good may come**? whose **damnation is just** [Paul says that this foolish thinking is justly damned. He mentions this slander experience in order to warn the saints that they most likely will encounter it also.].

9 ¶ What then? are we [Jews] better than they? No, in no wise: for we have before **proved both Jews and Gentiles, that they are all under sin**; [in the previous two chapters. Paul now lists several OT verses to show man's total sinfulness]. **10** As it is written, There is none righteous, no, not one [Psa. 14:1]: **11** There is none that understandeth, there is none that seeketh after God [Psa. 14:2]. **12** They are all gone out of the way, they are together become unprofitable; there is none that doeth good, no, not one [Psa. 14:3, says "filthy" [with sin] instead of unprofitable]. **13** Their throat is an open sepulcher [Psa. 5:9]; with their tongues they have used deceit [Psa. 140:3]; the poison of asps is under their lips [Psa. 140:3. **Deceit, concealing or misrepresenting the truth, begins in the heart (Jer. 17:9)**. Without Christ people are selfish, self-centered, and evil. "For **from within**, out of the heart of men, proceed evil thoughts . . ." (Mark 7:21)]: **14** Whose mouth is full of cursing and bitterness [Psa. 10:7]: **15** Their feet are swift to shed blood [Prov. 1:16]: **16** Destruction and misery are in their ways [Isa. 59:7, they are the evil children of disobedience like we used to be "Wherein in time past [before we were saved] ye walked according to the course of this world, according to the prince of the power of the air [Satan], the spirit that now worketh in the children of disobedience" (Eph. 2:2)]: **17** And the way of peace have they not known [Isa. 59:8]: **18** There is no fear of God before their eyes [Psa. 36:1. People do not **fear** God's judgment. So unsaved people are helpless to improve themselves because they lack any respect or knowledge of God. If God did not use the gospel in His word to seek us, we would be helplessly lost and no one would be saved].

19 ¶ Now we know that what things soever the law saith, it saith to them who are under the law [Who were under the law? Yes, the Jews. But so are the Gentiles because they have the law written in their hearts (2:15). The only ones that are not under the law are the believers (6:14). God is not imputing sin in this age of grace. But the law is still in effect for unbelievers to bring them to Christ. "Wherefore the **law was our schoolmaster to bring us unto Christ**, that we might be **justified by faith**" (Gal. 3:24). "Knowing this, that the law is not made for a righteous man, but for the lawless and disobedient . . ." (1 Tim. 1:9)] that **every mouth may be stopped, and all the world may become guilty before God** [Paul has put the closing remark on his case proving mankind's total sinful depravity. The final verdict – the whole world is guilty before God]: **20** Therefore **by the deeds [works] of the law there shall no flesh be justified in his sight** [even if someone could keep the law it could not save anyone]: **for by the law is the knowledge of sin** [Paul just stated the purpose of the law. The legitimate use of the law today in this age of grace is to show a person their sin and need for a Saviour. God cannot ignore sin. Every sin will be paid for, either by the sinner or by Christ.].

21 ¶ But now the righteousness of God **without the law** is manifested [now Christ has revealed to mankind through Paul how God can be righteous in declaring a sinner just apart from the law], being witnessed by the law and the prophets [the law verified that Christ's blood legally paid the price for our sin as the law demanded (Lev. 5:6) and the prophets predicted (Isa. 53:11)]; **22 Even the righteousness of God** [Adam was created sinless but disobeyed and sinned. Christ was born of a virgin and did not inherit the sin nature. Having perfect faith was still difficult. He was tempted by Satan but overcame in the wilderness. In the garden of Gethsemane, the temptation not to go to the cross was very strong Jesus prayed: "Saying, Father, if thou be willing, remove this cup from me: nevertheless not my will, but thine, be done . . . being in an agony he prayed more earnestly: and his sweat was as it were great drops of blood falling down to the ground" (Luke 22:42-44). But unlike Adam the faith of Jesus was perfect. He yielded His will and trusted the Father's plan of redemption and obeyed. "And being found in fashion as a man, he humbled himself, and became obedient unto death, even the death of the cross" (Phil. 2:8)] which is **by faith of Jesus Christ <u>unto all</u> and <u>upon all</u> them that believe** [It took Jesus Christ's faith to manifest God's righteousness to man. <u>Paul just gave everyone the solution to our sin problem – faith in what Christ has done by His faith.</u> We are "justified by the faith of Christ" (Gal. 2:16). It is by the faith "of" Jesus Christ (Phil. 3:9). The modern Bibles replace "of" with "in" putting the emphasis on the believer instead of on Christ. God's righteousness is offered "unto all and upon all" but only bestowed on them that believe. So how do we get the righteousness of God? By believing in Jesus! Christ "gave himself a ransom for all" (1 Tim. 2:6) and "he tasted death for every man" (Heb. 2:9). **<u>God substituted Himself and died in every man's place!</u>** (2 Cor. 5:21). God's will is "to save them that believe" (1 Cor. 1:21). He is the "Saviour of all men, specially of those that believe" (1 Tim. 4:10). Notice that today during Christ's ministry to us from heaven through Paul salvation does not require going through Israel. Is this the same gospel mankind had to believe during Christ's earthly ministry? No! Our gospel is not in John 3:16-18, 20:31; nor Matt. 16:15, 16 because if you read those verses you see that it is talking about believing that Jesus is the name of Israel's Messiah the Son of God. Notice how the disciples did not understand about His death, burial, and resurrection for our sins in Luke 18:31-34. But what about Peter after Jesus rose what did he preach in Acts 2:22, 23, 36? Did Peter preach the good news of Christ death as payment for our sins and resurrection for our justification? No! He preached the cross as bad news, and repent and be baptized just like John the Baptist and Jesus had done. **The gospel of our salvation is not revealed until Paul** (Acts 9). Whenever Paul says "but now" it usually signals that God has changed His dealings with men, Eph. 2:11-16 is a good example of another "but now."]: for there is **<u>no difference</u>** [there is <u>no difference</u> in salvation]: **23 For all have sinned, and come short of the glory of God** [There is <u>no difference</u> in sin. Paul reminds us why we need a Saviour.]; **24 Being justified freely** by his **grace** through the **redemption that is in Christ Jesus [God graciously provided His Son and His Son's righteousness]: 25** Whom God hath set forth to be a

propitiation [perfectly satisfying sacrifice] **through faith in his blood** [Christ's perfect blood paid for all sins of all time. In the past the blood of animals atoned (covered) for sins but never took sins away, never paid for them completely (Heb. 9:15, 22, 10:1-4; Lev. 17:11).], **to declare his righteousness for the remission of sins that are past** [Forgiveness for all the sins of those in paradise or "Abraham's Bosom" (Luke 16:22). Christ went to paradise after paying for all sins and declared His payment and righteousness to them. Remember Jesus Christ told the thief on the cross that He would be with him in paradise that day Luke 23:43? God had passed over those sins in anticipation of the cross. They could not come into His presence without Christ's payment or righteousness because they would have incurred His wrath. His righteousness having been imputed He has taken those saints to heaven (2 Cor. 12:4)], through the **forbearance** of God [God's patient self-restraint and withholding of His wrath knowing that Christ would pay for their sins]; **26** To **declare**, I say [Paul], **at this time** his righteousness [We can have His righteousness imparted to us by faith at this present time (the dispensation of grace).]: that **he** [the Father] might be **just** and the **justifier** of him which **believeth in Jesus** [God can remain just and justify us when we agree with God to trust His sacrifice (provision) for our sin having imputed to our account the righteousness of Christ. Salvation is by faith ALONE in what He did. He paid our sin debt and rose. Many people who think they are saved may not be saved if they add anything of their own work to what Christ has done, which is an insult to God! If they think they also played a part in their salvation by saying a prayer, confessing their sin, asking forgiveness, being water baptized, walking the isle, dedicating their lives, or any other work on their part they have insulted God! It is critical to know precisely how to be justified by God. So you can be sure you are saved and can accurately help others to be saved**.**]. **27** Where is **boasting** then? It is excluded. By what law? of works? Nay: but by the **law of faith** [The "law of faith" does not look to ourselves, but to what Christ had done to save us. He gets all the glory and we have nothing to boast about.]. **28** Therefore we conclude that a man is **justified by faith without the deeds** [works] **of the law** [we are declared righteous or justified apart from doing any deeds or works of the law of any kind. **Salvation is a free gift** (Eph. 2:8, 9). Man's pride is our biggest problem so God set things up so that "no flesh should glory in his presence" (1 Cor. 1:18, 29; Jer. 9:23, 24). Any worthwhile thing that we think or do is because "Christ liveth in me" (Gal. 2:20) so boasting is excluded. The only thing we can glory in is "the cross of our Lord Jesus Christ" (Gal. 6:14). People in Israel's program are saved by faith but they are required to do works that are motivated by their faith (Matt. 7:21, 19:16-21; Mark 16:16; James 2:14-26) God hates works that are <u>not</u> motivated by faith (Amos 5:21-26; Isa. 1:10-14; Psa. 51:17-19). **All the confusion about how to be saved today comes from mixing Israel's program (which required works) with ours (which**

prohibit works for salvation).]. 29 Is he the God of the **Jews** only? is he not also of the **Gentiles**? Yes, of the Gentiles also [**In time past** Gentiles were "without Christ, . . . having no hope, and without God in the world (Eph. 2:11-14. But **now**, Israel has been concluded in unbelief like the Gentiles, so God can offer mercy to all equally (11:32). In the future, God will still keep His special promises to Israel of ruling together with their King in His Kingdom on earth forever. But God has temporarily interrupted Israel's program (11:11-15, 25-30) ever since they **fell** in Acts 7:51-53 when the nation rejected the renewed offer of the King and His kingdom by stoning the Holy Ghost filled Stephen. God has begun a new program revealed through the apostle Paul (Eph. 3:1-6) so that He can call out a special people (the body of Christ) to rule with Him in the heavenly places]: **30** Seeing it is one God, which shall justify the **circumcision by faith**, and **uncircumcision through faith** [Paul reveals that both groups of people (Israel and Gentiles) are justified by faith. Gentiles are the uncircumcision. Since Israel has fallen to our level they are also considered Gentiles today. Gentiles are saved by believing Christ's sacrifice and doing nothing (3:28; Rom. 4:5). Gal. 2:7 shows that the gospel of the uncircumcision was committed and limited to the apostle Paul. While the gospel of the circumcision was committed to Peter. Do you see the difference between the two gospels in Gal. 2:7-9? Peter and His group died out because of Israel's unbelief demonstrated in Acts 7. Today there is only one gospel that saves and that is Paul's. In the body of Christ circumcision is unimportant: "For in Jesus Christ neither circumcision availeth any thing, nor uncircumcision; but faith which worketh by love" (Gal. 5:6]. **31** Do we then make **void** [empty, meaningless] the law through faith? God forbid [No! the purpose of the law is to prove guilt so that people will seek forgiveness for their sins through a blood sacrifice, not to give eternal life]: yea, we **establish the law** [Faith in God's ultimate sacrifice establishes the law, not void it.] "I do not frustrate the grace of God: for if righteousness come by the law, then Christ is dead in vain" (Gal. 2:21). Faith comes "by hearing, and hearing by the word of God" (10:17)]. "Is the law then against the promises of God? God forbid: for if there had been a law given which could have given life, verily righteousness should have been by the law. But **the scripture hath concluded all under sin, that the promise by faith of Jesus Christ might be given to them that believe.** But before faith came, we were kept under the law, shut up unto the faith which should afterwards be revealed. Wherefore the **law was our schoolmaster to bring us unto Christ**, that we might be **justified by faith**. But after that faith is come, we are no longer under a schoolmaster. **For ye are all the children of God by faith in Christ Jesus"** (Gal. 3:21-26). When we trust Christ and receive His righteousness it is as if we kept the law perfectly. Salvation is 100% what God has done, and 0% what man has done!

Romans Chapter 4 – Imputation – The Case of Abraham
How to be totally forgiven and free of the fear of death.
Blessings of Abraham, not Israel. A series of contrasts
4:1-8 Faith, not works – When did David know he would not have his sin imputed to him? 2 Sam. 12:9, 13. Faith is not a work (4:5).
4:9-12 Grace, not law
4:13-17 Life, not death
4:18-25 Justification by imputed righteousness of Christ – born of a virgin (no inherited sin nature), lived a perfect life, no blemish or sin (2 Cor. 5:21; 1 Peter 1:18, 19, 2:22; Heb. 4:15), because He had not sinned death could not hold Him (Rom. 6:23; Psalm 16:10). We are saved by faith in what Christ has done. **The most important verse in the Bible is <u>Gen. 15:6</u>.**

The double justification of Abraham. He was justified before circumcision (Gen. 15:6, Rom. 4:3), and after circumcision (Gen. 22:12-18; James 2:21-24). Gen.12:3 "a nation" Gen. 17:4, 5 "many nations" (believers). Seed as the "stars" and "sand" (Gen. 22:17). Seed which is Christ (Gal. 3:16). Christ's imputed righteousness (4:23-25) 2 Cor. 5:21; Philemon 18; Phil. 3:9.

Transaction of imputation.
When we believe the gospel (1 Cor. 15:1-4), we receive His righteousness. "For he [the Father] hath made him [Christ] to be <u>sin for us</u>, <u>who knew no sin [He was perfect]</u>; that <u>we might be made the righteousness of God in him</u> (2 Cor. 5:21).

There is no salvation outside Christ and Abraham because he is the "father of all them that believe" (4:11) and Jesus is his "**the SEED**" that we need to believe. "Now to Abraham and his seed were the promises made. He saith not, And to seeds, as of many; but as of one, And to thy seed, which is Christ" (**Gal. 3:16**). IN chapter 4 the word "promise" is mentioned four times and was that Abraham would be "heir of the world" (4:13, 14) "the father of all them that believe" (4:11) "the father of us all" (4:16) in both heaven and earth (Gen. 22:17). The "promise of God" (4:20) is a seed-line and eternal life with God.

The result is peace with God "through our Lord Jesus Christ" (Rom. 5:1). This is not true for the nation of Israel today, but the individual Jew. This is why we have to rightly divide. Heb. 8:6-12 they are not righteous until His second coming (Acts 3:19; 1 Peter 1:13). Abraham had hope. Hope is confident expectation.
Without the righteousness of Christ, we cannot come before the holy Father.
But because we have His righteousness by faith in what He has done alone and not by anything we have done God can declare us righteous. We cannot look to God

and say "wait a minute, I know you died and rose again for my sin, but let me just say a prayer, or get wet so I can have a part in what You did" because that is an insult to God. **We cannot add one molecule of our own works to what Christ has done for us or we cancel our salvation.** Christ's perfect blood was sufficient payment for our sin. By His grace, God imparts His righteousness to the believer, God does not have to do it, it is a gift which results in justification. Once we have Christ's imputed righteousness God sees Christ in us and us in Christ, we are perfect and "complete in him" (Col. 2:10). Now we have been made perfect in God's sight and nothing can ever change that. Salvation is 100 % what God has done, and 0% what we have done. As completely forgiven, we can trust God and loose our fear of death. The <u>scarlet thread of the redeeming blood is a continual theme throughout the Bible which culminated in the perfectly satisfying sacrifice of God the Son upon the cross</u> (Romans 3:24-26; 1 Peter 1:18-19).

Romans 4:1 What shall we say then that Abraham our father, as pertaining to the flesh, hath found [How was Abraham justified]? **2** For if Abraham were justified by works, he hath whereof to glory; but not before God [if Abraham had earned His own salvation then he could boast, but no man can boast before God]. **3** For what saith the scripture? Abraham **believed God**, and it was counted unto him for righteousness [Gen. 15:6, because of his faith God made him righteous]. **4** Now to him that worketh is the reward not reckoned of grace, but of debt [if someone earns his salvation by working for it God owes it to him and it is not a free gift]. **5** But to him that **worketh not**, but believeth on him that justifieth the ungodly, **his faith is counted for righteousness** [the person who simply trusts what God has told him and believes God, his faith is counted for righteousness in God's sight but anyone who adds their own work to what Christ has done insults God.]. **6** Even as David also describeth the blessedness of the man, unto whom God imputeth righteousness without works [Psa. 32:1, 2], **7** Saying, Blessed are they whose iniquities are forgiven, and whose sins are covered. **8** Blessed is the man to whom the Lord will not impute sin [When did David know that he would not have his sins imputed to him? 2 Sam. 12:9,13]. **9** Cometh this blessedness then upon the circumcision only, or upon the uncircumcision also? [Gal. 3:6. Does God impute righteousness only to the Jews?] for we say that faith was reckoned to Abraham for righteousness. **10** How was it then reckoned? when he was in circumcision, or in uncircumcision? Not in circumcision, but in uncircumcision [God did not reckon Abraham as righteous when he obeyed God and left Ur because that would have been a work that made him righteous, but God waited to pronounce Abraham righteous after he believed that God would give him descendants before he was circumcised.]. **11** And he received the sign of circumcision, a seal of the righteousness of the faith which he had yet being uncircumcised: that he might be the father of **all** them that **believe**, though they be not circumcised; that righteousness might be imputed unto them also [In His foreknowledge, God made provision for us in the body of Christ]: **12** And the father of circumcision to them who are not of the circumcision only, but who also walk in the steps of that faith of our father Abraham, which he had being yet uncircumcised. **13** For the promise, that he should be the **heir of the world** [everyone is saved in faithful Abraham], was not to Abraham, or to his seed, through the law, but through the righteousness of faith [Everyone must have faith to be saved, Heb. 11:6]. **14** For if they which are of the law be heirs, faith is made void, and the promise made of **none effect** [if keeping the law can save someone then faith in God to save would not be necessary. Similarly, if we add our own doings to what Christ has done, such as believing that a saying a prayer or being water baptized contributed to our salvation we void our salvation or make it of none effect]: **15** Because the law worketh wrath: for where no law is, there is no transgression [the purpose of the law is to condemn and to show our sin and need for a Redeemer].

16 Therefore it [imputed righteousness, v.11] is of faith, that it might be **by grace** [salvation is by faith, that God may impart the gift of his righteousness]; to the end the promise might be sure to all the seed [all believers]; not to that only which is of the law [the written law was given to the Jews], but to that also which is of the faith of Abraham; who is the **father of us all**, **17** (As it is written, I have made thee **a father of many nations**,) before him whom he believed, even God, who quickeneth the dead, and calleth those things which be not as though they were [In His foreknowledge God knew both earthly and heavenly people would believe]. **18** Who against hope believed in hope [hope of the promised seed (child)], that he might become the father of many nations; according to that which was spoken, So shall thy seed be [God would make his nation the seed-line to His Son]. **19** And being not weak in faith, he considered not his own body now dead, when he was about an hundred years old, neither yet the deadness of Sara's womb [God waited till he was too old to have children and had proved that his wife Sarah was barren before miraculously giving them a child by making them reproductively alive]: **20** He staggered not at the promise of God through unbelief; but **was strong in faith**, giving glory to God; **21** And being **fully persuaded** that, what he had promised, he was able also to perform [Abraham had faith that God could and would do what He said]. **22** And therefore it was imputed to him for righteousness [the righteousness of God was imputed to Abraham]. **23** Now it was **not written for his sake alone**, that it was imputed to him; **24 But for us also, to whom it shall be imputed**, if **we believe on him that raised up Jesus our Lord from the dead** [God said that His righteousness was imputed to Abraham in Gen 15:6 so that all believers would know that they would receive God's righteousness if they believed Him.]; **25** Who was **delivered for our offences, and was raised again for our justification. [**We need to believe that God delivered Christ to die for our offences and raised Him for our justification. When a person believes this they receive Christ's imputed righteousness and can stand before holy God.**]**

Romans Chapter 5 – Result of Justification
5:1-5 Result of justification.
5:6-11 God's immense love for us.
5:12-21 Justification compared with condemnation.
<u>Sin</u> = sin nature, while <u>sins</u> are the results of having the sin nature.

In chapter 5 we learn that **Christ died for us**, GOD DIED IN OUR PLACE, and then HE gave us His righteousness. **We gained so much more in Jesus Christ than we lost in Adam**. Because of Adam's sin, sin and death passed to all men. Adam was innocent before he fell into sin but he did not have God's imputed righteousness. Adam was not justified. Adam did finally receive this righteousness by faith in God as evidenced when he called Eve the mother of all living. Then after Christ paid for his sin on the cross His righteousness was applied to Adam.

Justification is the judicial act of God by which He justly declares and treats as righteous the one **who believes in Jesus Christ** resulting in **peace with God**.

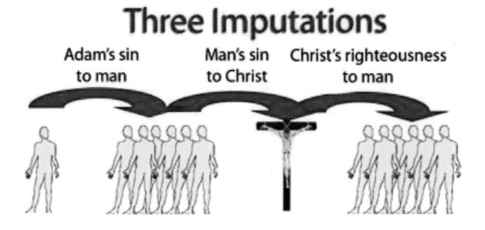

Three Imputations

Adam's sin to man   Man's sin to Christ   Christ's righteousness to man

Romans 5:1 Therefore being **justified by faith** [having Christ's imputed righteousness by faith], **we have peace with God through our Lord Jesus Christ**: **2** By whom also we have **access** by faith into this grace wherein we **stand** [our position or standing in Christ], and rejoice in **hope** of the glory of God [rejoice in our hope to be with God eternally]. **3** And not only so, but we glory in **tribulations** also [external and internal tribulations - circumstances, bad decisions, the enemy, stress and fears give us a chance to live by faith]: knowing that tribulation worketh patience; **4** And **patience, experience** [skill in living and control over our sinful bodies 1 Cor. 9:27, let Christ live through us Gal. 2:20 which gives God the glory because it was Him in us, not us, 2 Cor. 4:7 <u>God leaves us in the flesh so that He can perform a work in us Phil 1:6 and conform us to Christ</u>, and we do not think we are something when we are not]; and experience,

hope [confident expectation awaiting our glorified bodies]: **5** And hope maketh not ashamed; because the love of God is shed abroad in our hearts by the **Holy Ghost** which is given unto us. [we have received the Holy Ghost, who teaches us about God's love through His word 1 Cor. 2:9-13] **6** For when we were yet without strength [when we were helpless and could do nothing to save ourselves], **in due time Christ died for the ungodly** [at the right time God died for the ungodly (us)]. **7** For scarcely for a righteous man will one die: yet peradventure for a good man [a great leader] some would even dare to die. **8** But God commendeth [approved] his love toward us, in that, **while we were yet sinners** [when there was nothing good in us], **Christ died for us [HE TOOK OUR PLACE! Paul, as a prosecuting attorney, tells us that the Judge died for the accused! What a love story! God substituted Himself in our place and then He gave us His righteousness! What love! Greater love has no man! What a great and loving God He is! Thank You, LORD!].** **9** Much more then, being now **justified by his blood** [the price of redemption cost God enormously], we shall be **saved from wrath** through him [Christ saved us from the Second death and the Tribulation 1 Thess. 1:10]. **10** For if, when we were **enemies** [no one but God dies for His enemies], we were **reconciled to God by the death of his Son** [8:32, spared not His own Son], much more, being reconciled, we shall be **saved by his life** [His life in us saves us as we live now]. **11** And not only so, but we also **joy** in God through our Lord Jesus Christ, by whom we have **now** received the **atonement** [we have been reconciled to God now, while Israel receives their atonement at His return to earth].

12 ¶ Wherefore, as by one man sin entered into the world, and death by sin; and so death passed upon all men [**all inherited the sin nature**], for that all have sinned: [We have much more in Christ, than what we lost in Adam. Both men were born without the sin nature. The word "one" occurs "eleven times" in this chapter. Adam is the federal head of lost mankind, while Christ is the federal head of saved mankind. When God looks out over mankind He sees us in one or the other of these two men. We are either spiritually dead or spiritually alive. The next section is parenthetical] **13** (For until the law sin was in the world: but sin is **not** imputed when there is no law. **14** Nevertheless **death reigned from Adam to Moses** [people died because the "wages of sin is death"] even over them that had not sinned after the similitude of **Adam's transgression** [did not have a direct command from God not to sin and the ability to choose], who is the figure of him that was to come [the last Adam, Christ 1 Cor. 15:45]. **15** But not as the offence [Adam choosing to sin], so also is the free gift [imputed righteousness of Christ]. For if through the offence of one many be dead, much more the grace of God, and the gift by grace, which is by one man, Jesus Christ, hath **abounded** unto many. **16**

And not as it was by one that sinned, so is the gift: for the judgment was by one to **condemnation** [condemned to eternal spiritual death (separation from God)], but the **free gift** is of many offences unto **justification** [declared righteous by God]. **17** For if by one man's offence death reigned by one; much more they which receive abundance of grace and of the **gift of righteousness** shall reign in life by one, **Jesus Christ** ["abundance of grace" more than Adam's death, in Christ is eternal life now, and greater than Adam's death].) **18** Therefore as by the offence of one judgment came upon all men to condemnation; even so by the righteousness of one the free gift came upon all men unto justification of life. [Paul continues to compare Adam and the Lord Jesus Christ] **19** For as by one man's disobedience many were **made sinners**, so by the obedience of one shall many be **made righteous** [those who believe]. **20** Moreover the **law entered**, that the offence might abound ["by the law is the knowledge of sin" 3:20]. But where sin abounded, grace did **much more abound**: [Christ's righteousness "abounds" does not only cancel out Adams sin but is stronger than it] **21** That as sin hath reigned unto **death**, even so might grace reign through righteousness unto **eternal life by Jesus Christ our Lord** [Rom. 6:23].

Comparing and contrasting Adam with ……… Christ (5:15-21):
sin ….. righteousness
death …. life
offence ….. free gift
transgression …. abounding grace
condemnation ….. justification
death reigned …… reign in life by Jesus
inherited sin nature …. gift of righteousness
judgement on all men …….. all men unto justification
disobedience many made sinners ……. obedience many made righteous
then the law entered . . .
that offences might abound to sin …. but grace abounded much more
sin reigned to death. But ... grace reigned unto eternal life by Jesus Christ our Lord.

Adam chose to sin by eating of the tree of the knowledge of good and evil. Christ chose not to sin. The question is: are you in Adam? Or are you in Christ? **All Adam's descendants inherited his sinful nature and are under judgment and are condemned.** Christ was "obedient unto death, even the death of the cross" (Phil. 2:8; Mat. 26:39, 42). He freely offers His righteousness and eternal life to any and all men who believe. If you are **in Adam**, you are under [subject to] **sin and condemnation**. If you are **in Christ**, you have **His righteousness and eternal life.** **"For as in Adam all die, even so in Christ shall all be made alive."** (1 Cor. 15:21, 22, 45-49).

Romans Chapter 6 – Our new position in Christ

6:1-13 Our <u>identity</u> in Christ (baptized into His death, **dead to sin,** newness of life)
6:14-23 Free from sin, servants of righteousness and gift of eternal life.

To sanctify means simply "to set apart." Sanctification is two-fold: It is our "<u>position or standing</u>" in Christ **and** our "<u>practice or state</u>" with His life in us. In 5:12-21 we learned that we were taken out of Adam and put into Christ. We have a secure position in Christ. In chapters 6-8 we learn **how we can now live above sin**.

Our "state" is the process of learning who we are in Christ, our growth as we gain maturity in our practical "walk." Our day-by-day and moment-by-moment victory over sin as we <u>know</u> who we are in Christ, <u>reckon</u> that what God says "to us" and "about us" is true, and <u>yield</u> ourselves to God. We constantly have an opportunity to choose to make the right decision to grow in godliness, by the "renewing of our minds" (Rom. 12:1) as we "live by faith" (Rom. 1:17) in what God has told us in the Bible. As we spend time in God's word <u>we learn to know, reckon, and yield</u>.

In Romans 5 Paul explained that we have so much more "in Christ" than we had being "in Adam." Paul writes that "where sin abounded, grace did much more abound" (Rom. 5:20). Paul now asks an absurd question that he had been asked before (Rom. 3:8) "shall we continue in sin that grace may abound?" (6:1). He answers: "God forbid. How shall we, that **are dead to sin**, live any longer therein?" We are dead to sin, and its power so we do not need to sin anymore.

Romans 3-5	Romans 6 and 7
1. Christ died for us	1. We died with Christ
2. Substitution	2. Identification
3. Christ died for our sins	3. Christ died unto sin
4. He paid sins' penalty	4. He broke sin's power
5. Justification	5. Sanctification
6. Righteousness imputed	6. Righteousness imparted

In Romans 6 we learn that not only did Christ die for our sins, but we died with Him. Satan wants to keep this truth from us. When we were "baptized into Jesus" (6:3) we were buried with Him and raised in newness of life. This is how we are "in Christ." So Satan tries to add water to this baptism to make it fleshly and take away the powerful truth of the crucifixion of our old sin nature and our new life in Christ. <u>The only solution for our sinful flesh, our old Adam, is crucifixion. Adding water ruins this truth.</u>

Romans 6 "dead to sin." Romans 7 "dead to the law." Romans 8 "walk not after the flesh, but after the Spirit." In chapter 6, the problem is how to avoid doing bad (evil) when we have sinful natures. In Romans 7, the problem is - how can we do good when we have sinful natures.

Baptized means placed into, identified with (Rom. 6:3; 1 Cor. 10:2, 12:13; Gal. 3:27). We cannot tell that we were baptized into Christ but we know this happened by reading God's word. We have a total union - his death, life, and future glory. The old self is crucified and Christ now lives in us (Gal. 2:20). We have put off our "old man" and have put on the "new man" (Col. 3:9, 10). To live in sin is now contrary to who we are in Christ, our identity. Baptism is not a symbol for anything but a real operation of God (Col. 2:12). We walk in "newness of life" having Christ's life in us. Our baptism is spiritual (Eph. 4:5) and water baptism is not part of Paul's gospel (1 Cor. 1:17). We were baptized "into one body" (1 Cor. 12:13).

Paul uses the word "know" or "knowing" 5 times (6:3, 6:6, 6:9, 6:16, and 7:1) in this section. Paul asks another question. "Shall we live in sin, because we are not under the law but under grace?" (6:15). Again the answer is "God forbid."

What fruits had ye when you were servants of sin of which you are now ashamed? (Rom. 6:21). We are ashamed of some of the things we used to do (Gal. 5:19-21). But, Paul says that we should move forward now because we are no longer who we used to be, "forgetting those things which are behind, and reaching forth unto those things which are before" (Phil. 3:13). Now we should have "fruit unto holiness" (Rom. 6:22; Gal. 5:22-26).

Christ not only died "for our sins" (paid the penalty), but "unto our sins" (6:10). Christ broke the power of sin and destroyed the old sin nature (6:6). The old sin nature is still present in our bodies (7:18), as we know, but it has been robbed of its power by His cross. We no longer have to let the old nature have power over us.

Paul gives the example of a master and a servant. No one can serve two masters. **We now have a new master that we serve and a new nature**. The unsaved person is a slave to sin (Eph. 2:1-3) and could do nothing but sin. Now we can serve righteousness instead of sin. <u>Since the power of sin is broken, people who sin after being saved do so deliberately.</u> They yield to the old sin nature instead of the Holy Spirit. They live beneath their exalted position is Christ. They continue to live as slaves instead of joint-heirs.

God did not force us to believe the gospel. Similarly, after we are saved, God does not force us to live by faith. We can let "sin reign in our mortal bodies"

(6:11), or we can believe God that we are "dead to sin" (6:2). It takes Christ living through us to serve God right. We cannot do it in ourselves. We walk by faith (2 Cor. 5:7) in who God says we were and are in His word. When we "let the word of Christ dwell in you richly in all wisdom" (Col. 3:16), God's Spirit helps us to have the "mind of Christ" (1 Cor. 2:16). **We automatically do what pleases and delights God when we have Christ's mind.**

It is not enough to know that Christ died for us, we must know that we died with Him. It is not enough to know that we have new natures within, we must know that our old natures were dealt with on the cross.

The formula: "know-reckon-yield" are not "emergency measures" but something we must do continually. As we spend time in the word of God rightly divided we will <u>know</u> our position and walk in Christ. By faith <u>reckon</u> ourselves dead to sin and <u>yield</u> ourselves to the indwelling Spirit, obtaining victory. **The answer to the problem of our sin nature is not rules, regulations, self-discipline, or anything else that we do, but crucifixion and newness of life in Christ as we walk by faith in what God tells us in His word. Now we obey and live right, not because we have to, but because as sons of God, we want to.** The Law says do and be blessed, but grace says you are blessed now so do. Grace and law do not mix. <u>**When we allow the love of Christ to live through us, then He receives all the glory. When He is manifested to the world through us believers others want what we have – which is Him in us**</u>. We are to KNOW what God says about us is true, RECKON that we are dead in Christ, and YIELD ourselves to righteousness and allow Christ to live through us.

Romans 6:1 What shall we say then? Shall we **continue in sin**, that **grace** may abound? **2** God forbid [May it not be]. How shall we, that **ARE dead to sin**, live any longer therein? [sin has no power over a dead man]. **3** Know ye not, that so many of us as were **baptized into Jesus Christ** were baptized **into his death** [identified with His death]? **4** Therefore we are **buried with him** by baptism into death: that like as Christ was raised up from the dead by the glory of the Father, even so we also should **walk in newness of life [His life in us]. 5** For if we have been **planted together** in the likeness of his **death**, we shall be also in the likeness of his resurrection [raised to live in our new identity in Christ]: **6 Knowing** this, that **our old man is crucified with him** [Gal. 2:20], **that the body of sin** might be **destroyed** [Christ broke the power of sin], that henceforth we should not serve sin. **7** For he that is dead is **freed from sin [a corps does not sin]. 8** Now if we be **dead with Christ**, we believe that we shall also **live with him** [our eternal life began at salvation]: **9** Knowing that Christ being raised from the dead dieth no more; death hath no more dominion over him. **10** For in that he died, he died **unto sin ONCE** [once is all that it took for Jesus Christ to finish paying for our sin on the cross]: but in that he liveth, he liveth unto God [Christ lives unto God and so shall we]. **11 Likewise reckon ye also yourselves to be dead indeed unto sin, but alive unto God through Jesus Christ our Lord. 12** Let not sin **therefore reign** in your **mortal body**, that ye should obey it in the **lusts** thereof. **13** Neither **yield** ye your **members [hands, feet, voice, skills, talents]** as instruments of unrighteousness **unto sin**: but **yield** yourselves **unto God**, as those that are **alive from the dead**, and your **members as instruments of righteousness unto God [chose to do right]**.

14 For **sin shall not have dominion** over you: for **ye are not under the law, but under grace. 15** What then? **shall we sin, because we are not under the law,** but under grace? God forbid. **16** Know ye not, that **to whom ye yield yourselves servants to obey, his servants ye are** to whom ye obey; whether of **sin unto death, or of obedience unto righteousness? 17** But God be thanked, that ye **were the servants of sin, but ye have obeyed from the heart that form of doctrine which was delivered you [the sound doctrine given to us through Paul]. 18 Being then made free from sin, ye became the servants of righteousness. 19** I speak after the **manner of men because of the infirmity of your flesh**: for as ye have yielded your members servants to uncleanness and to iniquity unto iniquity; even so now yield your **members servants to righteousness unto holiness. 20** For when ye were the **servants of sin**, ye were **free from righteousness. 21 What fruit had ye** then in those things whereof ye are **now ashamed**? [We are now ashamed of those things we did 1 Cor. 6:9-11; Gal. 5:19-21] for **the end of those things is death. 22 But now being made free from** sin [because Christ destroyed the power of sin, it no longer has power over us], **and become servants to God, ye have your fruit unto holiness** [fruit that is acceptable to God and will stand the test of fire at the judgment seat of Christ 1 Cor. 3:12-15], **and the end everlasting life. 23 For the wages of sin is death; but the gift of God is eternal life through Jesus Christ our Lord**.

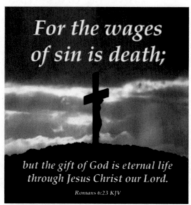

For the wages of sin is death;

but the gift of God is eternal life through Jesus Christ our Lord.

Romans 6:23 KJV

Romans Chapter 7 – Our new problem in the flesh

7:1-6 dead to the law
7:7-14 the law condemns
7:15-25 the sin nature is still in our flesh, so in it we can do nothing good

In Romans 4, Paul used Abraham and David as examples, in Romans 7, **Paul uses himself as an example of how not to serve God after we are saved.** Paul is our "pattern" (1 Tim. 1:16). Notice how many times in chapter 7 Paul uses the pronoun "I" (31 times). **Paul also mentions sets of twos: two husbands, two natures, and two laws** (in Ch. 8). Ch. 7 is vital for understanding our problem in the flesh while Ch. 8 helps us to live above sin. Ch. 8 will reconfirm and elaborate on the truths of Ch. 6, how to be servants to God and have righteous fruit unto holiness, making Ch. 8 the most important chapter in the Bible for the believer.

Many Christians wonder why Paul moves from the victory in Chaper 6 to the defeat in chapter 7 instead of the blessings of chapter 8. But Paul, under the inspiration of the Holy Spirit, knows that there is something vital that the believer needs to know first in our desire to live "unto God."

Paul answered the question "Shall we continue in sin that grace may abound?" The answer is that we shall not continue in sin because we are "**dead to sin**" (6:2). The only cure for sin is crucifixion. We have to know-reckon-yield to this truth. At the end of chapter 6, Paul answers another question. "Shall we sin because we are not under the law but under grace?" (6:15). The answer is that we shall not continue in sin but yield ourselves to be servants of righteousness unto holiness.

Then in chapter 7 Paul explains that we have another problem - **we are not able to produce "good works" in the flesh**. **We are dead to sin, but sin still lives in our flesh**. If we go back to living under the law, we actually make the sin nature worse because the law magnifies sin in us. But now that we are "in Christ" we are dead to the law because we are "married" (or joined) to Him. Christ triumphed over sin on the cross and "condemned sin in the flesh" (Rom. 8:3). The solution is not to go back to the law, but to walk in the Spirit. We must realize that we are "**dead to the law**" (7:4). Now that we are saved by faith, we should not think that we can control the flesh by trying to follow a performance-based-acceptance-system (PBA or religious rules). We were saved by faith, and must live the same way, by faith.

Paul had found out that after salvation both the Galatians and the Corinthians tried to become perfect in the flesh by keeping rules and regulations, the law. These people noticed that they were still sinning after salvation and didn't know how to have victory through grace so they were deceived into trying to be "made perfect by the flesh" (Gal. 3:3) as a result they began following "another Jesus, whom we have not preached" (Christ's earthly ministry) "another spirit, which ye have not received" (legalism, not grace) or "another gospel, which ye have not accepted" (the gospel of the kingdom on earth, not grace - see 2 Cor. 11:4).

These two groups of believers had been beguiled or tricked by **false ministers that teach false doctrine** (either Christ's earthly ministry, or a mixture of Christ's earthly ministry and His heavenly ministry through Paul. We must remember that law and grace do not mix, they must be divided by applying 2 Tim. 2:15). The letters to the Corinthians and Galatians were written before Paul wrote Romans so Paul wanted to address this issue and show how he had been able to secure victory over the flesh so that the believers in Rome could do the same without going back to the law. The law had brought them to Christ by showing them their need for the Saviour, but once they are saved the law is not necessary because "the law is not made for a righteous man" (1 Tim. 1:9). "For sin shall not have dominion over you: for ye are not under law [its power], but under grace" (6:14).

Two Husbands
Paul uses the marriage analogy. Marriage is a contract for life which can only be broken when death do us part. We are dead to our **old husband, the law** when we identified with Christ and were baptized into Him at our salvation. "For I through the law am dead to the law, that I might live unto God" (Gal. 2:19). So now we can be **married to Christ** (or joined to Him) as a member of the body of Christ (Christ being the Head). Christ's body is married or joined to Himself. In marriage, two become one, and His identity is now ours. Our "life is hid with Christ in God" (Col. 3:3). So now when God looks at us, He does not see us, but Christ. We are "accepted in the beloved" (Eph. 1:6). *Note that Paul never calls us the "Bride of Christ," that is Israel who will dwell in the New Jerusalem (Rev. 21:2, 9, 10).

Two Natures
Notice in verse 5 how the flesh, sin, and law bring on "the motions of sins" to produce "fruit unto death," and NOT unto God! We cannot serve God in our flesh, we must serve Him in the Spirit. The law is holy, just, and good (7:12) but we still have the sin nature. The law only magnifies sin making it "exceedingly sinful" (7:13). In our "flesh, dwelleth no good thing: for to will is present with me; but how to perform that which is good I find not. For the good that I would I do not: but the evil which I would not <u>that I do</u>" (7:17, 18). Paul found that even after salvation, the sin nature was still in his body (Rom. 7:22, 23). **<u>There is a war inside the believer between our two natures</u>**. The sin nature (or flesh) cannot keep the law, and the new nature does not need the law because the new nature

wants to do righteousness out of love (2 Cor. 5:14). Therefore, we must die to our flesh daily (1 Cor. 15:31). At the end of chapter 7, Paul demonstrates his feeling of self-condemnation and frustration "O wretched man that I am! Who shall deliver me from the body of sin and death?" All the flesh can do is sin. The law magnifies sin, and the result is self-condemnation and unpleasing fruitless work to God.

So now the question is: **how can I do good works for God?** The answer is that we must allow Christ to do the work through us. Then He receives all the glory because it was He who did the work through us. "For who maketh thee to differ from another? and what hast thou that thou didst not receive? now if thou didst receive it, why dost thou glory, as if thou hadst not received it?" (1 Cor. 4:7).

Therefore, we can pray to God and say: I would like to do this thing, a good work for You, please will You do it through me? Only the work done by Christ working through us is pleasing to God. I am married (joined) to Christ, so I let Him live through me. Therefore, the **most important verse on Christian living** is this one: "I am crucified with Christ: nevertheless I live; yet not I, but **Christ liveth in me**: and the life which I now live in the flesh I live by the faith of the Son of God, who loved me, and gave himself for me" (Gal. 2:20). I could only receive the imputed righteousness of Christ by faith in what He had done because my weak flesh could not keep the law. "I do not frustrate the grace of God: for if righteousness come by the law, then Christ is dead in vain" (Gal. 2:21).

We are to choose to walk in the Spirit every moment of every day. So with Christ's Spirit working in us, we serve the law of God, automatically bearing good fruit. **We must realize that the only good thing in us is Christ.**

Two Laws (unchangeable rules, facts)
"For the **law of the Spirit of life in Christ Jesus** hath made me free from the **law of sin and death**" (Romans 8:2). This verse summarizes chapters 6-8. There is life in Christ (6:23), He is our resource now. Romans 6-8 deal with how believers can and should live for God, our "reasonable service" (Romans 12:1). The victory is not by forcing ourselves to keep the law, but by reckoning that **we died with Christ** and now can allow **Christ to live through us** (Gal. 2:20).

In summary, living in a way that pleases God is our "state" the process of sanctification. As we learn what we have in Christ by what God says in His word and let Him live through us. Today, Christ is manifesting Himself to the world through the believer. We are set apart unto Him. We cannot be saved or sanctified by keeping the law. The law revives our sinful natures. The "law was our schoolmaster to bring us unto Christ, that we might be justified by faith. **But after** that faith is come, we are no longer under a schoolmaster" (Gal. 3:24, 25). **We are dead to the law.** We cannot serve God by self-effort, it must be the Holy Spirit working through us. **We walk by faith in what God tells us in His word.** The flesh is just as vile after salvation, as it was before. The flesh can never be improved but will remain "vile" until we receive our glorified new bodies at the Rapture (Phil. 3:21). <u>**Now we obey the law of the Spirit of life in Christ Jesus**</u>.

There is therefore now no self-condemnation (7:24, 25; 8:1-4) for those who walk not after the flesh, but after the Spirit. **We were saved by faith and must walk the same way.** "And they that are Christ's have **crucified the flesh** with the affections and lusts. If we live in the Spirit, let us also walk in the Spirit" (Gal. 5:24, 25).

Now with Christ in us we can do "good works." "For we are his workmanship, created in Christ Jesus unto good works, which God hath before ordained that we should walk in them" (Eph. 2:10). As we will learn in chapter 8, **His Spirit in us helps us until our work on earth is done.**

Romans 7:1 Know ye not, brethren, (for I speak to them that know **the law** [are familiar with the law],) how that the law hath dominion over a man **as long as he liveth**? **2** For the woman which hath an husband is bound by the law to *her* husband so long as he liveth; but if the husband be dead, she is loosed from the law of *her* husband. **3** So then if, while *her* husband liveth, she be married to another man, she shall be called an adulteress: but if her **husband be dead, she is free from that law**; so that she is no adulteress, though she be married to another man. **4** Wherefore, my brethren, ye also are become **dead to the law** by the body of Christ; that ye should be **married to another**, *even* to him who is raised from the dead, **that we should bring forth fruit unto God [Gal 3:12-14]. 5** For **when we were [past tense] in the flesh, the motions of sins** [evil working in us], which were **by the law**, did work in our members to bring forth fruit **unto death. 6 But now** we are **delivered from the law**, that being dead wherein we were held; that we should **serve in newness of spirit [Christ's righteous nature in us]**, and not *in* the oldness of the **letter [the law]**.

7 ¶ What shall we say then? *Is the law sin*? God forbid. Nay, I had not **known sin, but by the law [Gal. 3:24-28]**: for I had not known **lust**, except the law had said, Thou shalt **not covet. 8** But sin, taking occasion by the commandment [rules, ordinances], **wrought** in me **all manner of concupiscence** [lust for what is forbidden]. For **without the law sin** *was* **dead. 9** For I was **alive without the law once** [he was alive under grace]: but when the commandment came [when he placed himself back under the law, sin came alive again and he died], **sin revived,**

and I died. **10** And the **commandment**, which *was ordained* to **life**, I found *to be* unto **death**. [Life was not in the law]. **11** For **sin**, taking occasion by the commandment, **deceived** me [tricked], and by it **slew** *me*. **12** Wherefore the **law** *is* **holy**, and the **commandment holy**, and just, and good. **13** Was then that which is **good** [the law] **made death** unto me? God forbid. But **sin**, that it might appear sin, working death in me by that which is **good**; that sin by the commandment might become exceeding sinful. **14** For we know that the **law is spiritual**: but **I am carnal** [present tense, flesh in verse 18], sold under sin [tainted by sin]. **15** For that which **I do I allow not: for what I would, that do I not; but what I hate, that do I** [wrong actions and motives]. **16** If then I do that which I would not, I consent unto the law that *it is* good. **17** Now then it is no more I that do it, but **sin that dwelleth in me**. **18** For I know that in me (that is, **in my flesh**,) **dwelleth no good thing**: for **to will is present with me; but** *how* **to perform that which is good I find not. 19 For the good that I would I do not: but the evil which I would not, that I do**. **20** Now if I do that I would not, it is no more I that do it, **but sin that dwelleth in me**. **21** I find then a law, that, **when I would do good, evil is present with me**. **22** For I delight in the **law of God** [the perfect standard of God in the Law given through Moses] after the inward man [our spirit and soul]: **23** But I see another law in my members, **warring** [the war between the flesh and the Spirit in the believer] against the law of my mind [desire to live perfectly unto God], and bringing me into captivity to the law of sin which is in my members [truth that sin dwells in me]. **24** O wretched man that I am! who shall deliver me from the body of this death? [the sin in our flesh is magnified by the law which condemns us] **25 I thank God through Jesus Christ our Lord** [with Christ working in us we can win this war]. So then with the **mind** I myself serve the law of God [our minds desire to serve God perfectly]; but with the **flesh** the law of sin [our flesh only produces sin continually, with wrong motives and deeds so we cannot do what is "good" or pleasing to God].

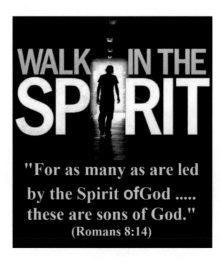

Romans Chapter 8 – Our new power in the Spirit

8:1-39 Life in the Spirit; or Living the Victorious Grace Life

The main emphasis in Romans 8 is NOT salvation, but walking in the Spirit. Walking in the Spirit results in a life and fruit pleasing to God. As we **"walk not after the flesh, but after the Spirit" (8:4).**

To be perfectly honest a few years ago it seemed to me that I did not have any of the fruit of the Spirit in my Christian life, even after 25 years of being His. I could not understand what was wrong. Ashamed and perplexed, I told God about my problem, my lack. "But the fruit of the Spirit is love, joy, peace, longsuffering, gentleness, goodness, faith, Meekness, temperance: against such there is no law" (Gal. 5:22, 23).

I was a mixer, but after I became a Bible believer and a right divider I started having some fruit automatically. I became less legalistic and more gracious, joyful, and loving. What changed? I trusted the word of God and understood it more clearly as I studied it rightly divided. As Christ lives through me I am able to walk in the Spirit by faith much of the time. I began following my "pattern" **Paul as he follows Christ** (1 Cor. 11:1; 1 Tim. 1:16). My family has noticed a real difference. The Holy Spirit is in me, Christ lives in me, and I am beloved of God.

Because of **Christ's Spirit and life in us** we can live on a higher plane above sin and self. "There is therefore now no condemnation to them which are in Christ Jesus, who walk not after the flesh, but after the Spirit. For the law of the Spirit of life in Christ Jesus hath made me free from the law of sin and death" (8:1, 2). We have victory as we walk by faith with Christ's Spirit working in us, we then have His life manifested through us.

The words "Holy Ghost" appear in the King James Bible 90 times and in Paul's writings 14 times. The word **"Spirit"** with a capital "S" appears in the Bible 172 times and **in Paul's writings 80 times.** In the letter to the Romans, it appears 21 times, 19 of those times are in Romans 8. This tells us that Romans 8 has a lot to do with the Spirit. The word "Spirit" does not always refer to the Holy Ghost. Jesus (who was the only Person of the Godhead to put on human flesh) said, "God *is* a Spirit: and they that worship him must worship *him* in spirit and in truth" (John 4:24). The Holy Father is Spirit, the Son is Spirit, and the Holy Ghost is Spirit. When the King James Bible says the Holy Ghost it is referring specifically to the Holy Ghost, but when the Bible says "Spirit" then it could be referring to any one of the three Persons of the Godhead, and the context must help us decide which one. *Please note that all modern Bibles eliminate the name "Holy Ghost" and replace it with the "Holy Spirit" and therefore the distinction between them is lost. In summary, we find that the "Spirit" in Romans 8 is often the Spirit of Jesus Christ in the believer (Rom. 8:2). Therefore, sometimes the Spirit in us is Christ's, sometimes the Holy Ghost's and sometimes the Father's because all three live in us.

Background Review
The theme of Romans is the "righteousness of God." The key verses are 1:16, 17. God through Paul demonstrates mankind's need for righteousness in Romans Ch. 1, 2, and most of 3. Mankind needs "the righteousness of God which is by faith of Jesus Christ unto all and upon all them that believe" (Rom. 3:22).

In Romans 4, we learn that when a person believes God, God out of His grace freely imputes His righteousness to that person and they are justified – declared righteous. Remember a person is justified by believing God, but God says different things to different people at different times. As an example, Abraham believed God would begin a seed-line through him (Rom. 4:16-22).

Then in Romans 5, we have the result of the justification we received in Romans 3 (salvation was settled in chapter 3, the imputed righteousness was explained in Romans 4) – The result of justification stated in chapter 5 **is peace with God through our Lord Jesus Christ** (because of our reconciliation by Him). We have access to God, hope, and have been given the Holy Ghost. God commended His love to us **while we were yet sinners** (5:8). So "being now justified by his blood, we shall be saved from wrath through him [hell and eternal death in the Lake of Fire]" (5:9). "For if, when we were enemies, we were reconciled to God by the death of his Son, much more, being reconciled, **we shall be saved by his life** [from the power of sin since Christ now lives in us]" (5:10). Christ's life is in us.

Sin entered the human race by Adam's disobedience and all mankind inherited his sin nature that results in death. But then in 5:15-21 we find out that what we gained in Christ is much more than we lost in Adam. The gift (mentioned 7 times in this section, including 6:23) is imputed righteousness **"the gift of righteousness"** (5:17) and results in eternal life "even so might grace reign through righteousness unto **eternal life** by Jesus Christ our Lord" (5:21).

Paul answers a series of questions in chapters 6 and 7 and then returns to discuss all that we have gained in Christ and God's great love in chapter 8. Questions: Shall we continue in sin that grace may abound? (6:1); Shall we sin because we are not under the law? (6:15). The answer two both is God forbid! Know ye not . . . how that the law hath dominion over a man as long as he liveth? (7:1), Is the law sin? God forbid! (7:7). Was then that which is good made death to me? God forbid! (7:13). Culminating in: "who shall deliver me from the body of this death? (7:24).

<u>**Good news**</u> of chapters 6 and 7: <u>We are dead to sin and the law</u>, and have become:
6:18 servants of righteousness
6:22 servants of God

<u>**Bad news**</u> in chapter 7 is that the sin nature still resides in the body after salvation:
7:17 sin dwelleth in me.
7:21 evil is present with me.
7:23 war "But I see another law in my members warring against the law of my mind and bringing me into captivity to the law of sin which is in my members."
7:24, 25 O wretched man that I am! who shall deliver me from the body of this death? I thank God through Jesus Christ our Lord. So then with the <u>mind</u> I myself serve the law of God; but with the <u>flesh</u> the law of sin. **The battle is for the mind.**

In chapter 7, we discovered that Paul was condemned by the law when he tried to do "good things" in the flesh. Doing works in the sin-filled flesh brought on legalism and amplified sin in Paul. The purpose of the law is to condemn. The law magnifies and then condemns sin in us. The law condemns us when we try to make our flesh conform to God's standards. We cannot do "good things" in the flesh because we have the wrong motives, thoughts, and actions. If we think we can keep the law or do good in our flesh we will fail like Paul demonstrated using himself as an example. Paul explained that we are **dead to the law**. However, the bad news is that <u>our sin nature still resides in our bodies</u>, although it has lost its power and we are dead to it. The old man, the flesh, is sort of like a headless chicken that still runs around in us. The old man, our sin nature, cannot be reformed, it will remain vile until the Rapture (Phil. 3:20, 21). In chapter 7, we learned that the only good thing in us is Christ.

God says, ". . . the **gospel of Christ** is the **power of God**. For therein is the **righteousness of God revealed** from **faith to faith**: as it is written, **The just shall live by faith**" (Rom. 1:16, 17). <u>We were saved by faith and shall live the same way, by walking after the Spirit.</u> However, we can still make the wrong decision from time to time, especially if we regress to living in the flesh. "For he that soweth to his flesh shall of the flesh reap corruption; but he that soweth to the Spirit shall of the Spirit reap life everlasting" (Gal. 6:8).

Now in chapter 8, Paul tells us how to live without condemnation by walking in the Spirit. While works in the flesh brought fruit unto death, works done in and through us by Christ's Spirit brings life and fruit unto God.

There is a new law working in us after salvation, "the law of the Spirit of life in Christ Jesus" (8:2). We **"walk not after the flesh, but after the Spirit" (Rom. 8:1 and 4).** The Spirit lives in us and takes the word of God and applies it to our spirit (1 Cor. 2:9-16). Read His word until you believe it. "So then faith cometh by hearing and hearing by the word of God" (Rom. 10:17). Christ said that "the words I speak are Spirit and they are life" (John 6:63). Therefore, **not** reading God's word is the most foolish thing a person can do. Jesus said, "God *is* a Spirit: and they that worship him must worship *him* in spirit and in truth" (John 4:24). His word is our spiritual food, "though our outward man perish, yet our inward man is renewed day by day" (2 Cor. 4:16).

The Holy Spirit takes the word of God and helps us to live by faith in what God says. He teaches our spirit God's word. Our sin nature still resides in our flesh and is enmity against God. There is a war inside the believer between the two natures, the flesh and the Spirit (Gal. 5:16, 17). The flesh has been rendered without power, so if we yield to it we choose to sin deliberately and live beneath who we are in Christ. So live after the Spirit, the old sinful self is not who we are anymore. As we let His word dwell in us richly (Col. 3:16), and have "the mind of Christ" (1 Cor. 2:16), then we automatically do what pleases God. When we notice any sinful thought creep in we bring it "into captivity . . . to the obedience of Christ" (2 Cor. 10:5) before we act on it. We decide that is not who I am or what I do anymore – now I live a life that is pleasing to God, blessing others.

We are to study His word (2 Tim. 2:15). We must come to His word knowing that the perfect God has preserved His word perfectly for us in the King James Bible. **Just like we were saved by faith in what Christ did for us, we must believe the King James Bible is perfect, and not waste our time checking "the Greek." The Holy Spirit is able to give us more <u>illumination</u> in His word if we have made the King James Bible our final authority by faith.** If you have not been persuaded to trust the KJB then it is wise to research the textual issue until you do. KJVtoday.com is a good website to learn from. After becoming a Bible believer, the **third step** is to learn how to rightly divide the word of God.

Our attitude in studying the Bible is also important, it should be "For what saith the scripture?" (Rom. 4:3). What does God want me to know? What is God revealing to me in His word? To study His word simply means to read it carefully, attentively and thoughtfully. Eventually, His word rightly divided, starts to become very clear to us.

8:14-23 Sons of God, Spirit of adoption, children of God, joint-heirs, and the redemption of the body. The moment we believe we are considered as adult sons of God because Christ lives in us (8:10). The Spirit in us is the guarantee or the down payment of the future redemption or adoption of the body (Eph. 1:13, 14). Those who are the sons of God will be revealed at the Rapture (in our glorified bodies). Do not miss the Rapture and be left behind to go through the 7-year Tribulation! The other group of believers who will enter Christ's earthly kingdom will also be called the sons of God (John 1:12). When they are revealed and come out of their graves (Ezek. 37:12, 13) to enter into the restored creation, then the creation will not groan anymore, but be like Eden. There is one Redeemer, but two groups of human sons of God. The believing angels are also called sons of God (Job 38:7). So, sons of God refer to believers. Therefore, in the future New Heaven and New Earth there will only be believers. The kingdom on earth believers, the believers that go to the heavenly places, and the believing angels.

8:18 We live in a sin cursed world but God has a wonderful future plan. God has predestinated (predetermined) that those who love Him will be conformed to the image of His Son. God will accomplish His **purpose** which He had from the beginning when God said, "Let us make man in our own image" (Gen. 1:26).

8:28 All Things – The sufferings of this world. When God says "all things work together for good for them that love God" it means He will use all (physical and spiritual things, even the enemy's attacks) to conform us to Christ. This does not mean that God will provide a parking spot, or health, wealth, or a happiness for us, but that He will develop patience, gratefulness, joy, experience (maturity, wisdom, or skill in living) and hope within us in our tribulations (Rom. 5:3, 4). As we read God's word and begin to use Paul as our "pattern" to follow Christ (1 Cor. 11:1). We start to have small successes in our Christian walk. We must remind ourselves daily that life is not about us, but about Christ. The Spirit helps us to say no to the flesh and yes to God. Now we beseech others instead of commanding them. We forgive others "even as God for Christ's sake hath forgiven us" (Eph. 4:32). We stop murmuring and decide to be content in all things.

8:34-39 God's great love – Abraham was a father willing to sacrifice his son, but his son Isaac was also willing to be offered up. God stopped Abraham from slaying his son, Isaac. But as we will learn, God spared not His own Son. Also, our Lord Jesus Christ was "obedient unto death, even the death of the cross" (Phil. 2:8).

Abraham proved that he loved God more than his son. Christ proved that He loved the Father more than Himself. Christ trusted in His Father's plan of redemption. He knew that His friends Abraham and Moses and all who love Him could not be redeemed any other way. The tree in the Garden was very different from the tree of the cross (1 Peter 2:24). First, Christ suffered and now He is glorified, and will yet be more glorified (Luke 24:25, 26). <u>Once we are "in Christ" by faith, we cannot be un-justified, un-adopted, un-reconciled, un-accepted, or un-sealed</u>. We are joint-heirs (which is what husbands and wives are) and we cannot be separated from our union with Him. No member of the body of Christ can be "amputated." **<u>Once saved, always saved</u>**. We can rest in this truth. We have no fear, only bold confidence in what God told us through Paul. We are in Christ, and the Father loves His Son. We are secure because we are "hid with Christ, in God" (Col. 3:3).

Romans 8:1 *There is* therefore now **no condemnation** to them which are **in Christ Jesus**, who **walk not after the flesh, but after the Spirit**. **2** For the **law of the Spirit of life in Christ** Jesus [the unchangeable truth that the Spirit of life of Christ living through us that is ours after we identified with Him (Rom. 6:3, 4). We now have His life see <u>5:10</u>] hath made me **free** from the **law of sin and death [we are unshackled from the power of sin that results in death]**. **3** For what the law **could not do**, in that **it was weak through the flesh** [no one could keep it, except Christ], God sending **his own Son in the likeness of sinful flesh**, and for sin, **condemned sin in the flesh** [Christ destroyed sin, 6:6]**: 4** That the **righteousness of the law might be fulfilled in us** [now we can live right if it is His Spirit working in us], who **walk not after the flesh, but after the Spirit**. **5** For they that **are after the flesh do mind the things of the flesh** [selfish pride, having wrong motives, thoughts, and deeds]; but they that **are after the Spirit the things of the Spirit** [pleasing God]. **6** For to be **carnally minded** [in the flesh] *is* **death**; but to be **spiritually minded** *is* **life and peace** [confidence in Him]. **7** Because the **carnal mind** *is* **enmity against God** [the enemy of God]**: for it is not subject to the law of God** [does not want to obey God], **neither indeed can be** [totally incapable]. **8** So then **they that are in the flesh cannot please God**. **9** But ye are **not in the flesh, but in the Spirit, if so be that the Spirit of God dwell in you**. Now **if any man have not the Spirit of Christ** [the Spirit here is clearly the Spirit of Christ]**, he is none of his. 10** And **if Christ** *be* **in you, the body** *is* **dead because of sin** [the flesh, the body of sin, our old self, has been crucified with Christ, Gal. 2:20. The soul was redeemed, but not the flesh, the spirit was made alive.]**; but the Spirit** *is* **life because of righteousness** [the Spirit of Christ works righteousness in and through us]. **11** But if **the Spirit of him that raised up Jesus from the dead dwell in you** [all three members of the Godhead, the Father, Son, and Holy Ghost, raised Christ from the dead, Gal. 1:1, John 10:18, 1 Thes. 1:10 so all three live in us], he that raised up Christ from the dead **shall also quicken your mortal bodies by his Spirit that dwelleth in you** [in the future, believers will receive a glorified body like Jesus has because of the down payment of the Spirit, 2 Cor. 1:22]. **12** Therefore, brethren, we are **debtors, not to the flesh**, to live after the flesh [we are not under obligation to the flesh]. **13** For **if ye live after the flesh, ye shall die** [not bear fruit that pleases God]: but if ye through the Spirit do **mortify the deeds of the body** [put the deeds of the flesh to death, Gal. 6:8], **ye shall live** [bear God fruit and please God]. **14** For as many as are **led by the Spirit of God** [Gal. 5:18], **they are the sons of God** [we believers ARE sons of God now. It is interesting that God calls the good angels sons of God in Job 38:7, also the believing remnant in John 1:12. We function as adult sons now. Sons want to please their fathers and labor with them out of love when no one is looking. Not as hired people who serve because they have to, but because they want to.] **15** For ye have **not received the spirit of bondage again to fear** [we are not under sin or the law that condemns us, 6:14]; but **ye have received the Spirit of adoption** [Sonship, the Spirit in us is the guarantee or down payment of the redemption of the future redemption of the body Eph. 1:13, 14 when the sons of God will be revealed, 8:19], whereby **we cry, Abba, Father** [we can call Father God "Daddy" like Christ did Mark 14:36, "Abba" is also mentioned for the third and last time in Gal. 4:6]. **16** The **Spirit itself beareth witness with our spirit, that we are the children of God** [the Holy Spirit confirms with our spirit that we are God's children, since we are in His Son Jesus Christ]: **17** And **if children, then heirs; heirs of God, and joint-heirs with Christ** [being in Him we share in Christ's inheritance, everything Christ has is ours and everything we have belongs to Him]; **if so be that we suffer with *him*, that we may be also glorified together** [we suffer internally because of the lifelong war between our flesh and the Spirit, "we are partakers of the afflictions of the gospel" 2 Tim. 1:8; "we suffer with him" 2 Tim. 2:12; we are also persecuted by unsaved people, Gal 4:29, but we "glory in tribulation" Rom. 5:3 because then we will depend more on Christ in us].

18 ¶ For I reckon that the sufferings of this present time *are* not worthy *to be compared* with the glory which shall be revealed in us [We suffer because we live in a sin cursed world (Gen. 3 and Gal 1:4) but God has a wonderful future plan for those who love Him]. **19** For the earnest expectation of the creature [all living things, creation] waiteth for the **manifestation of the sons of God** [to see who will be revealed to be the true sons of God, in the body of Christ at the Rapture and in the kingdom at that resurrection Ezek. 37:12]. **20** For **the creature was made subject to vanity, not willingly** [God cursed creation when Adam sinned, Gen. 3:17], but by reason of him who hath subjected *the same* in hope [God has promised to redeem creation, Isa. 11:6-10; Acts 3:21], **21** Because **the creature**

itself also shall be delivered from the bondage of corruption into the glorious liberty of the children of God [at Christ's Second Coming]. **22** For we know that **the whole creation groaneth and travaileth in pain together until now** [in the meantime, all creation suffers because it is not as God intended it to be. Satan and his host have not been cast out of the Second heaven yet.]. **23** And not only *they*, but ourselves also, which have the **firstfruits of the Spirit** [down payment, promise of redemption because of the Holy Spirit in us, Eph. 1:13, 14], **even we ourselves groan within ourselves** [we and all creation are not as we were meant to be], **waiting for the adoption, *to wit*, the redemption of our body. 24** For we are **saved by hope** [the confident expectation of being redeemed from the presence of sin at the Rapture]: but hope that is seen is not hope: for what a man seeth, why doth he yet hope for? **25** But if we hope for that we see not, *then* do we with **patience wait for** *it*. **26 Likewise the Spirit also helpeth our infirmities: for we know not what we should pray for as we ought: but the Spirit itself maketh intercession for us with groanings which cannot be uttered** [we do not know how to pray we need to learn how as members of the body of Christ]. **27** And he that searcheth the hearts knoweth what *is* the mind of the Spirit, because he maketh intercession for the saints according to *the will of* God [Prayer is us talking with God. The "he" is the Word of God (John 1:1-3, 14) using His word (Heb. 4:12). The mind of the Spirit is Christ. Then the Holy Spirit helps us understand His word and to pray]. **28** And we know that **all things work together for good to them that love God** [The "sufferings of this present time." (8:11) God uses everything that happens to us to mature us and make us choose the right thing as we follow our "pattern" Paul to follow Christ (1 Cor. 11:1). We learn to beseech others instead of commanding them, to be content in all circumstances, to forgive as God in Christ Jesus has forgiven us. I am still not sure if I would sing at midnight after being tortured, or have enough love in my heart to stop a jailer from committing suicide. The Spirit helps us to say no to the flesh and yes to God. To not grumble or complain. To not be talebearers, to study to be quiet and mind our own business. To be kind and say uplifting things. "Being confident of this very thing, that he which hath begun a good work in you will perform *it* until the day of Jesus Christ" (Phil. 1:6). "For our light affliction, which is but for a moment, worketh for us a far more exceeding *and* eternal weight of glory" (2 Cor. 4:17)], **to them who are the called according to *his* purpose** [God's purpose is to conform us to Christ] **29** For **whom he did foreknow** [God, the Creator of the Heaven and the Earth is outside of time and forknew who would believe but still gave us free will], **he also did predestinate** [predetermined] *to be* **conformed to the image of his Son** [God is working in us to conform us to His Son, "holy and without blemish" (Eph. 5:27)], **that he might be the firstborn among many brethren** [Christ was the first to be in a glorified body prepared for Him, Heb. 10:5]. **30** Moreover **whom he**

did predestinate, them he also called [how does God call us? See 2 Thes. 2:14]: and whom he called, them he also **justified**: and whom he justified, them he also **glorified** [past tense our eternal life is a done deal, Rom. 4:17]. **31 What shall we then say to these things?** [what shall we say to all these glorious things] **If God *be* for us, who *can be* against us?** [five questions follow] **32 He that spared not his own Son, but delivered him up for us all, how shall he not with him also freely give us all things?** [Abraham was a father willing to sacrifice his son, but his son Isaac was also willing to be offered up. God stopped Abraham from slaying his son, Isaac. But God spared not His own Son. Also our Lord Jesus Christ was "obedient unto death, even the death of the cross" (Phil. 2:8). This great love of the Father and the Son is more precious and wondrous than our hearts and minds can comprehend. If God gave us His beloved Son what else shall He not freely give us? Abraham proved that he loved God more than his son. Christ proved that he loved the Father more than Himself. Christ trusted in His Father plan of redemption. He knew that His friends Abraham and Moses and all of us who love Him could not be redeemed any other way.] **33 Who shall lay any thing to the charge of God's elect?** [Christ is God's elect Isa. 42:1 and we, the body of Christ are in Christ and are called "the elect of God" (Col. 3:12)] *It is* God that justifieth [God decided to justify us based upon the perfect sacrifice of His Son and our faith in Him]. **34 Who *is* he that condemneth?** *It is* Christ that died, yea rather, that is risen again, who is even at the right hand of God, who also maketh intercession for us [Satan cannot condemn us, nor the dead flesh. Christ won the victory. His blood atonement satisfied the Father, He rose, and now He is seated **at His right hand as proof that it is finished**. He paid the sin debt mankind owed **in full**. We have trusted in Him.]. **35 Who shall separate us from the love of Christ?** [it is interesting that Paul says who instead of what, then mentions 7 things that Paul himself endured including the beheading] *shall* tribulation, or distress, or persecution, or famine, or nakedness, or peril, or sword? **36** As it is written, For thy sake we are killed all the day long; we are accounted as **sheep for the slaughter** [This is how Satan sees us]. **37** Nay, **in all these things we are more than conquerors through him that loved us** [Christ is the One who is the Conqueror but as we allow Him to live through us we are conquerors with Him. This is how the Father sees us now, in Christ]. **38** For **I am persuaded**, that neither **death**, nor **life**, nor **angels**, nor **principalities** [evil or otherwise], **nor powers, nor things present** [in the dispensation of grace], nor **things to come** [in the future], **39** Nor **height**, nor **depth**, nor **any other creature** [not Satan or even ourselves], **shall be able to separate us from the love of God which is in Christ Jesus our Lord.** [***Note v. 31 the <u>power of God</u> is "for us" v. 32 the <u>grace of God</u> is "for us" vs. 33, 34 the <u>justice of God</u> is for us, and vs. 35-39 the <u>love of God</u> is "for us."]

Romans Chapter 9 – Election and Rejection of Israel

9:1-5 Paul had a strong burden for Israel's salvation.

9:6, 7 They had all the privileges of God yet they are not all "seed of Abraham" who is "the father of all them that believe" (4:11). The children of the flesh are not the children of God, but the children of faith are. Paul under the inspiration of the Holy Spirit says that in the past God elected the nation of Israel to come through Isaac the child of promise that God provided miraculously. The seed-line continued through Isaac. Also, before Rebecca's twins were born, God said that His nation would come through Jacob, not Esau (the elder who would serve the younger). To fulfill His purpose, God as the potter made Israel (a lump of clay in His hands) a vessel of honour.

9:8-21 God decides who He will have compassion and mercy on. So then, just as God had hardened Pharaoh's heart, now God has hardened unbelieving nation Israel's heart. The "thing formed" (Israel) cannot blame their Creator for making them first a "vessel unto honour" and now deciding to make them a "vessel of dishonor." **God has decided to show mercy to the Gentiles**.

9:22, 23 God was willing to postpone His wrath. God has endured with much longsuffering the "vessels of wrath fitted for destruction" (unbelievers) so He can "make known the riches of his glory" on the vessels of mercy (believers) which were "afore prepared unto glory." God had chosen the body of Christ "before the foundation of the world" (Eph. 1:4).

9:24 "Even us, whom he hath called, not of the Jews [believing remnant] only, but also of the Gentiles" so that God could show His power.

9:27 God always had a remnant of believers in the nation of Israel.

9:29 God always "left them a seed" of believers otherwise the nation would have been destroyed like Sodom and Gomorrah.

9:30 So the Gentiles "attained the righteousness of God . . . which is of faith."

9:32 But the nation of Israel did not follow after righteousness by faith but "by works of the law."

9:33 "For they stumbled at that stumblingstone: As it is written, Behold, I lay in Sion a stumblingstone and rock of offence: and whosoever believeth on him [**the Lord Jesus Christ**] shall not be ashamed."

Our effectiveness in the body of Christ depends on our understanding of what happened to Israel and how that relates to us. In Romans 9, Paul explains how God could be just in setting aside His privileged nation, save a remnant of Israel, and offer the Gentiles salvation. **It is important to notice that Paul is speaking to groups of people: the nation, the remnant and the Gentiles, and NOT about individual salvation**.

After declaring that nothing can separate the body of Christ believers from the love of God (8), Paul addresses **another series** of unstated (but anticipated) **questions**. What about Israel? Will God still keep His promises to them? Is God finished with Israel? Has God cast away His people? The underlying thought is: if God has not kept His promise to Israel, will He keep His promises to us?

The next three chapters 9-11 are a parenthesis in Paul's letter to the Romans. Paul is very logical, and everything builds on the previous information. This section answers the question: What about Israel? Paul speaks of Israel's past election and rejection (9) present salvation opportunity for the individual Jews (10) and glorious future restoration of the nation (11). Paul's purpose is to explain how God temporarily set aside His chosen people and saved the Gentiles, and how He will restore the nation in the future. **The body of Christ's effectiveness depends on our understanding what happened to Israel.** However, to think that Paul stops talking to the Gentiles in these chapters leads to error, Paul never stops speaking primarily to the Gentiles about Israel, but he also speaks to the Jews. **Paul explains what happened to Israel at the cross and in Acts 7, and how the salvation has now come to the Gentiles apart from Israel.**

Romans 9-11 in a nutshell: Is there unrighteousness with God because He has a new agency (the body of Christ)? Will He still keep His promise to Israel?
Rom. 9 is about how the privileged nation of Israel who rejected their Messiah has been formed into a vessel of dishonor by God, but in the future, God will reform it into a vessel of honor again.
Rom. 10 Paul urges his kinsmen, the Jews, living today to be saved by the gospel he preaches.
Rom. 11 Israel's temporary blindness was a mystery, but in His great wisdom, God made a way so that anyone who believes what Christ has done can be saved apart from going through the nation of Israel and join together with Gentile believers as members of the body of Christ. God is not finished with Israel.

In chapter 9, Paul explains how God is just in setting aside His privileged nation, has saved a remnant of Israel, and is saving Gentiles. It is important to notice that Paul is speaking to groups of people (there are three main players): the nation of Israel, the remnant, and the Gentiles, NOT individual salvation.

Rom. 9:1-3 Paul had an exceptional burden for Israel even saying that he would be willing (if it were possible) to suffer eternal punishment if they could be saved. That is love! But this is impossible since he is so secure in Christ. Paul's words remind us of Moses in Ex. 32:31, 32 when he pleaded with God - forgive Israel or blot me out of Your book.

The first words **Jesus** said on the cross were: "Father, forgive them; for they know not what they do" (Luke 23:34). **Stephen** also said, "Lord, lay not this sin to their charge" (Acts 7:60). Now **Paul** also reveals his love for Israel and says he is willing to trade places with Israel if he could. Even though Paul says, "Of the Jews five times received I forty *stripes* save one [a total of 195 stripes]" (2 Cor. 11:24).

Israel had received many privileges as a nation. God made them covenants and promises – God did not pick one of the nations that was formed when God "confounded their language" (Gen. 11:7). He waited 5 generations which is 175 years (Job 42:16 REVEALS THAT A GENERATION IS 35 YEARS) and then chose Abraham to make His own nation from. "And I will make thee a great nation" (Gen. 12:2). From Abraham God made a special people. God made promises and covenants: they were promised a special land, I will bless those who bless you and curse those who curse you. God gave circumcision as a token of the covenant between Him and Israel (Gen. 17). Most of the covenants (except for the law) were one-sided - an agreement God told them He would keep.

Through Moses God gave Israel the Law. "And God spake all these words, saying, I *am* the LORD thy God, which have brought thee out of the land of Egypt [Israel], out of the house of bondage. Thou shalt have no other gods before me" (Ex. 20:1-3). The **law** (613 laws) **further distinguished Israel from the Gentiles**. "Keep therefore and do *them*; for this *is* your wisdom and your understanding in the sight of the nations, which shall hear all these statutes, and say, Surely this great nation *is* a wise and understanding people. For what nation *is there so* great, who *hath* God *so* nigh unto them, as the LORD our God *is* in all *things that* we call upon him *for*? And what nation *is there so* great, that hath statutes and judgments *so* righteous as all this law, which I set before you this day?" (Deut. 4:6-8). In the future Israel will be this kingdom of priests (Isa. 61:6).

Israel was to be a kingdom of priests so they could be a CHANNEL OF BLESSING to the Gentiles. "Now therefore, if ye will obey my voice indeed, and keep my covenant, then ye shall be a peculiar treasure unto me **above all people**: for all the earth *is* mine: And ye shall be unto me a **kingdom of priests, and an holy nation**. These *are* the words which thou shalt speak unto the children of Israel" (Ex. 19:5,6). But before Moses got down from Mount Sinai, Satan had corrupted the people and they were worshipping the golden calf (a calf is one of the faces of the Cherubs, Rev. 4:7). Aaron said about the molten calf, "These be thy gods, O Israel, which brought thee up out of the land of Egypt" (Ex. 32:4). No wonder God was upset. So Israel became Satan's "lawful captive" (Isa. 49:24).

Then God promised a future King to be a descendant of David to rule forever (Christ). *Notice in 9:5 that the fathers are God blessed forever, it cannot be Christ because He is God. In the Bible, the pronoun is not always followed by the closest antecedent.

Rom. 9:4, 5 No other nation had these **8 wonderful privileges**; yet Israel took them for granted and ultimately rejected the righteousness of God by their **unbelief** in what He said and their **self-righteousness**. Therefore, **God has not fulfilled this list yet**. Israel's privileges will now be compared and contrasted with those of the body of Christ:

The 8 privileges of Israel:

1. **adoption** (son-ship, sons of God John 1:12). Israel will not receive their adoption as sons of God until Christ's Second Coming (Rev. 21:17, because they do not receive the atonement until then (Acts 3:19-21). Therefore, "the adoption" for them refers to the national day of atonement for the nation of Israel. We have the spirit of adoption now, and will be adopted at the Rapture (Rom. 8:23). Plus, we have received the atonement NOW (5:11).

2. **glory** (God's glory in the tabernacle, temple, and in the future Kingdom when "the glory of the LORD will rise upon thee" Isa. 60:1-3). We have a future glory with Christ (Col. 3:1-4).

3. **covenants** The covenants belong to Israel, not the Gentiles (Eph. 2:11, 12), therefore we cannot be spiritual Israel. [The covenant are the Old and New Covenants, plus Abrahamic (Gen. 12:1-3), Mosaic (Ex. 19:5, 6), Palestinian (Deut. 30:3, the regathering into the land still future, and did not happen in 1948 because this will be a time when Israel knows that Jesus is their Messiah), Davidic (2 Sam. 7:16). Those under the future New Covenant (Jer. 31:31) will never sin "I will cause [Israel] to walk in My statutes, and shall keep My judgments, and do them" (Ezek. 36:27). This is why 1 John 3:9 says "whosoever is born of God doth not commit sin . . . he cannot sin." (This does not apply to us today because we still sin.) Although we never had any covenants, God freely gives us all spiritual blessings in the heavenly places (Eph. 1:3). But in time past, we were "strangers from the covenants of promise, having no hope, and without God" (Eph. 2:12).

4. giving of the law God's law at Mount Sinai was only given to Israel, Ex. 20:2. The law was given to Israel "the oracles of God" (Rom. 3:2) and was a major difference between Israel and all other nations. As mentioned under the future New Covenant, Israel will keep the law perfectly. Our operating system is grace. Today, by choosing to walk in the Spirit, using the word of God which gives us the mind of Christ we can fulfill God's law (Rom. 8:4-6, 13:8-10).

5. service of God The only religion given by God was given to Israel. Their law showed in detail how to worship and serve God. In the future, Israel is to be God's royal priesthood teaching the world how to serve God (Ex. 19:5, 6; Isa 2:2, 3; Rev. 5:10; Deut. 32:8; 1 Peter 2:9, 10; Rev. 5:10). Right now the members of the body of Christ are ambassadors in this present evil world (2 Cor. 5:20, Gal. 1:4).

6. promises God promised to perform physical signs and wonders (Ex. 34:10) for Israel, and physical blessings for keeping the law (Deut. 7:12-15). God promised Abraham and the nation to be a seed-line, cursings and blessings, land forever (Gen. 12:1-3, 7; 13:15). We have been sealed with "that Holy Spirit of promise" (Eph. 1:13, 14) and will be raptured (as promised). We have received all spiritual blessings in heavenly places (Eph. 1:3; 1 Thes. 4:16, 17; 1 Cor. 15:42-44).

7. the fathers (Abraham, Isaac, Jacob and his 12 sons). God chose to make His nation out of Abraham. God will never permanently cast off Israel because of His love for the fathers. We have no fathers, but believers today are spiritually children of Abraham, not Israel (Rom. 4:9-12; Gal. 3:14, 29).

8. of whom concerning the flesh Christ came (Matt. 1-17; Gal. 4:4). Christ came to set Israel free from being Satan's lawful captive (Isa. 49:24, 25) and to "save his people [Israel] from their sins" (Matt. 1:21). Paul says Christ ransomed all (1 Tim. 2:6). There is one Redeemer who has two different ministries: one earthly, and one heavenly. There are two groups of people: the earthly kingdom believers, and the body of Christ. They will live in two different places: the Earth and the Heaven. Jesus, our Redeemer, is 100% God and 100% man. Jesus was a Jew concerning the flesh (John 4:22). As a human, He is a kinsman to all mankind (Phil. 2:7).

Not all Israel is saved just because they are the seed of Abraham. Only those with **faith** are saved, not those who try to be saved by acts of their flesh. God chose (**elected**) the nation to come from Abraham, Isaac, and Jacob. While God accomplished His purpose in forming the nation He still allowed for free will. Now God has decided to harden Israel just like He did Pharaoh. God like a potter can formed the nation of honour into a vessel of dishonour if He wants to. But God in

His mercy has always saved a remnant. Is God unjust? If God did not show mercy no one could be saved and everyone would be wiped out like Sodom and Gomorrah. God was faithful to Israel but they rejected Him so He has **rejected** them for a season because He is wise. God set Israel aside for their own good. God is not unjust because He has mercy on some. God has endured for a long time the vessels of wrath (wicked unbelievers like Caiaphas and Annas and the other religious rulers who crucified Christ, and the many idol worshipers in the nation over the ages. God was longsuffering and did not obliterate them at that time.) on whom He was willing to show His wrath, but instead God chose to make known the riches of His glory on the vessels of mercy (the Gentiles) which He "afore prepared unto glory" (9:23, Eph. 1:4). "Even us, whom he hath called [the believers, 2 Thess. 2:14] not the Jews only [the believing remnant or little flock], but also of the Gentiles?"

Then Paul continues to speak about how God has saved a remnant. The "not my people" is the remnant. God will make a short work in the earth, and finish the prophetic program after this dispensation is over. The Gentile believers have shown faith, while the nation of Israel "sought it not by faith, but . . . by the works of the law. For they stumbled at that stumblingstone [Christ] . . . the rock of offence: and whosoever believeth on him shall not be ashamed" (9:33). The nation did not believe in their Messiah so they are now Lo-ammi (not My people). As we will see in chapter 11, in the future God will pick up where He left off in Acts 7 and Israel will again be a nation of honour with a believing remnant in the Tribulation. Then at Christ Second Coming, God will reshape Israel making a nation out of the believing remnant, which will be a nation of 100% Honour. But first Paul explains how a Jew can believe and be saved at this present time.

At the Tower of Babel God set the Gentiles aside. In Acts 7, God set Israel aside for a season (it has been nearly 2,000 years so far in this dispensation). He has also postponed His day of wrath (the Tribulation, Jacob's trouble, Jer. 30:7). The Gentiles, who previously had nothing to do with God, "Wherefore remember, that ye being in time past Gentiles in the flesh, who are called Uncircumcision by that which is called the Circumcision in the flesh made by hands; That at that time ye were without Christ, being aliens from the commonwealth of Israel, and strangers from the covenants of promise, having no hope, and without God in the world" (Eph. 2:11, 12) can now have God's righteousness by faith in Christ apart from Israel. God has revealed a new purpose in showing mercy to the remnant of Israel (the Little Flock) and all nations (including Israel who has fallen to the level of all other nations) in the dispensation of the grace of God. God's purpose in the future is to set up His Kingdom on the earth. He will use Israel as a royal priesthood to be a CHANNEL of BLESSING to the Gentiles. God wants to reclaims the Earth from Satan and to populate it with believers. But right now God is showing mercy to all nations so that He can reclaim the Heavenly Places from Satan and populate them with the body of Christ believers.

Again, in Acts 7, the nation committed the blasphemy of the Holy Ghost and God, as the potter, made them a vessel of dishonour (Lo-ammi). In the future, after the Rapture, God will make Israel a vessel of honour again out of a remnant of believers in the Tribulation. After the Tribulation, at his Second Coming all believing Israel (the remnant, "little flock") will be saved. God will give them who were not a people, the nation of Israel (Isa. 65:8, 9; Hosea 1:8-10, 2:23; 1 Peter 2:10; Matt. 21:43; Luke 12:32) in the Kingdom. Peter and the 11 (which includes Matthias) will be raised to sit on the 12 thrones (Matt. 19:28) and **God will reshape the nation into a 100% honourable vessel without a remnant.**

Interestingly, on a side note, the body of Christ can also be vessels of value to God as 2 Tim. 2:20 says. Humans cannot tell God what to do. If we purge ourselves of false doctrine (2 Tim. 2:16-19), then God can use us for honourable purposes "prepared unto every good work" (2 Tim. 2:21).

In election, God exercises His sovereign will to accomplish His purpose based on His foreknowledge, while at the same time allowing for free will. Keep in mind that this election (Rom. 9-11) is national, not individual. The future hope of the world depended on Israel receiving God's blessings and passing them on to the Gentiles (Gen. 12:1-3; Matt. 15:24-27; Zech. 8:20-23). Paul very carefully points out that he is speaking about Jews and Gentiles as peoples, not individual sinners. In Matt. 4:17 the promises were "at hand," but in Acts 1-7 they were offered to Israel by the Holy Ghost through Peter, and "the little flock" (Luke 12:32; Acts 2:4; 3:19-21). The fulfillment of the 2000-year prophecy that began with Abraham was that close. But Israel refused the offer to receive and believe in their Messiah through the "little flock." Their rejection culminated the stoning of Stephen, the blasphemy of the Holy Ghost (Acts 7:51-53; Matt. 12:31, 32).

Instead of sending His prophesied WRATH, in His mercy **God interrupted "prophecy" and inserted the "mystery"** so that Paul and other individual Jews and Gentiles could still be saved. God delayed His judgment, the Tribulation, so He could demonstrate His mercy on the Gentiles (the vessels of mercy, 9:23).

This interruption of prophecy was not expected, it was not revealed until Paul (Rom. 16:25; Gal. 1:11, 12; Eph. 3:1-6). This delay of Israel's program is so that God can form the body of Christ in this dispensation of the grace of God.

God had to endure Israel's unbelief and reshape them many times. In Exodus, after promising to keep the Ten Commandments, Israel forsook God and worshipped the golden calf while Moses was receiving them and became **Satan's lawful captive** (Isa. 49:24). Moses intervened and asked God to not blot them out. In Numbers 13 and 14, Israel's unbelief prevented them from entering into the promised land, so they wandered in the wilderness 40 years till the unbelievers died.

Will God still keep His promises to Israel? Yes, He will resume His dealings with Israel after the body of Christ have been caught up (raptured). There will be a 7-year Tribulation period that begins when Antichrist signs the 7-year covenant with apostate Israel (Dan 9:26; Matt. 24:21; Jer. 30:7; Zech. 14:1-11). The apostate nation will offer animal sacrifices because they do not believe Jesus is their Redeemer and will believe Antichrist, but the remnant will believe Jesus, not the false religion.

9:6, 7 Just because people are descendants of Abraham doesn't mean they will believe God. In God's foreknowledge, Isaac was chosen to be the seed of promise, not Ishmael.

9:8-13 Before the children were born. God said that the older shall serve the younger. Why? To show that God's foreknowledge in forming the nation would be fulfilled. God knew Jacob would believe Him, while Esau would not "Esau despised his birthright [double portion/seed-line]" (Gen 25:34). "Jacob have I loved, but Esau have I hated" (Mal. 1:2, 3). **"And the LORD said unto her [Rebecca], Two nations** *are* in thy womb, and two manner of people shall be separated from thy bowels; and *the one* people shall be stronger than *the other* people; and the elder shall serve the younger" (Gen. 25:23). God knew that Esau (the nation of Edom) would not believe Him but that Israel (Jacob) finally would (during the Tribulation). God's purpose does not depend on man's decision.

9:14 Is God unrighteous? No, because election has nothing to do with justice, but rather with free grace. Ignorant people may say that God is unjust because he picks one and not the other. But God is not unjust, because if God only did what was just no one would be saved. Nobody deserves His mercy. God can dispense grace and mercy as He chooses.

Paul uses Moses (Ex. 33:19) and Pharaoh (Ex. 9:16) to show that God can do as He wants in showing His grace and mercy. <u>Nobody deserves God's mercy, and no one can condemn God for His choice of forming Israel and not choosing another nation.</u> <u>Nor can anyone condemn God for deciding to show mercy to the Gentiles.</u>

9:16 God chose to have mercy on Jacob, not Esau (and make him the seed line).

9:18 Pharaoh was hardened by God so that he would not believe God and would not let His people go for a long time so that God could show His power in the 10 plagues. Now Paul will essentially say that the nation of Israel has been hardened because of their unbelief so God can show mercy to the Gentiles. Israel has been in unbelief throughout its whole history "Which of the prophets have not your fathers persecuted?" (Acts 7:52).

9:20, 21 The "thing formed" is Israel. Israel is "marred in the hand of the potter" (Jer. 18:1-12, Isa. 64:7-10). God is the potter; the lump is Israel. Israel was an honorable vessel before the fall, but after their fall in Acts 7 they were dishonorable. So God shaped the nation of Israel to be **Lo-ammi** (not my people, Hosea 1:8-10) but in the future (after the Rapture) the nation of Israel will be a reshaped lump of clay and they will be called "the sons of the living God" (Hosea 2:23, 2 Peter 2:9, 10).

To review, before the fall Israel received God's blessings and were a lump of honour with a continuous remnant of true believers, presently they are a lump of dishonor. (<u>There is no remnant today because individual Jews today who believe become members of the body of Christ</u>). After the Rapture, the nation of Israel will become a vessel of honour (preferred) with a remnant during the Tribulation. After the Tribulation God will give the Kingdom to the believing remnant making the lump and the vessel of 100% pure honour with the New Covenant and His Spirit in them (so no remnant, as 1 Peter 2:10 indicates along with Matt. 19:28, 21:43; Luke 12:32).

9:22 Cannot God chose to make Israel a nation of honour for a time and then a nation of dishonour for a time? God has been ready to judge righteously, but God has endured patiently for a long time all those vessels ready for wrath and destruction.

9:23 Gentiles and "little flock" believers are the vessels of mercy.

9:25, 26 These verses are speaking about the apostate nation of Israel that are Lo-ammi (not my people) being called my people again after the Tribulation.

9:27 God has always had a remnant of believers even in Elijah's day. God had a remnant at Christ first coming "the little flock" of Luke 12:32 and will have another remnant of believers in the Tribulation before His Second Coming.

9:28 Short Work I believe the short work is twofold, referring to both Daniel's 70th week, the Tribulation and His work calling believers on earth. God is calling out two groups of people to populate the Heaven and the Earth in a mere 7,000 years. After Christ rules for the last 1,000 years of the 7,000 years, there will be a final rebellion when Satan is loosed, and then the Great White Throne Judgment of the lost. During these 7,000 years God is calling out those who will believe the instructions He gives them to determine the true believers that will be in the New Heaven and the New Earth by faith. God gives all people free will. All people are saved by faith. **<u>Where we will spend eternity is all that really matters</u>**. God's purpose in election by His gospels makes it possible to save both groups by His grace. No one could be saved apart from faith and the grace of God.

In the future, God will "finish the work" (9:28). **Paul quotes Isa. 10:22** that says that the remnant of Israel will be saved (Isa. 4:2-4; Zech. 13:8, 9). The context is the Tribulation when the Antichrist is trying to convert all of Israel to his **apostate religion**. <u>It is important to note this context because there is no "remnant of Israel" right now since Israel's program was set apart nearly 2,000 years ago.</u>

God "endured with much longsuffering the vessels of wrath [Israel]" (9:22, 23) so that He could save the Gentiles. Why will He cut the work short? Because "except those days should be shortened, there should no flesh be saved" (Matt. 24:22). This is why Jesus says that He will "come quickly" (Rev. 22:20), not soon. When Israel is ready He will come quickly to bring them into the kingdom.

9:29 Paul quotes Isa. 1:9-11 when God calls Israel "Sodoma" and "Gomorrah." Israel would have been completely destroyed if God did not always have a remnant who believed. God is not pleased with Israel because they have replaced following Him with their own traditions. At Christ's Second Coming, Israel will be in the same condition they were in at Christ's first coming, Mark 7:9. Believing Israel in the Tribulation will have hope because they know of God's salvation of Gentiles. God was not unfaithful to Israel, but rather Israel was unfaithful to God.

9:30-33 The great <u>paradox</u> of history is that the Jews tried to be righteous and were rejected, while the Gentiles who did not have the same privileges were received. <u>The reason is that the Jews tried to be righteous by their works, while the Gentiles received righteousness by faith through the grace of God.</u> Many Gentiles knew they were evil and in need of a Saviour, therefore many of them believed when

Paul preached the gospel to them. Israel's righteousness was like "filthy rags" (Isa. 64:6) but in the future it will be like "fine linen" (Rev. 19:8).

Christ is "a precious corner stone, a sure foundation" (Isa. 28:16). The Jews stumbled at the cross by crucifying their Messiah **in unbelief** (Isa. 8:14; 28:16; Mat. 21:42, 1 Cor. 1:23; 1 Peter 2:6-8). They did not receive and believe in their Messiah (John 1:11). They were looking for a Messiah who would set them free from their Roman captors. They did not realize that they had to be redeemed from bondage to sin and Satan.

Isa 28:16 says "he that believeth shall not make haste" while Paul quotes it and by the holy Spirit says "whosoever believeth on Him shall not be ashamed." The builders of the temple were the religious Jewish leaders, who left out the corner stone. The further revelation of Paul shows a dispensational change. It is not "he" but "whosoever" this change indicates that there is no difference between the Jew and the Gentile today. In the past Jews were above the Gentiles (Deut. 7:6). Make "haste" has been changed to "ashamed" meaning if they trust God to provide the corner stone they will not have to try to find it themselves and they will be approved of God. Furthermore, "on him" is added in Romans because we now know that the corner stone is the Lord Jesus Christ.

Israel was an elect nation that failed to believe God and receive His Son. But in the future, God will make a believing Nation out of the remnant (Matt. 21:42-43). Christ will grind the Gentile nations to powder (Dan. 2:34, 35) and set Himself up to rule as the "head of the corner." God is able to be sovereign and still allow free will. Because in His foreknowledge He knew who would believe. God's purposes will prevail regardless of human disobedience.

Romans 9:1 I say the truth in Christ, I lie not, my conscience also bearing me witness in the Holy Ghost [Paul's conscience bore witness with the Holy Ghost that Paul truly had a strong burden for Israel], **2** That I have **great heaviness** and continual sorrow in my heart. **3** For I could wish that myself were **accursed from Christ** [eternal separation from Christ] for my brethren, **my kinsmen according to the flesh** [He was willing to trade places with the unbelieving Israelites]: **4** Who are Israelites; to whom *pertaineth* the **adoption**, and the **glory**, and the **covenants**, and the **giving of the law**, and the **service** *of God*, and the **promises** [the Israelites had a list of privileges going for them]; **5** Whose *are* **the fathers** [Abraham, Isaac, Jacob], and **of whom** as concerning the flesh **Christ** *came* [Gal. 4:4], who is over all, God blessed for ever [the fathers, since Christ is God]. Amen.

6 ¶ Not as though the **word of God** hath taken **none effect** [some have been saved, a remnant]. For they *are* **not all Israel, which are of Israel** [Rom. 2:28, true Israel are those that did believe God]: **7 Neither, because they are the seed of Abraham**, *are they* **all children**: but, **In Isaac shall thy seed be called** [God promised Abraham a son when he was old, and Sarah was barren so that He could fulfill His purpose. God sovereignly decreed by whom the nation's the seed-line would come because they would be believers. The seed-line led to Christ (Gal. 3:16), the promised Redeemer of Gen. 3:15]. **8** That is, They which are the children of the **flesh** [Ishmael, Abraham's son begotten in the flesh by self-effort], these *are* **not the children of God**: but the children of the promise are counted for the seed [begotten by faith]. **9** For this *is* the word of promise, At this time will I come, and Sara shall have a son. **10** And not only *this*; but when Rebecca also had conceived by one, *even* by our father Isaac; **11 (For *the children* being not yet born**, neither having done any good or evil, **that the purpose of God according to election might stand**, not of works, but of him that calleth;) **12** It was said unto her, **The elder shall serve the younger** [not only the nation of Edom but all nations will serve Israel in the kingdom]. **13** As it is written, **Jacob have I loved, but Esau have I hated** [Jacob produced twelve sons, the twelve tribes of Israel. From Esau came the nation of Edom, Mal. 1:1-4].

14 ¶ What shall we say then? *Is there* **unrighteousness** with God? God forbid [No, God is merciful. God is not unrighteous because he will accomplish His purpose based on His foreknowledge]. **15** For he saith to Moses, I will have **mercy** on whom I will have mercy, and I will have compassion on whom I will have compassion [Moses pleaded with God for the nation after they worshipped the golden calf, Ex. 33:19. God had mercy and did not kill all of them]. **16** So then *it is* **not** of him that willeth, **nor** of him that runneth, **but of God** that sheweth mercy [God decides to show mercy to those He chooses. This verse is not talking about individual salvation, but nations]. **17** For the scripture saith unto Pharaoh, Even for this same **purpose** have I raised thee up, that I might **shew my power** in thee, and that my name might be declared throughout all the earth [God put Pharaoh in power knowing he would not let Israel go right away so that God could show His power, Ex. 9:16]. **18** Therefore hath he mercy on whom he will *have mercy*, and whom he will he **hardeneth** [Currently, Israel is temporarily hardened, with a vail over their heart 2 Cor. 3:13, 14; 2 Peter 3, 4, 9, 10, 15, 16]. **19** Thou wilt say then unto me, **Why** doth he yet find fault? For who hath **resisted** his will? [Some will say it is God's fault if someone is not saved since He is in control] **20** Nay but, O man, who art thou that repliest against God? Shall **the thing formed** say to him that formed *it*, **Why** hast thou made me thus? [shall someone blame God because he is an unbeliever instead of a believer?] **21 Hath not the potter power over the**

clay, of the **same lump** to make one **vessel unto honour** [preferred nation], and another **unto dishonour** [not preferred see 9:6, 7]? **22** *What* if God, **willing** to shew *his* wrath, and to make his power known, **endured** with much longsuffering the **vessels of wrath** fitted to **destruction** [unbelieving Israel]: **23** And that he might make known the **riches of his glory** on the **vessels of mercy** [Gentile and "little flock" believers are the vessels of mercy], which he had **afore prepared** unto glory [since before the foundation of the world we were prepared for His glory Eph. 1:4, 2:7; 1 Cor. 2:7, 8; Col. 1:25-27], **24** Even us [the Gentile believers], whom he hath called, not of the **Jews** only, but also of the **Gentiles?** [the believing remnant was saved out of the Jews and Gentiles have God's mercy today and if they believe and become members of the body of Christ] **25** As he saith also in **Osee**, I will call them my people, which were not my people [God will call believing Israel His people again, Osee is Greek for Hosea be sure to read Hosea 1:8-10, 2:23, 1 Peter 2:9, 10]; and her beloved, which was not beloved [God will reform Israel to be a vessel of honor again]. **26** And it shall come to pass, *that* in the place where it was said unto them, **Ye** *are* **not my people**; there shall they be called the children of the living God. **27** Esaias [Greek for Isaiah] also crieth concerning **Israel**, Though the number of the children of Israel be as the sand of the sea, **a remnant shall be saved** [God has always had a Jewish remnant of believers even in Elijah's day. God had a remnant at Christ first coming "the little flock" of Luke 12:32 and will have another remnant of believers in the Tribulation before His Second Coming]: **28** For he will **finish the work**, and cut *it* short in **righteousness**: because a **short work** will the Lord make **upon the earth** [I believe the short work is twofold, referring to both Daniel's 70th week, the Tribulation and God's work calling believers on earth. God is calling out two groups of people to populate the Heaven and the Earth in a mere 7,000 years. Why will He cut the work short? Because "except those days should be shortened, there should no flesh be saved" (Matt. 24:22). After Antichrist signs the covenant with apostate Israel mentioned in Dan. 9:26 there will be a seven-year Tribulation with much destruction.]. **29** And as Esaias said before, Except the Lord of **Sabaoth** [Lord of armies] had left us **a seed**, we had been as **Sodoma**, and been made like unto **Gomorrha** [Unless God left Israel a remnant they would have been completely destroyed, Isa. 1:4-9, 4:2-4; 10:21-23, God will bring forth "a seed out of Jacob" 65:8, 9; Zech. 13:8, 9. God will never totally destroy Israel. God will finish regaining back the earth from Satan and to rule it in righteousness]. **30** What shall we say then? That the **Gentiles**, which followed not after righteousness, have attained to righteousness, even the righteousness which is of **faith** [**the Gentiles, who previously had nothing to do with God (Eph. 2:11, 12), can now have God's righteousness by faith in Christ**. They believed Paul's gospel Rom. 3:22-26, 4:5, were saved and became members of the body of Christ because they had faith to believe what Christ had done for them]. **31 But Israel**, which followed after the law of righteousness, hath not attained to the law of righteousness. **32** Wherefore? Because *they sought it* **not by faith**, but as it were **by the works** of the law [Israel did not seek righteousness by faith in Christ, but tried to be righteous in themselves, by trying to keep the law]. For they stumbled at that **stumblingstone** [Christ is the stumbling stone (Gen. 49:24, Isa. 8:13-16; 28:16 1 Peter 2:4-10; Matt. 21:42-44, and Israel's Rock 1 Cor. 1:23, 10:4; Deut. 32:18, 30, 31). Israel did not receive and believe their Redeemer. They were looking for a Messiah who would set them free from their Roman captors. They did not realize that they had to be redeemed from bondage to sin and Satan. Instead, in their ignorance, Israel demanded His crucifixion.]; **33** As it is written, Behold, I lay in **Sion** [capital of Israel, where Christ was crucified] a stumblingstone and **rock of offence**: and **whosoever believeth on him** shall not be **ashamed.** [Isa. 45:17-25, The builders of the temple were the religious Jewish leaders, who left out the corner stone. Jesus was an offence to Israel's corrupt religious system, Matt. 23, but those who trust that He was Israel's Christ are not ashamed]. At Christ's Second Coming Israel will say that He is their potter, their Creator "But **we are all as an unclean thing, and all our righteousnesses are as filthy rags** [the believing remnant of Israel will **confess** their **sins** in the Tribulation and believe God]; and we all do fade as a leaf; and our iniquities, like the wind, have taken us away . . . **But now, O LORD, thou art our father; we are the clay, and thou our potter; and we all are the work of thy hand**" (Isa. 64:6-8). That is so wonderfully amazing!

We are not Israel – we are the body of Christ.

Comparing Israel with the Body of Christ

Israel	Body of Christ
• Gospel of Kingdom	• Gospel of the grace of God
• Earthly Promises, hopes and blessings	• Heavenly promises, hopes and blessings
• Christ is King	• Christ is Head
• Physical	• Spiritual
• National Salvation	• Individual Salvation
• 12 Apostles	• 1 Apostle
• Under Law	• Under Grace
• Water Baptism	• Spirit Baptism
• Christ's return to earth	• Christ's meeting in the air

Romans Chapter 10 – Present Salvation Opportunity for Individual Jews

10:1-13 The nation stumbled, but individual Jews can believe Christ is the end of the law for righteousness as proved by the Father raising Him from the dead; and then that Jew can have Christ's righteousness by faith, not by keeping the law. **10:14-21** God saved a believing remnant, but the nation rejected Him. *The "no people" and "a foolish nation" in 10:19 are the little flock (Isa. 65:1).

In Romans 10, Paul speaks about the present opportunity of salvation for the Jew. Let me just say plainly from the start that all Jewish people today are saved the same way as everybody else by believing Paul's gospel. The Jew who believes then becomes a member of the body of Christ. He uses many scriptures from the Old Testament to prove his point. I am constantly, amazed at God the Holy Spirit's economy of words through Paul. The Spirit uses the quoted verses to deepen His message. To understand His word better just kept reading and studying every day until the Holy Spirit helps you to understand God's word better. Increased clarity is so thrilling. Romans 10:9, 10 will be examined closely.

Let us compare the salvation verses in Rom. 10:8b-10, often used in the Romans Road witnessing tool, but I include 8b with that of 1 Cor. 15:3, 4. ". . . that is, **the word of faith, <u>which we preach</u>** [Paul]; That if thou shalt **confess** with thy mouth the Lord Jesus [agree with God with the mouth of your soul that Jesus is Lord this has nothing to do with speaking audibly, so no work is being done salvation is purely by faith in what Christ has done], and shalt **believe** in thine heart that God hath raised him from the dead [He was resurrected because His payment for your sins was accepted by the Father and so He proved to be the Son of God, the LORD], **thou shalt be saved** [from the penalty of your sins]. For with the heart man **believeth** unto righteousness [with our spirit we believe God and receive His righteousness]; and with the mouth confession is made **unto salvation** [saved from eternal death because of sin, because with the mouth of your soul you agree with what God says about His Son by faith]" (Rom. 10:8b-10). * Paul uses these verses for saving the Jews during his Acts ministry. The salvation that Paul is speaking about in these verses is not from hell but from Israel's apostasy (lack of faith that Jesus is their Messiah). The Jew first needs to trust that Jesus is the Messiah, the Son of God and then they can trust the same gospel as the Gentiles: His death, burial and resurrection for their sins (1Cor. 15:3, 4). **<u>Romans 10:9, 10 leave out Christ dying for our sins</u>**. However, Paul has already talked about Christ's death for sins earlier in the letter: Rom. 3:22-26 and Rom. 4:5, 24, 25, 5:8. The fact that Christ died for sins was mentioned often in Israel's program but the fact that Christ would die for OUR (Gentiles) SINS was not revealed until Paul.

All have sinned. **Therefore, since Rom. 10:9, 10 is talking about salvation from apostasy and not from eternal death, for the purpose of witnessing 1 Cor. 15:3, 4 are superior for both Jews and Gentiles. There is no distinction between Jew and Gentile in the body of Christ (Gal 3:27, 1 Cor. 12:13).**

"For I delivered unto you first of all that which I also **received** [Paul received this gospel by revelation from the risen Christ in heaven], how that [by crucifixion] Christ died for **our sins [that Christ died for OUR (all people's) SINS was not revealed until Paul]** according to the scriptures [as prophesied in the OT]; And that he was buried, and that he rose again the third day according to the scriptures [the third day is the sign of Jonah in Matt. 12:39, 40]" (1 Cor. 15:3, 4).

Romans 10:1 Brethren, **my heart's desire and prayer** [Paul was burdened and prayed for them because he wants Israel to be saved] to God for **Israel** is, that they might be **saved** [salvation from sin and eternal death]. **2** For I bear them record that they have **a zeal** of God [like Paul when he persecuted the "little flock" and was "zealous toward God" Acts 22:3], but not according to **knowledge** [that <u>Jesus of Nazareth</u> (Acts 22:8) was their Messiah]. **3** For they being **ignorant of God's righteousness**, and going about to establish their own righteousness, have not submitted themselves unto the righteousness of God. **4** For **Christ** *is* the end of the law for righteousness to every one that believeth [10:10, The law ends for the believer because the law was our schoolmaster to bring us to Christ, and once He is in us we can keep the law be walking after the Spirit (Gal. 3:12, 24, 25; Rom. 8:4)]. **5** For Moses describeth the righteousness which is of the **law**, That the man which **doeth** those things shall **live by them** [Lev. 18:5]. **6** But the righteousness which is of faith speaketh on this wise, Say not in thine heart, Who shall ascend into heaven? (that is, to bring Christ down *from above*:) **7** Or, Who shall descend into the deep? (that is, to bring up Christ again from the dead.) [Deut. 30:12-14] **8** But what saith it? **The word is nigh thee,** *even* in thy **mouth**, and in thy **heart**: that is, the **word of faith** [4:24, 25], **which we preach; 9** That if thou shalt **confess** with thy mouth the Lord Jesus [agree with your soul's mouth that Jesus Christ is **the "Stone"**], and shalt **believe** in thine heart [in your spirit] that God hath raised him from the dead [He proved that He is the Son of God and finished the work of the cross by rising from the dead, it is faith in His work ALONE that saves. The apostate nation of Israel did not believe Jesus was the Christ], thou shalt be **saved. 10** For with the heart man believeth unto righteousness [the sinner receives the gift of the imputed righteousness of Christ, 10:4]; and with the mouth confession is made unto salvation. **11** For the scripture saith, Whosoever **believeth** [*Notice the present tense] on him shall not be **ashamed** [at the Great White Throne Judgment, Isa. 28:16]. **12** For there is **no difference between the Jew and the Greek** [Rom.

3:23, 11:23 the ground is level at the foot of the cross in this dispensation, Gal. 3:28]: for the same Lord over all is **rich** unto all that call upon him [Everyone is saved the same way today. God will save all individuals who believe the gospel, Rom. 4:24, 25; 2 Thess. 2:14; 1 Cor. 15:3, 4, Therefore, individual Jews who believe become members of the body of Christ]. **13** For **whosoever** shall **call** upon the name of the Lord shall be saved [in the Tribulation also, **Joel 2:32** but to follow Paul's gospel will be error after the Rapture]. **14 How** then shall they **call** on him in whom they have not believed? and how shall they believe in him of whom they have not heard? and how shall they hear without a preacher? **15** And how shall they preach, except they be sent? as it is written, How beautiful are the feet of them that preach the **gospel of peace** [Isa. 52:7, once they are saved they can tell others so they can also have "peace with God" Rom. 5:1], and bring **glad tidings of good things**! **16** But they have not all **obeyed** [believed] **the gospel**. For Esaias saith, Lord, who hath **believed our report**? [Isa. 53:1, just like in Isaiah's day Israel is resistant to believing the gospel] **17 So then faith** *cometh* **by hearing, and hearing by the word of God** [The sinner cannot be saved apart from the word of God, so show them the word. The power is in His word!]. **18** But I say, Have they not heard? [Psa. 19:4; Col. 1:23] **Yes** verily, their sound went into **all the earth**, and their words unto the ends of the world [Israel heard the gospel]. **19** But I say, Did not Israel know? First Moses saith, I will provoke you [unbelieving Israel] **to jealousy** by *them that are* no people [the "little flock" told them about Jesus Christ, Isa. 65:1], *and* by **a foolish nation** ["a" singular, Deut. 32:21, the remnant, the "little flock"] I will anger you [unbelieving Israel]. **20** But Esaias is very bold, and saith, **I was found of them that sought me not**; I was made manifest unto them that **asked not after me** [the nation should have believed Isaiah 53 and the remnant, Isa. 65:1, 2]. **21 But to** Israel [the unbelieving nation] he saith, All day long I have stretched forth my hands unto a disobedient and gainsaying people [God has had His arms wide open to Israel for them to run into but they have resisted and opposed His many offers while others have believed].

The Times of the Gentiles (Luke 21:24) is different **from the fullness of the Gentiles** (Rom. 11:25 at the Rapture) and it is also different from Daniel's 490 years (Dan. 9:24-27). Daniel's timeline begins later. It began with the decree to return to the land (as mentioned in Neh. 2:6 while some say Ezra 1:1) to complete the wall around Jerusalem (which took 52 days, Neh. 6:15) and build the temple (which took 46 years). However, the times of the Gentiles began earlier with the Babylonian captivity of Israel and ends at the Second Coming of Christ. Daniel's Timeline also ends at the Second Coming of Christ. The prophetic clock stopped at the cross, but then Israel was given a bonus year (Luke 13:6-9).

Romans Chapter 11 – Has God Cast Away His People?

11:1-6 Paul continues to talk about the remnant saved by God's grace.
11:7-10 the election (a remnant of Peter and Paul saved) the rest were blinded
11:11, 12, 15, 25 The nation of Israel has temporarily fallen and been postponed
11:13 Paul is the apostle of the Gentiles.
11:17 Gentiles are graft into the root Abraham's "thy seed" Christ (Gal. 3:14-16).
11:25 Israel is blinded in part so that God can show mercy to all and save all who will believe Paul's gospel both individual Jews and Gentiles. The **"fulness of the Gentiles" is the fulfillment of the promise to the Gentiles, the Rapture.**
11:26 After the Rapture, God will resume His prophesied dealings with Israel.
11:31-36 Paul is jubilant because by joining in the Gentiles' mercy, individual Jews may also be saved in this age. God has declared all people to be in unbelief so that He can show mercy to anyone that does believe.

By having a clear understanding of Romans 11 we will understand what God is doing today, and **why we are not "spiritual Israel" like some Replacement Theologians like to say.** We already know that **the covenants all belong to Israel and not to the Gentiles today (Rom. 9:4).** Therefore, not only is Replacement theology wrong, so is **Covenant Theology.** Today we will learn the truth of what God says in His word about who the "wild olive tree" (Rom. 11:17) is/are. Then we can know from this chapter what God has done, is doing, and will do.

As we study Romans chapter 11, keep in mind that in Romans 9-11 there are three main groups of people: 1) the apostate nation of Israel, 2) the remnant (Peter and the "little flock" that believed Christ in His earthly ministry) and 3) the Gentiles (all people including the apostate nation in the dispensation of grace). ***It is very important to realize that Gentile means all people and is not the same as the body of Christ unless they are a believing Gentile.** In this lesson, we will learn that the Gentiles (the wild olive tree branch) is grafted in, and **NOT** the body of Christ. Furthermore, they are grafted into the blessings of Abraham, the root being Christ "thy seed" (Gal. 3:7, **14**, **16**, 29; Rom. 4:11), **NOT** Israel.

So before we start please remember that 9:25, 26 speaks about the **apostate nation of Israel** that are Lo-ammi (not my people) being called my people again after the Tribulation when God reshapes the lump to be honorable. Also 9:27, the **remnant** is Peter and the "little flock" (Luke 12:32).

As mentioned, Romans 9-11 is a parenthetical explanation by Paul in his letter to the Romans that answers the question, what about Israel? Knowing this information helps the body of Christ to better understand what God is doing for the Gentiles today and what He will do for Israel in the future.

Before Paul, no one knew that God had planned to form the body of Christ to fill the heavenly places by giving Gentiles a direct salvation opportunity apart from going through the nation of Israel.

In Romans 11, **Paul will explain the mystery (a previously undisclosed secret plan of God) of Israel's judicial temporary blindness**. They have been blinded by God as a nation for nearly 2,000 years. The blinding of Elymas, the Jewish sorcerer (recorded in Acts 13:6-13) is a miniature picture of Israel's blinding. Paul told him, ". . . the hand of the Lord is upon thee, and thou shalt be blind, not seeing the sun for a **season**" (Acts 13:8).

In **chapters 1-5 Justification** We learned how Jesus Christ paid the sin debt of all mankind and freely gives imputed righteousness to all who believe so that we can be justified by what He has done even though we were guilty, helpless, and sinful.

Then in **chapters 6-8 Sanctification** Paul said that we are dead to sin, dead to the law, but alive unto God so we can live for Him if we walk in the Spirit, not in the flesh. "For I know that in me (that is in my flesh), dwelleth no good thing" (7:18).

Chapters 9-11 What about Israel? Through Paul, Christ revealed the mystery of Israel's national blindness because of their lack of faith in Christ. God has delayed Israel's prophetic program and His wrath until after the Rapture of the Church (the Gentile believers, the body of Christ) which He is now forming. God is showing mercy to all Gentiles (which includes the individual Jews since they are considered to be Gentiles today). The blindness is "in part" for two reasons: first the individual Jew can be saved today when God is displaying His amnesty to all (2 Cor. 5:19), and second the remnant also "saw" and "perceived" (understood) the grace that had been given to Paul. *Remember Gentiles in Prophecy are different from Gentiles in Mystery, but God wants to save them in both programs.

Besides the Gentiles, the believing remnant was also a vessel of God's mercy. It was necessary for the little flock to be notified of the dispensational change ushered in by Paul's ministry. Paul did not meet Peter until three years after he began his ministry. Then 14 years later Paul attended the Jerusalem Council. By then Paul had been in the ministry for 17 years. The ascended Lord Jesus Christ waited until Paul had a firm grasp of the doctrine committed to him before he shared it with the 12 apostles to Israel. By that time many were asking the 12

"Where is the promise of his coming?" (2 Peter 3:4). Paul went up by revelation of the Lord to communicate to them "**that** gospel which I preach among the Gentiles" (Gal. 2:2). When Peter, and the other Holy Spirit filled leaders at Jerusalem, understood that Christ had begun a new ministry to the **Gentiles** from heaven through Paul, they **loosed** themselves from carrying out their commission. At the Jerusalem Council (Acts 15; Gal. 1, 2) they realized that Christ had given Paul a different gospel and ministry so they gave Paul and Barnabas their approval.

Peter had the "**keys of the kingdom**" (Matt. 16:19) that allowed for binding and loosing, but notice the plural for "hands" meaning that all the leadership agreed with the decision to **loose** themselves. "But **contrariwise**, when they **saw** that the **gospel of the uncircumcision** was committed unto **me**, as the **gospel of the circumcision** was unto **Peter [*notice the two different gospels]** ; (For he that wrought effectually in Peter to the apostleship of the circumcision, the same was mighty in me toward the Gentiles:) And when James, Cephas, and John, who seemed to be pillars, **perceived** the grace that was given unto me, they gave to me and Barnabas the **right hands of fellowship**; that we *should go* unto the **heathen** [all unbelievers including Jews, 1 Chr. 16:24, Gal. 1:16], and they unto the circumcision" (Gal. 2:7-9).

The "circumcision" refers to true spiritual believers in Israel's program that have a circumcision of the heart. Israel stumbled at the cross, then they fell in Acts 7 with the stoning of Stephen. After the fall of the nation of Israel, the little flock continued in the 12 apostle's doctrine (the gospel of the kingdom) to the circumcision, those saved by John the Baptist, Christ's earthly ministry and through the "little flock" which includes the 120 in the "upper room" and the seven (Philip, Stephen, etc.). The remnant wrote Hebrews through Revelation (during Acts) before they died out. There is only one gospel that saves today, Paul's (see "my gospel" Rom. 2:16, Rom. 16:25: 2 Tim. 2:8; see also "our gospel" 2 Cor. 4:3; 1 Thess. 1:5; 2 Thess. 2:14).

Summary overview: This chapter answers the question – has God cast away His people? No, not permanently. While the nation of Israel has been cast off, spiritual believers of the remnant of Israel have not been cast off. In fact, in God's plan He is actually continuing to show mercy to Israel. It is important to keep in mind that Paul is primarily speaking of groups of people. Paul explains that God has extended mercy to both a remnant of Israel (that existed at the "present" time when Paul is writing this letter, there is no remnant today because it diminished) and to the Gentiles (Israel is considered to be just like any other nation today, Gentile). After using the olive tree to describe what God is doing, Paul discusses

Israel's future, and God's current mercy to all. God has a dispensational purpose behind the temporary fall, blindness in part, and casting away of His people, and the salvation opportunity of the Gentiles apart from Israel's prophecy program.

In the past Christ was to die for "the transgression of my people was he stricken" (Isa. 53:8). Again, the angel told Joseph, "thou shalt call his name JESUS: for he shall save his people [Israel] from their sins" (Matt. 1:21). However, to Paul, Christ from heaven revealed that "Christ died for **OUR (Gentiles) SINS**" (1 Cor. 15:3). Jesus told His 12 apostles that they would be "in Him." In John 17:23, Jesus prayed, "I in them, and thou in me [the Father] . . ." From Paul we learn the Gentile believers are also to have this privilege: He is in us "**Christ in you** the hope of glory" (Col. 1:27, 28). We are in also in Him "hid with Christ in God" (Col. 3:3).

We learn that we have **OUR own words of God** specifically "to us" from Christ in heaven through Paul **OUR APOSTLE**. We also learn through Paul that **Abraham is OUR spiritual father, too**. He is "father of all them that believe" (Rom. 4: 11) so like Abraham (who was a Gentile when He trusted God) we can receive God's imputed righteousness by faith. **In 11:17,** Jesus is the **root**, and the **fatness** is His blessings. Christ is Abraham's "thy seed" (Gal. 3:16) and Jesus Christ is the "root of Jesse" (Rom. 15:12). **Not until Paul do we find out that God has a plan for the Gentiles apart from going through the nation of Israel.**

Romans 11: 1 I say then, **Hath God cast away his people**? God forbid. For I also am an Israelite, of the seed of Abraham, of the tribe of Benjamin [the fact that individual Jews like Paul can still be saved from the penalty of their sin, proves that God has not cast off His people Israel. Rather, He has given them another opportunity to be His people, along with Gentiles, in the body of Christ]. **2** God hath **not** cast away his people which he **foreknew** [Before God formed Israel, He had a plan for them to be His holy nation of priests, ruling on earth (Ex 19:6; Isa. 2:1-4, 60:1-3, 12]. Wot ye not what the scripture saith of **Elias**? how he maketh intercession to God against **Israel**, saying, **3** Lord, they have killed thy prophets, and digged down thine altars; and I am left alone, and they seek my life. **4** But what saith the answer of God unto him? I have reserved to myself seven thousand men, who have not bowed the **knee *to the image* of Baal. 5** Even so then **at this present time** also there is a **remnant** [just like in Elijah's day when it seemed that all of Israel was against God (1 Kings 19), God knows those that are His, even if they were not standing with Elijah. These have not "bowed the knee *to the image* of Baal" man's religion. God has saved a remnant of Jews who are still alive during the beginning of the dispensation of grace.] according to the **election of grace** [salvation is always by grace. God freely imputes His grace]. **6** And if by

grace, then is it no more of **works: otherwise grace is no more grace**. But if it be of works, then is it **no more grace**: otherwise work is no more work [This verse is not talking about salvation but refers to Rom. 9:11 when Paul pointed out that God chose to elect Jacob by whom His nation would come, not Esau before they were born. It was by God's grace entirely, not of works. God chose. Grace is unearned kindness].

7 ¶ What then? **Israel** [the nation] hath **not obtained** that which he seeketh for [* notice not called she, because that Israel is not His Bride at this time. They were seeking for eternal life with God]; but **the election** [Peter and the "little flock," the remnant] **hath obtained it**, and **the rest were blinded** [the apostate nation of Israel] **8** (According as it is written in Psalm 69:13-28 [Jesus Christ prayed to the Father on the cross, He looked for pity but there was only reproach, so He prays that these unbelieving enemies will not receive righteousness but be blotted out from eternal life], **God hath given them the spirit of slumber**, eyes that they should **not see**, and **ears** that they should **not hear**;) unto this day. **9** And David saith, Let their **table be made a snare** [all the provisions of God including their Deliverer], and **a trap**, and a **stumblingblock**, and **a recompence** unto them [let them get what they deserve]: **10** Let their **eyes be darkened**, that they may **not see**, and bow down their back always ["loins to continually shake" (Psalm 69:23) under the burden of their sin]. **11** I say then, Have they stumbled [They stumbled over Christ, their rock of offence at the cross Rom. 9:31-33; Isa. 8:13-15; 28:16] that they should fall? [Christ prayed on the cross that "father forgive them" (Luke 23:34). Even after Christ's resurrection, during Acts 1-7 God was still speaking only to Israel (for example Acts 2:5, 14, 22, 36, 3:12, 25, 5:30, 31)] God forbid: but **rather through their fall salvation is come unto the Gentiles** [So they did fall after they had stumbled at the cross they fell at the stoning of Stephen in Acts 7. The Holy Ghost had come down in Acts 2 and filled all the remnant believers. Stephen summarized Israel's rebellion when he called them "uncircumcised (Acts 7:51). This meant that they had broken God's covenant, and were no better than the Gentiles (Gen. 17:10-14; Rom. 2:25-27). Israel fell when the religious leaders (who represented the nation) demonstrated that they refused to believe that Jesus was their Messiah by stoning Stephen to death], **for to provoke them to jealousy** [God's favor to the Gentiles causes the Jews to be jealous so that they may be saved in this new dispensation]. **12 Now if the fall of them be the riches of the world, and the diminishing of them the riches of the Gentiles** [The riches of the world is direct access to God without having to go through Israel. Israel diminished during the Acts period. They rejected Peter and the Holy Spirit filled remnant of believers that had trusted that Jesus was their Messiah when He was on earth committing the unforgivable blasphemy of the Holy Ghost, Matt. (12:31, 32). And then they rejected the Holy Spirit filled Paul (Acts 13:46, 18:6, 28:28). **Paul's frequent visits to the synagogues were to notify the lost Jews that they now needed to be saved through his ministry]; how much more their fulness**? [They have fallen temporarily but when God resumes His dealing with them it will be a grand revival for the world after Israel is saved at Christ's Second Coming.]

13 ¶ For I speak to you Gentiles, inasmuch as **I am the apostle of the Gentiles, I magnify mine office** [Paul's motive for magnifying his office is to win his kinsmen. *Notice the mini-timeline: stumbled at the cross, fell at the stoning of Stephen, then Paul saved on the road to Damascus. His office as apostle of the Gentiles was given to him by Christ after his unique salvation on the road to Damascus in Acts 9. Paul is the only one to write to the body of Christ about the dispensation of grace . . . that was kept secret (Eph. 3:1-6; Rom. 16:25, 26]: **14** If by any **means I may provoke to emulation them which are my flesh, and might save some of them [Paul had a distinct ministry, and hoped to save his kinsmen]. 15** For if the **casting away of them** [those in the apostate nation who did not believe were cast away] **be the reconciling of the world** [the world has an opportunity to be saved directly by believing the gospel of grace, apart from their prophetic program of Israel, keeping their laws, believing what they believe, being water baptized, and circumcised, and so on], **what shall the receiving of them be, but life from the dead?** [God will bring Israel back to life. They will have their sins atoned at the Second Coming (our sins are atoned now, 5:11), and will have eternal life. The kingdom saints will be resurrected and flourish in the kingdom and there will be a great revival in the earth] **16** For if the **firstfruit** be holy [The remnant (Peter's group) also a holy beginning of the nation through Abraham and his seed through Isaac, Jacob, and the 12], **the lump is also holy** [Num. 15:20]: and if the **root be holy, so are the branches. 17** And if some of the branches be broken off, and **thou** [the Gentiles], being a **wild olive tree**, wert graffed in among them, and **with them partakest of the root [Jesus the "root of Jesse" (Rom. 15:12)] and fatness of the olive tree** [the blessing of a chance for eternal life (Gal. 3:14-16)]; **18** Boast not against the branches [unbelieving Israel]. But if thou boast, thou bearest not the root, but the root thee [you have been made part of their goodness]. **19** Thou wilt say then, The branches were broken off, that I might be graffed in. **20** Well; because of unbelief they were broken off, and thou **standest by faith** [those who take the opportunity to trust in the gospel of grace become members of the body of Christ]. **Be not highminded, but fear: 21 For if God spared not the natural branches [the nation of Israel], take heed lest he also spare not thee. 22 Behold therefore the goodness and severity of God: on them which fell, severity** [the nation of Israel has been postponed for nearly 2,000 years]; **but toward thee, goodness, if thou continue in his goodness: otherwise**

thou also shalt be cut off [the dispensation of grace will end at the Rapture]. **23 And they also, if they abide not still in unbelief, shall be graffed in: for God is able to graff them in again** [when they believe in the future, God will graft them in]. **24 For if thou wert cut out of the olive tree which is wild by nature, and wert graffed contrary to nature into a good olive tree** [a graft is usually a better branch cut in from a good olive tree NOT a wild inferior one, Gal. 3:26-29]: **how much more shall these, which be the natural branches, be graffed into their own olive tree** [Israel will naturally take to their own olive tree]?

25 ¶ For I would not, brethren, that ye should be ignorant of this mystery, lest ye should be wise in your own conceits; that blindness in part is happened to Israel, until the fulness of the Gentiles be come in [fulness is the promise of the Rapture. Israel is partially (not totally) blinded in two ways: first Paul communicated to the leaders of the little flock that God had begun a new dispensation and was forming the body of Christ through his ministry in Acts 15 and in Galatians, they "saw" and "perceived" (Gal. 2:7-9). Second, since individual Jews can be saved today the nation is blinded, but not the individual. However, a vail is over their hearts which is taken away when they believe (2 Cor. 3:13-16). The **"fulness of the Gentiles"** is the fulfillment of the promise to the Gentiles] **26 And so all Israel shall be saved: as it is written, There shall come out of Sion the Deliverer [Christ], and shall turn away ungodliness from Jacob** [Psa. 14:7, 53:6; Joel 3:16; Isa. 2:3; 59:20]: **27 For this is my covenant unto them** [This is a covenant that God has promised to Israel that He will not be angry with them forever. God will make them His people again. Then at that time He will implement His New Covenant, (Jer. 31:31-34, Heb. 8:8-12, Isa. 59:20, 21, and Ezek. 36:24-28) God will supernaturally cause Israel to keep the law by putting it in them, so they will keep the law and stop sinning. Therefore, God will can give them all physical blessings and promises for obedience, instead of curses (Ex. 23:25-27; Duet. 7:12-16; 28:1-28], **when I shall take away their sins [God will take away Israel's sins at Christ's Second Coming. No one is sin free currently so we are not under the New Covenant now. But the body of Christ believers have already been forgiven all trespasses at salvation (Col. 2:13, Ep. 4:32)]. 28** As concerning the gospel, they are enemies for your sakes [Jews generally do not want to believe that Jesus of Nazareth is the Christ who died for their sins, was buried and rose again the third day according to the scriptures]: but as touching the **election**, they are beloved for the **fathers' sakes** [God will keep His promises to their fathers (Duet. 4:37, 7:6-8, 10:15)]. **29 For the gifts and calling of God are without repentance** [God will not change His mind about giving them the gift of eternal life with Him]. **30 For as ye in times past have not believed God** [Rom. 1:18-32; Eph. 2:11, 12, 13], yet have now obtained mercy through their unbelief:

[Israel was to be a blessing, but now the Gentiles are.] **31** Even so have these also now not believed, that **through your mercy they also may obtain mercy** [While God is dispensing grace and mercy on the Gentiles the Jews can be saved also, especially if the Gentiles share the gospel with them. This is the **opposite** of Israel's program. Paul committed the **blasphemy of the Holy Ghost** which would not be forgiven (Matt. 12:30, 31) yet because God has interrupted Prophecy and inserted the Mystery, Paul was forgiven and became the first member of the body of Christ, our pattern (1 Tim. 1:12-17)]. **32** For **God hath concluded them all in unbelief**, that he might have mercy upon all [Today, in the dispensation of grace, God is not imputing sins to anyone (2 Cor. 5:19). <u>Sins do not keep a person from eternal life, it is unbelief that keeps a person from eternal life.</u>].

33 ¶ O the depth of the riches both of the wisdom and knowledge of God! how **unsearchable** are his judgments, and **his ways past finding out!** [Paul marvels at the wisdom of God. His great plan was so unsearchable that no one knew it, not even Satan, "for had they know it, they would not have crucified the Lord of glory" (1 Cor. 2:8). If Satan would have known that God would not only reclaim the earth, but also the heavenly places, and give the Israelites another chance in a new dispensation then Satan would not have crucified our Saviour. Paul is ecstatic because he is so thrilled that God has introduced a new dispensation so that not only he (who was a former blasphemer see 1 Tim. 1:11-17] can be saved but also his kinsmen, and anyone who would believe the gospel of grace.] **34** For **who hath known the mind of the Lord? or who hath been his counsellor?** [No one knew "the things that God hath prepared for them who love him. But God has revealed *them* unto us by his Spirit" through His word (I Cor. 2:9, 10). "Wherein he hath abounded toward us in all wisdom and prudence" (Eph. 1:8). God is a giver. He had no counsellor. No one was in on God's plan, it was a complete secret until He revealed it to us through Paul (Eph. 3:1-9] **35** Or **who hath first given to him, and it shall be recompensed unto him again?** [God came up with His plan on His own so He does not owe anything to anyone.] **36 For of him, and through him, and to him, are all things: to whom be glory for ever.** [Paul brakes out in a jubilant praise of God's magnificent wisdom. God "worketh all things after the counsel of his own will" (Eph. 1:11). <u>Paul is so happy because he has realized that God has made a way to save both Jews and Gentiles in this age of amnesty in which we live</u> (2 Cor. 5:19). (<u>Interestingly, in the future Millennial Kingdom, Gentiles will have a 1,000-year opportunity to be saved.</u>) All things are of God, through Him, and to Him. To Him be all glory forever!] Amen.

When we understand the difference between God's dealings with the nation of Israel and the body of Christ, then we begin to understand the Bible much better.

The Wild Olive Branch Explained

Paul is speaking to Gentiles (11:13). The "thou" (11:17) is the "Gentiles" NOT the Body of Christ. The Gentile opportunity to stand by faith ends at their fullness.

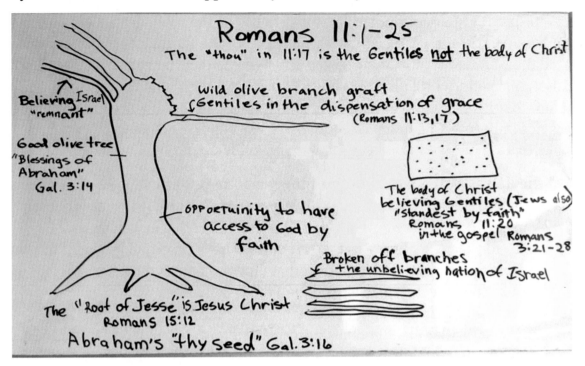

The Trees of Israel (Judges 9:7-15)

Olive Tree – represents the spiritual life of Israel (access and communication with God). Spiritual advantages (imputation, justification, forgiveness, sanctification, etc.) not physical promises about a land and a nation (Gen.12:2, 13:15) and spiritual promises (resurrection and eternal life). <u>The root is Abraham's "thy seed" (Gal. 3:14-16) which is Christ "the root of Jesse" (Romans 15:12), the fatness is blessings through Christ.</u>

Vine – represents Israel's national life (Psa. 80:8-16; Isa. 5:1-7; John 15:1-5).

Fig – Israel's legal-religious system (faith) (Luke13:6-9).

Bramble – represents Israel when in rebellion against God.

It is significant that Paul uses the olive tree (access opportunity to God) in his illustration in Romans 11. It is the **only** one of the four trees that can apply to us since Abraham was a Gentile when he trusted that God would give him an heir (a son) and received the imputed righteousness of God by faith (Gen. 15:6). <u>We receive the righteousness of Christ, there is no salvation apart from being in Christ.</u>

Romans Chapter 12 – How do we live a life of service to God?
12:1-8 How to live a life of Christian service for the **glory of God.**
12:9-16 How to serve all men especially those in the faith.
12:17-21 How to treat those outside the body of Christ and our enemies.

In Romans chapters 12-16, the last section of his letter to the Romans, Paul demonstrates **how to live a life of service to God out of gratitude (righteousness practiced)** based on what He has done and said in chapters 1-11. It is our practical daily living guide for our "reasonable service." **We are to present our bodies a living sacrifices unto God and know how to deal with those inside and outside the faith, and our enemies.** In this study, we will not only discover how to serve God but also distinguish between talents, spiritual gifts, and Christ living in us as our resource. This chapter is about our service (practicing righteousness) consecrating our bodies to God as mentioned in the Romans Outline. Paul ends the chapter by saying we believers should heap coals of fire on our enemy's head. Do you know what Paul means? This interesting quote will be explained.

I pray that these Bible Studies, which cover an entire chapter at a time will edify and equip us all. After we have been enlightened and come to the "knowledge of the truth" (1 Tim. 2:4) by "rightly dividing the word of truth" (2 Tim. 2:15) many of us feel compelled to share this knowledge with anyone who will listen. We want others to have the clarity, joy, and peace we have come to appreciate from understanding God's word rightly divided. We all need to be **ambassadors** and **teachers for Christ** in these last days of the dispensation of the grace of God.

In addition, for a clear understanding of scripture, it is important to keep the 12 apostles separate from the one apostle to the body of Christ. The 12 are NOT in the body of Christ. We must not mix law and grace, prophecy and mystery, nor Christ's ministry on earth through Israel with His ministry from heaven through the body of Christ (1 Tim. 3:16). GOD HAS TWO PROGRAMS IN THE BIBLE: ONE FOR THE EARTH AND ONE FOR HEAVEN. Shawn Brasseux has posted 50 reasons why the 12 are not in the body of Christ on his very informative website Forwhatsaiththescriptures.org I have a link to it on God's Secret Facebook Page.

It is interesting to note that Peter's first apostolic miracle was to heal the lame man who sat at the gate Beautiful of the temple to show Israel that they could be healed as a nation, and be a royal priesthood if they believed (Acts 3:6-11; Isa. 35:5, 6). Paul's first apostolic miracle was the blinding of Elymas the Jewish sorcerer for "a season" (Acts 13:11) is a snapshot of the present temporary blinding of the nation of Israel (Rom. 11:25, 2 Cor. 3:14).

In summary, with the power of Christ living in us "the righteousness of God" (Rom. 1:17) can be revealed through us from His faith to our faith, "as it is written, The just shall live by faith" (Rom. 1:17). We present our bodies (earthen vessels) as living sacrifices to Him. Christ is our treasure, our life, our All in all. His life in us is our power source. Life is about Him and His people (the body of Christ), not us. At the judgment seat of Christ, the only thing that will count is what we have allowed Christ to do through us, His wisdom, knowledge, and understanding are the gold, silver, and precious stones. Sign gifts stopped at the end of Acts. We do not need spiritual gifts today because we have His word and Christ living through us. So now we want to "make all men see what is the fellowship of the mystery, which from the beginning of the world hath been hid in God . . ." (Eph. 3:9).

Romans 12:1 I beseech [we live in the dispensation of God's grace so Paul is not commanding us, but urging us] you **therefore** [Because God is so merciful (as demonstrated by all that we learned in chapters 1-11) we want to serve Him. What should be our motive? (Eph. 5:1, 2; 2 Cor. 9:15; He purchased us with His blood, Rom. 3:25, 5:9; Eph. 1:7. Our motive is love and gratitude, and to glorify God], **brethren** [speaking to the saints, 1:7], by the **mercies of God** ["For God hath concluded them all in unbelief, that he might have **mercy** upon all" (11:32) both Jews and Gentiles] that ye **present your bodies a living sacrifice** [A sacrifice is dead so how can we be a living sacrifice? Because we are dead and have been crucified with Christ, so now Christ who is our life, can live through us (Gal. 2:20, Rom. 6:4, 8:2, 10, 11). **Our bodies are earthen vessels that house a treasure, the life of Jesus in and through us.** Some of us are cracked pots so that more of Jesus can shine through us (2 Cor. 4:7-11) The magnitude of what it means to have Christ living through us is hard to understand. But by faith, we believe what the Bible says. When we get our glorified bodies and fly around in heaven the light that shines in us will be His light. **This life is not about us, but about Christ and what He has done and serving Him and His people**], **holy** [Christ in us is holy], **acceptable unto God** [we are accepted because of him (Eph. 1:6)], **which is your reasonable service** [since God has done all this for us, it is only reasonable that we should want to serve Him (1 Cor. 6:19, 20; 2 Cor. 5:14, 15)]. **2 And be not conformed to this world** [Satan is the "god of this world" (2 Cor. 4:4), and the "prince of the power of the air" (Eph. 2:2) we need to make sure that we are not sucked into watching TV (the airwaves) or wasting our time on social media or on other pursuits that have no eternal value. We are to be conformed to "the image of his Son" (Rom. 8:29). We conform to Christ by reading, studying and meditating on His word (Col. 3:16, 17)]: **but be ye transformed by the renewing of your mind** [we renew our minds by reading the Bible (Eph. 4:22-24; Col. 3:6-13) so we can have the "mind of Christ" (1 Cor. 2:16) and make the right decisions because we think like Christ. We need to control our minds moment by moment (2 Cor. 10:5). We need to reprogram our minds with the truth of His word rightly divided], that ye may prove what is that **good, and acceptable, and perfect, will of God** [We need to join into what He is doing, and promote His good, and acceptable, and perfect will (1 Tim. 2:4; Phil. 1:9-11; Eph. 1:9, 10; Col. 1:9, 10, 25 28). We need to walk by faith and be led by the Spirit (2 Cor. 5:7; Gal. 5:16) God's word is complete now, so we do not expect God to speak to us in any other way (2 Tim. 3:16, 17). Remember Christ is our resource (Col. 1:27)].

3 ¶ For I say, through the grace given unto **me [Christ made Paul our apostle]**, to every man that is among you, not to think of himself more highly than he ought to think [Romans has taught us that we are eternally saved from the penalty of our sin, justified by the faith of Jesus, having received His imputed righteousness, we will spend eternal lives with Him in glory – all because of what our Lord Jesus Christ did for us. We have no goodness or merit apart from Him (Rom. 3:10-12). This means that no one is any better than anyone else. We have what we have because we have received it of Him (1 Cor. 4:3, 7)]; but to **think soberly** [realistically], according as God hath dealt to every man the **measure of faith** [We all had faith to believe, now by studying God's word our faith grows (10:17)]. **4** For as we have many members in **one body**, and all members have not the same office [A body is made up of different parts, fingers, toes, eyes, and ears that function differently but together, controlled by the brain. Likewise, each believer has a different function in the body of Christ in their service for God.] **5** So we, being many, are **one body in Christ**, and every one members one of another [We are one organism or agency, the one new man (Eph. 2:15)] **6** Having then **gifts differing according to the grace that is given to us, whether prophecy, let us** *prophesy* **according to the proportion of faith;** [We learn from each other because everyone is valuable but have different strengths, capabilities, and functions. There is so much confusion today about spiritual gifts. Let us distinguish between talents, spiritual gifts, and the life of Christ in us as our resource. Talents are skills in things like music, art, sports, and so on, they are a result of heredity, environment, and hard work. Talents are not spiritual gifts and even unsaved people who are dead to God have talents. Some spiritual gifts were promised to Israel as a sign of their impending kingdom on earth (Isa. 35:5, 6; Mark 16:17, 18; Luke 9:1, 2). When God postponed the kingdom these gifts were briefly carried over into our time period to verify to the Jews that Paul's ministry was from God (Acts 15:12, 19:11, 12, 28:9). Other gifts were given to inform and edify the **new** body of Christ when there was little or no scripture written for it yet (1 Cor. 12:7-11, 28, 14:26; Eph. 4:8, 11-14). All these sign gifts **ceased** when the full revelation for the body of Christ was made known to Paul and written (1 Cor. 13:8-12). Now that the scripture is complete and fulfilled (Col. 1:25), it is everything we need to be edified and made "perfect, thoroughly furnished unto all good works" (2 Tim. 3:16, 17). Today we still have pastors, evangelists, and teachers (2 Tim. 2:2; 4:5) but they are not supernaturally filled with knowledge. Today they have to desire the office (I Tim. 3:1) and study the scriptures to be approved unto God (2 Tim. 2:15). Remember that Romans is one of Paul's early letters still written during the Acts period when he was still going to the Jews in the synagogues first and then to the Gentiles. By the end of Acts Paul stops going to the Jew first and just goes to the Gentiles (Acts 28:28) and the sign gifts stopped. Remember from the lesson on chapter 8 that all three Persons of the Godhead are Spirit. We have all three in us. Therefore, "Holy Spirit" can refer to any One of the Godhead, while Holy Ghost refers to the third member of the Godhead. The context will help us determine who the Spirit is referring to. The Holy Spirit uses His word to teach us and to work effectually in us (1 Thess. 2:13). There is power in His blood and there is power in His word. Knowledge is power. God wants us to use the power in His word, with His motivation, to edify His body, to help the body of Christ to **grow and thrive (Eph. 4:11-16 * There are no apostles or prophets today. There are evangelists, pastors, and teachers but they are not supernaturally gifted.)** We are to study and teach the things that we have learned from Paul's letters (2 Tim. 2:2; 1 Cor. 4:16, 17, 11:1, 14:37). **Therefore, the power of Christ living in us is far superior to having spiritual gifts**. We must allow Him to live out His life through us, this is how He manifests Himself to the world today (1 Tim. 3:16). We do not need spiritual gifts because we have His word and Christ living through us];

7 Or **ministry**, let us wait on our ministering: or he that teacheth, on teaching [The gifts in verses 7 and 8 apply to us today (but we are not supernatural endowed). Ministry (serving) and teaching are things that can be done by **every one of us** today because they depend on knowledge of the word of God, **not** on having a supernatural gift.]; **8** Or he that **exhorteth**, on exhortation [We encourage and comfort others with our blessed hope (2 Cor. 1:4, 4:16, 17; 1 Thess. 4:13-18)]: he that **giveth**, let him do it with simplicity [Let us give so others may be saved and know the truth. Whether it is time, treasure, talents, or whatever giving is meant for God to see and not men (2 Cor. 8:1-7, 9:7)]; he that **ruleth**, with diligence [This may refer to the "overseers" of the church (Acts 20:28), also called bishops and elders (1 Tim. 3:1-7; Titus 1:5-9). This could also be the ruling of the home, or over people]; he that sheweth **mercy**, with cheerfulness [cheerfully not giving someone what they deserve, but forgiving them (Eph. 4:32)].

9 ¶ Let **love** be without dissimulation [without hypocrisy, not false or with an ulterior motive]. Abhor that which is evil [hate evil, like God does. I must admit that I hate the modern bible versions. I, myself, was deceived by one of the counterfeit bibles, the NKJV which are devoid of the Holy Spirit for more than 15 years, until I learned better.]; **cleave** to that which is good [I am sticking to the King James Bible]. **10 Be kindly affectioned** ["walk in love as Christ also hath loved us" (Eph. 5:2)] one to another with **brotherly love** [show genuine love and care for each other like in a family]; in honour preferring one another [esteem others better than yourselves]; **11 Not** slothful [lazy] in business; fervent [enthusiastic] in **spirit**; serving the Lord ["And whatsoever ye do, do it heartily, as to the Lord, and not unto men" (Col. 3:23)]; **12** Rejoicing in **hope** [of the Rapture]; patient in tribulation [present sufferings]; continuing instant in prayer [pray (talk) to God immediately] ; **13 Distributing to the necessity of saints** [share, including financially to a worthwhile cause, person, or ministry]; given **to hospitality** [Welcome, invite and care for people in your home or restaurant, etc.]. **14 Bless them which persecute you** [speak well of]: **bless, and curse not** [speak badly of]. 15 Rejoice with them that do rejoice [(1 Cor. 12:25-27) have joy with those who have reason to rejoice], and **weep with them that weep** [show empathy with those who are sad]. **16 Be of the same mind one toward another [We in the body of Christ should be thinking the same thing. There is a seven-fold unity in the body (Eph. 4:3-6)** our common purpose is to exalt the Lord Jesus Christ]. **Mind not high things, but condescend to men of low estate** [meet people on their level]. **Be not wise in your own conceits** [Be humble. Don't think you are something (Pro. 26:12)]. **17 Recompense to no man evil for evil,** [1 Thess. 5:15, 22]. **Provide things honest in the sight of all men. 18 If it be possible, as much as lieth in you, live peaceably with all men. 19 Dearly beloved, avenge not yourselves, but rather give place** [make room for and trust that God will judge rightly] **unto wrath: for it is written, Vengeance is mine; I will repay, saith the Lord. 20 Therefore if thine enemy hunger, feed him; if he thirst, give him drink: for in so doing thou shalt heap coals of fire on his head** [This is a quote from Prov. 25:21, 22. When we do good to someone their sinfulness is pointed out to them, and they get a small reminder of the Lake of Fire that awaits them. So they have a chance now to do something about it before the Great White Judgment when it will be too late. This is why doing good is better for our enemy and more powerful than doing evil, because only more evil can come from evil] **21 Be not overcome of evil, but overcome evil with good.** [If we return evil for evil we have been overcome by evil. But if we do not seek revenge, but do good to all men (Gal. 6:10) including our enemies, then we have overcome evil with good. Then evil has failed to affect your inner peace (Gal. 5:22, 23) and to distract us from God's purposes (2 Cor. 4:5, 6, 6:4-10).]

Romans Chapter 13 – Living with Government

13:1-7 God has set up governmental structures in heaven and earth to maintain law and order for the believers good. Christians are to be good citizens.

13:8-14 How to show love to our neighbor. Love is seeking the other person's highest good. We should love our neighbor as ourselves. Our motive should be to edify others. When we love others we automatically fulfill the law.

Romans chapters **1-5** covers salvation (justification because of Christ's imputed righteousness), **6-8** sanctification (how to function), **9-11** is dispensational about Israel, and **12-16** is how a person lives and thinks with a **renewed mind** applying the doctrine learned in 1-11. In chapter 12, Paul addressed how the individual shall live and serve God, those in the Church, and those outside the Church (their enemies). In chapter 13, we learn how to live with government and to love our neighbor as ourselves.

Today we will answer several questions:
What does "knowing the time" mean?
According to prophecy, wasn't Jesus supposed to return about 2,000 years ago?
How can humans (who are selfish by nature) show love to a neighbor?

We are going to find out that WE CANNOT SERVE GOD, CHRIST MUST SERVE GOD THROUGH US. <u>Let us ask: "What can Christ do through me</u>?

"The higher powers" are governmental powers which are ordained by God to maintain law and order. God instituted human government after the flood, when He instituted capital punishment for murder. "Whoso sheddeth man's blood, by man shall his blood be shed: for in the image of God made he man" (Gen. 9:6). Therefore, people were needed to enforce that rule of law. At the Tower of Babel, in Genesis 11, God separated people into nations by making them speak different languages. God knew that it was best for mankind to live in sovereign nations so that they would not do evil continually. God did not choose one of these nations to be His, but about 175 years later He picked Abraham to be the man from whom He would make His own nation (Gen. 12:2). God then decided that Isaac and Jacob would be the fathers of the seedline of His nation, not Ishmael or Esau. Christ came through these fathers (John 4:22; Gal. 3:16).

It is the office of government that God has ordained, not the deeds of the men that fill the office. Christ has ordained governmental structures in heaven and earth. "For by him were all things created, that are in heaven, and that are in earth, visible and invisible, whether they be **thrones, or dominions, or principalities, or powers**: all things were created by him, and for him" (Col. 1:16). There are also might, and dominion. Christ is seated at the right hand of the Father: "Far above all **principality, and power, and might, and dominion, and every name that is named**, not only in this world, but also in that which is to come" (Eph. 1:21). Even Satan and the evil angels have governmental structure. "For we wrestle not against flesh and blood, but against **principalities, against powers, against the rulers of the darkness of this world, against spiritual wickedness in high places**" (Eph. 6:12). Satan and his fallen angels will be thrown out of the Second Heaven in the middle of the Tribulation (Rev. 12:7-9). At this time the heavens are not clean in God's sight (Job. 15:15). After Satan and his angels are evicted we will take their place.

Paul gives us an example of obeying government even though it is not doing right in Acts 23:5 (compare Exodus 22:28). Only in the rare case that government is going against God should we obey God rather than men (Acts 5:29).

We believers fulfil the commandments given of God with Christ living through us, NOT because we have to, but because we want to. All things are lawful for us but not all things are expedient or practical (1 Cor. 6:12). It is good for us to obey both the government and God. We are citizens of our country and of heaven. Grace doesn't free us to sin, it frees us from the penalty and power of sin (and later the presence of sin). The goal for the members of the Church, the body of Christ is "That ye may be blameless and harmless, the sons of God, without rebuke, in the midst of a crooked and perverse nation, among whom ye shine as lights in the world; Holding forth the word of life . . ." (Phil. 2:15, 16a).

Governmental law is not made for the righteous man but for the disobedient and the sound doctrine taught by Paul teaches obedience, right living against such things there is no law. **"Knowing this, that the law is not made for a righteous man**, **but for the lawless** and disobedient, for the ungodly and for sinners, for unholy and profane, for murderers of fathers and murderers of mothers, for manslayers, For whoremongers, for them that defile themselves with mankind, for menstealers, for liars, for perjured persons, **and if there be any other thing that is contrary to sound doctrine**" (1 Tim. 1:9, 10). We are to walk in the Spirit (Christ's Spirit) so that we can bring forth fruit as a result of Him living through us. "But the fruit of the Spirit is love, joy, peace, longsuffering, gentleness, goodness, faith, Meekness, temperance: **against such there is no law. And they that are Christ's have crucified the flesh with the affections and lusts. If we live in the Spirit, let us also walk in the Spirit.** Let us not be desirous of vain glory, provoking one another, envying one another" (Gal. 5:22-26).

Paul wrote Romans (circa AD 58) and all his epistles during the reign of the Roman Emperor Nero, who ruled from AD 54-68 (except Galatians, and the two Thessalonian letters which were written during the reign of Claudius (AD 41-54).

The saints in Rome were very well informed and knowledgeable because they had probably already read copies of Paul's pre-prison letters. Romans is the last of the Acts epistles even though it is first in the canon of scripture (canon means the sacred arrangement, the order of the list of books in the Bible) because it is the foundational book of doctrine following the pattern mentioned by Paul. "All scripture is given by inspiration of God, and is profitable for **doctrine**, for reproof, for correction, for instruction in righteousness" (2 Tim. 3:16).

Although there were three house churches in Rome (as mentioned in Romans 16) Paul wrote to the saints in the body of Christ as a whole, not to the individual groups. "Priscilla and Aquila my helpers in Christ Jesus" (Rom. 16:3) most likely had brought with them all of Paul's letter written by that time (Galatians, the two Corinthian letters, and the two to the Thessalonians). These ministers (Aquila and Priscilla) had been helping Paul for years in both Corinth and Ephesus and were able and willing to share all that they had learned, just like they had with Apollos (Acts 18:24-28). They used to talk while working together making tents (Acts 18:1-3). They knew that Paul was Christ's spokesman to His body of Gentile believers in the dispensation of grace and that he was progressively receiving new revelation from the ascended, glorified Lord Jesus Christ (Acts 26:16; 2 Cor. 12:1).

Christ had begun something new using a:
New Apostle (Paul)
New Gospel (of Christ)
New Dispensation (of grace)
New Agency (the Church, the body of Christ)
New Audience (all people)
New Operating System (Grace, not Law)
New Destiny (Heaven)

Romans 13:1 Let every soul be subject unto the **higher powers** [governmental powers Titus 3:1, 2; 1 Peter 2:13-15]. For there is no power but of God: the powers that be are **ordained of God** [God has set up governmental structures in heaven and on earth (Col. 1:16; Eph. 1:21). It is the office of government that God has ordained, not the deeds of the men that fill that office. Men misuse the office of government to do awful things, like Hitler and Stalin], even Christ while on earth as a man was subject to the brutal Roman government Matt. 22:17]. **2** Whosoever therefore **resisteth** the power, resisteth the **ordinance of God** [governmental structure arranged by God]: and they that resist shall receive to themselves **damnation** [punishment from government for doing wrong, not going to hell]. **3** For **rulers** are not a terror to **good** works, but to the **evil**. Wilt thou then not be afraid of the power? do that which is **good**, and thou shalt have **praise of the same** [If we do good, we are not likely to get in trouble with our government (1 Peter 3:13; Prov. 16:7)]: **4** For he is the **minister of God** to thee **for good**. **But if thou do that which is evil, be afraid**; for he beareth not **the sword in vain**: for he is the minister of God, a revenger to **execute wrath** upon him that doeth evil. [God created government for our good, to protect us. Evil is deterred and restrained by strong rules that are reinforced with punishments. Therefore, Theodore Roosevelt said, "Talk softly, but carry a big stick." The stick is the "wrath" or punishment that fits the crime. We are to pray for our governmental officials 1 Tim. 2:1-3. The right to bare arms, the Second Amendment is a deterrent to evil government.]

5 Wherefore ye must **needs be subject, not only for wrath,** but also for **conscience sake** [We should not only obey because the government says so, but because our conscience tells us what is right and wrong]. **6** For for this cause **pay ye tribute** [tax]: for they are **God's ministers**, attending continually upon this very thing [our taxes go to attendants who keep law and order]. **7** Render therefore to all their dues: **tribute** to whom tribute is due; **custom** [import and export fees] to whom custom; **fear** [respect] to whom fear; **honour** [our leaders who do their best to rule righteously] to whom honour [God is the highest authority, therefore there are exceptions when government disobeys God we should obey God rather than men, Acts 4:19, 5:29; Daniel's friends decided not to worship the statue (Dan: 3:10-18), and also Daniel chose to pray (Dan. 6:5-10)]. **8 Owe no man any thing** [pay your bills, your monthly payment if you take a loan], **but to love one another:** [Love is seeking the other persons highest good. Notice how Paul opens and closes with love in verses 8-10, 1 Tim. 6:11; Phil. 1:9. When we love others we keep the law. God considers us as adult sons who can do what is right without having to follow a list of rules. More people are won to God by love than arguments. Christians who walk with the love of Christ in them have something that others recognize and want. They are the best citizens and the best witnesses] for **he that loveth another hath fulfilled the law**. **9** For this, Thou shalt not commit adultery, Thou shalt not kill, Thou shalt not steal, Thou shalt not bear false witness, Thou shalt not covet; and if there be any other commandment [Paul mentions the last 5 commandments here because they are the ones that deal with our relationship to others. He mentions all except keeping the Sabbath in his writings], **it is briefly comprehended** [we follow the basic principle, not a list of do's and don'ts] in this saying, namely, **Thou shalt love thy neighbour as thyself**.

10 Love worketh no ill to his neighbor [Gal. 5:13-16; 1 Thess. 2:7, 8; 1 Cor. 13:6-8a]: therefore **love is the fulfilling of the law** [God's law was given to show us our sin, Rom. 3:19, 20; Deut. 31:26. Human nature is self-centered Rom. 7:18, so the only way we can ever keep God's law is for Christ's Spirit to live through us Rom. 8:2, 7-10]. **11** And that, **knowing the time,** [1 Thess. 5:1-11 this age of amnesty in which we now live because God has interrupted and postponed Israel's prophetic program and inserted the dispensation of grace which He began with Paul, 2 Cor. 5:15-19: Rom. 8:23; 1Thess. 5:23; 2 Tim. 4:1, 8] that **now it is high time to awake out of sleep:** [notice the urgency, time is running out! (1 Cor. 7:29-31). We have a short life on earth (Psa. 90:10, 12; James 4:14) wake up and share the gospel with unbelievers and "knowledge of the truth" (1 Tim. 2:4) with wrongly dividing believers so they can join the body of Christ believers and not be left behind when the Rapture happens and know the truth (Thess. 4:13-18, 2 Tim. 4:1, 8). It has been the last days in the dispensation of grace for a long time, nearly 2,000 years (2 Tim. 3:1-5). Paul expected Christ return to come at any time. So now nearly 2,000 years later we are nearer than before] for **now is our salvation nearer than when we believed.** [We are looking for our Saviour Jesus Christ to catch us up in the air to Himself (Titus 2:13).]

12 The night is far spent, the **day is at hand** ["the night" is Christ's absence we are waiting for Him in this "present evil world" (Gal. 1:4) we are living in Satan's domain serving our Lord in heaven as His ambassadors waiting to be called home, "the day" refers to the time when Christ is present with us in heaven, the day of Christ]: let us therefore cast off the **works of darkness [Let us stop doing things that have no profit,** Eph. 5:8-11, 2 Cor. 4:3-6, 6:14; 1 Cor. 4:5; Eph. 6:12; **1 Thess. 5:4-10; Col. 1:13, 14]**, and let us put on the **armour of light [Put on Christ, He is the light, Col 3:12-17; Eph. 4:22-24, Christ is the "new man" Eph. 6:10-18]. 13** Let us **walk honestly [we should be honest, not wasting our time in unfruitful works of darkness], as in the day** [as we would if Christ was physically with us]; not in rioting [reveling] and drunkenness, not in **chambering** [sexual indulgence, lewdness] and **wantonness** [unrestrained, reckless], not in **strife and envying** [fighting against people, and wanting what they have]. **14** But **put ye on the Lord Jesus Christ**, and make not provision for the flesh, to fulfil the lusts thereof [Paul reminds us to keep the flesh in subjection and not let it have a chance to lust, 1 Cor. 9:24-27; Gal. 5:16, 25; Rom. 8:1, 4; Gal. 3:27, we are in Him and He is in us (Col. 1:27). Christ is the light John 1:9, 8:12, 14:6, and truth].

The armour of light is really the sound doctrine given to us through Paul and Christ living through us. The whole armour in **Eph. 6** has to do with the Person of our Lord Jesus Christ, His word rightly divided, and prayer to Him: be strong in the Lord, and in the power of **his** might (10).

Put on the whole armour of God . . . stand against the wiles of the devil (11).
having your loins girt about with truth (14) [Jesus is the truth, John 14:6]
breastplate of righteousness (14) [His imputed righteousness]
feet shod with the preparation of the gospel of peace (15) [with God, Rom. 5:1]
shield of faith (16) [faith of Christ and our faith in Him, Gal. 2:16]
helmet of salvation (17) [the battle is for the mind, our spirit, Eph. 4:23]
the sword of the Spirit, which is the word of God (17) [Heb. 4:12]
Praying always with all prayer and supplication in the Spirit (18) [part of the armour is being able to pray to God with help of the Spirit anytime, anywhere].

Christ defeated Satan on the cross and paid the sin debt for all humanity for all time, but He has not taken possession of what He has reclaimed yet. "And having spoiled principalities and powers, he made a shew of them openly, triumphing over them in it" (Col. 2:15).

The law that we follow now is: "the **law** of the Spirit of life in Christ Jesus" (Rom. 8:2). We have the "Spirit of Christ" (Rom. 8:9) in us.

Our salvation was settled at the cross, but now CHRIST IS OUR LIFE so that we can ". . . **walk in love**, as Christ also hath loved us, and hath given himself for us an offering and a sacrifice to God for a sweetsmelling savour" (Eph. 5:2).

Paul's 13 letters to the body of Christ – Romans to Philemon.

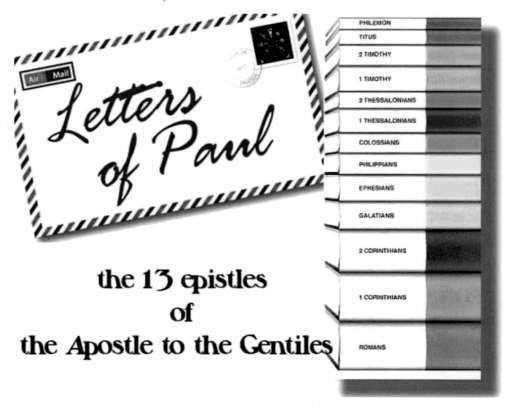

Romans Chapter 14 – Consideration for the weaker brother

14:1-15:7 How to deal "with him that is weak in the faith: (14:1) who does NOT know sound doctrine and is not rightly dividing the word of truth" (2 Tim. 2:15).

When we go to the market today we don't have to worry about if the best food has been offered to idols. But the weaker brother principle still applies today.

For years I went without eating my favorite part on my pizza, the sausage. I love the fennel seed and spices in Italian sausage. I also avoided the pepperoni and ham sandwiches. Because **I was a mixer and I thought Israel's dietary laws may apply to me too. I just wasn't sure. I was a "weaker brother/sister" and I did not know it. I was ignorant of my ignorance**. I had been taught by **ignorant** brethren that the body of Christ began in **Acts 2** with the coming of the Holy Ghost. So I was applying Israel's program to myself.

Now I know that a church was <u>NOT</u> "started" in Acts chapter 2. That a church was already in existence. In Acts 2, people were added to this existing Messianic Jewish church (Matt. 16:15-18; Acts 2:47). Now I know that Paul is my apostle (Rom. 11:13) and that his 13 letters (Romans to Philemon) written by revelation of the Lord Jesus Christ are directly to and about me. Now as a member of the body of Christ **I have** confidence knowing I can eat whatever I want giving thanks to God (1 Tim. 4:1-5; 2:4). The fact that Paul does NOT say that we should obey Israel's dietary laws is another indication that God began a new dispensation and the body of Christ with him. **I now have clarity, joy, grace, (not law) and freedom like I never had before.** I am still learning, but I want to share what I have learned so others can have this liberty and understanding too.

When did God change things? In Lev. 11 God tells His nation, Israel, that many animals such as swine "are unclean to you" (Lev. 11:7) then He tells Peter all kinds of animals are now considered clean. "What God has cleansed, that call not thou common" (Acts 10:15). In Lev. 11, the animals represented the Gentile nations who were unclean, but Israel was clean. But now God is telling Peter that he has cleansed them. What happened? God introduced a new dispensation in Acts 9 with the salvation of Saul of Tarsus on the road to Damascus. Peter is also astonished in Acts 10 when the Gentiles who bless Israel receive the Holy Ghost before being baptized (Acts 10:45). Peter will later use this event to help Paul's new gospel to be accepted at the Jerusalem Council (Acts 15, Gal. 1 and 2). We will be learning more about dealing with weaker brethren, those who have not come to the "knowledge of the truth" (1 Tim. 2:4) as we study Romans Ch. 14.

What is meant by "knowing the time" mentioned in Romans chapter 13? We live at a time of amnesty which is the reason for the delay of Tribulation. We can learn so much from understanding Israel's program from the vantage point of our own. Paul said, "Consider what I say; and the Lord give thee understanding in all things" (2 Tim. 2:7).

Many people are planning for their retirement, their financial future, but we need to prepare even more diligently for our eternal future, too. **The only thing that really matters is where and with whom we spend eternity. For this reason, I would like to spend some more time teaching on "knowing the time."** "And that, **knowing the time**, that now it is high time to awake out of sleep: for now is our salvation nearer than when we believed" (Rom. 13:11).

God is dispensing grace in this age because Christ has paid the sin debt of all mankind (2 Cor. 5:19; Col. 1:20-26). God is not imputing sin today. But, the only way to receive God's imputed righteousness is to believe what Christ has done for us. Only then are we forgiven and accepted by God. Paul is the "due time" apostle who explained the full scope of what Christ accomplished on the cross (Titus 1:3; 1 Tim. 2:6). We are living in the last days of the dispensation of grace. This time began in Paul's day and continues today. "This know also, that in the **last days** perilous times shall come" **(2 Tim. 3:1).** "Now the Spirit speaketh expressly, that in the **latter times** some shall **depart from the faith [Paul's sound doctrine], giving heed to seducing spirits, and doctrines of devils" (1 Tim. 4:1). This is what the ignorant and weaker brethren are doing when they mix dispensations.**

The dispensation of grace is holding back God's WRATH, Jacob's trouble (Jer. 30:7). Sometimes taking a look at Israel's program from the vantage point of Paul's doctrine gives us more clarity about our own program.

Jacob's trouble is the 7 years of Tribulation which is the last part of the installment of Israel's 5 courses of punishment which are mentioned in Leviticus 26. In Lev. 26:1-13, God promised Israel blessings if they worship and obeyed Him, but in Lev. 26:14-39 God warns Israel that He will punish them if they make idols (spiritual adultery) and do not obey His commands.

The first course of punishment is 26:16, 17 their enemies will eat of their harvest (Gideon, Judges 2:13).

The second course of punishment 26:18-20 is that the kingdom is divided because of Solomon's sins and God says He will punish them "seven times more" (God will not hear from heaven and famine, 1 Kings 11:12, 31, 32).

The third is punishment (26:21, 22) with wild beasts who will take their children, destruction of livestock, commerce and productivity and few in number (Elisha, 2 Kings 2:24) again it will be "seven times more."

The fourth course 26:23-26 is "yet seven times for your sins" and is pestilence (disease), famine, and sword (delivered into the hand of your enemies) the Assyrian Gentile captivity of the northern kingdom their land and people lost (2 Kings 17:6).

The fifth course of punishment is His "<u>fury</u>: and I, even I, will chastise you seven times for your sins" (26:27-39). There will be severe famine and destruction of their cities and sanctuary and God will not accept their sacrifices (the time of the Gentiles beginning with the Babylonian captivity of the southern kingdom and ending at the Second Coming of Christ, 2 Kings 25:4, 10, 21; 2 Chron. 36:17-21; Dan. 2:44, 45, 9:24-27; Ezek. 36:17-38). Remember that 7 times seventy is 490, and that in the Tribulation there will be 7 seals, 7 trumpets, and 7 vials of wrath poured out. At this time, the Jews and those who bless them will use the King James Bible to anticipate every event and Christ's return to the day.

However, **God will still keep the Abrahamic covenant with His people.** In Lev. 26:40-46, **God says that if they <u>confess their sins</u>** and humble themselves God will remember His covenant with Jacob, Isaac, Abraham and the land and not cast them away or destroy them utterly. God will remember why He brought His people out of Egypt and parted the **Red Sea for them that He might be Israel's God. The Tribulation will complete the 70 weeks of Daniel's timeline and finish the transgression of Israel (Dan. 9:26).**

Daniel interpreted king Nebuchadnezzar's dream which revealed that the "time of the Gentiles" is over when the smitting stone destroys those kingdoms (Christ at His Second Coming). The stone becomes a gigantic mountain, a great kingdom (with the King of the Jews, Jesus ruling). "Thou, O king, sawest, and behold a great image. This great image, whose brightness was excellent, stood before thee; and the form thereof was terrible. This image's head was of fine gold, his breast and his arms of silver, his belly and his thighs of brass, His legs of iron, his feet part of iron and part of clay. Thou sawest till that a stone was cut out without hands, which smote the image upon his feet that were of iron and clay, and brake them to pieces. Then was the iron, the clay, the brass, the silver, and the gold, broken to pieces together, and became like the chaff of the summer threshingfloors; and the wind carried them away, that no place was found for them: and the stone that smote the image became a great mountain, and filled the whole earth" (Dan. 2:31-35; Luke 21:24).

In Romans Ch. 9-11 Paul explained that <u>we are now living at the time of Israel's blindness as a nation until the fullness of the Gentiles</u>, the Rapture (Rom. 11:25). **We are not waiting for the kingdom to come, but for the Church to go.**

This dispensation is what is holding back the last part of the fifth course of punishment of Israel, or 70th week of Daniel, the WRATH. "And now ye know what [the dispensation of grace] withholdeth that he [antichrist] might be revealed in his time. For the mystery of iniquity doth already work: only he [the Holy Spirit] who now letteth will let, until he [the one new man, the body of Christ] be taken out of the way. And then shall that Wicked be revealed [antichrist], whom the Lord shall consume with the spirit of his mouth, and shall destroy with the brightness of his coming [Second Coming]. Even him, whose coming is after the working of Satan with all power and signs and lying wonders, And with all deceivableness of unrighteousness in them that perish; because they received not the love of the truth, that they might be saved. And for this cause God shall send them strong delusion, that they should believe a lie: That they all might be damned who believed not the truth, but had pleasure in unrighteousness" **(2 Thess. 2:6-11). We are looking for Christ to meet us in the air**. "Looking for that blessed hope, and the glorious appearing of the great God and our Saviour Jesus Christ" (Titus 2:13). "I charge thee therefore before God, and the Lord Jesus Christ, who shall judge the quick and the dead at his **appearing** and **his kingdom** [notice the Rapture and the Second Coming are both mentioned in this verse]" (2 Tim. 4:1). We are those who "**love his appearing**" (2 Tim. 4:8).

During their 70 years in Babylon the land of Israel enjoyed her Sabbath rests that the people should have allowed every 7 years but did not. The **7 times more times is the 70 weeks that are determined upon thy people to finish the transgression equals 490 years.** Sir Robert Anderson calculated that Palm Sunday when Christ rode into Jerusalem was exactly 69 weeks or 483 years from when the decree went forth to build the wall in Nehemiah 2:6 (there is debate over this, some say the decree went out in Ezra 1). Christ rose the following Sunday having been crucified on Passover. The prophetic clock stopped at the cross, but Israel received a one-year extension of mercy. Israel's clock will resume when antichrist signs the 7-year covenant with Israel.

After the Rapture, God will resume His dealings with the nation of Israel (Rom. 11:26), and the believing of Israel will be saved. "But we are all as an unclean thing, and all our righteousnesses are as filthy rags; and we all do fade as a leaf; and our iniquities, like the wind, have taken us away [Israel is confessing their sins in the Tribulation]. And there is none that calleth upon thy name, that stirreth up himself to take hold of thee: for thou hast hid thy face from us, and hast consumed us, because of our iniquities [(Isa. 64:6-9). The Tribulation was because of their iniquities but now they will believe God]. But now, O LORD, thou art our father; we are the clay, and thou our potter; and we all are the work of thy hand [Now they accept God as their Potter and Maker. God will have made them over to a vessel of honour.]"

Romans 14 continues to 15:3. Paul presents principles of guidance regarding how to deal with a brother weak in the faith and to minor debatable differences among believers. Although Paul uses the examples of meat offered to idols and ceremonial days, the principles are timeless and can apply to believers on other subjects in this age. The word "meat" in the KJB means "food" while "flesh" means animal meat.

We are to receive people who are weak doctrinally because God has accepted them since they trusted in Christ's death, burial, and resurrection for their sins. This chapter is also dealing with things that are not so clearly stated in scripture, such as what we eat, drinking alcohol, smoking, dances, movies, going to church on Sundays or not.

We are not to judge the practices of other Christians in respect to doubtful thing. There are many things that we should not divide over such as the "gap theory" "flat earth" and "the Lord's supper." If someone is saved they are a brother or sister in the Lord. Regardless of if they have come to "the knowledge of the truth" (1 Tim. 2:4) concerning when the body of Christ began and the distinctiveness of Paul's unique apostleship, or not. We still treat them as a brother and try to help them to come to this truth.

As mentioned, Paul said that we do not need to follow Israel's dietary laws, but can eat whatever we want with thanksgiving (1 Tim. 4:3-5). This fact in itself demonstrates that God has changed His dealings with mankind in this dispensation. God gave Israel a list of strict dietary laws in **a past** dispensation to show that they were different from other nations. But after Israel fell in Acts 7:51-53, then God set the nation of Israel aside and saved Saul of Tarsus making him Paul the apostle of the Gentiles in Acts 9.

A person who is weak in their understanding of the dispensation in which we now live (Eph. 3:1-3) may be trying to live under rules from a **past** dispensation. **We should not be critical of saints who do not have any dispensational understanding. We must keep in mind that we used to be like them.** Neither should they condemn the liberty that we have in the body of Christ (Gal. 5:1; 1

Cor. 6:12). We are part of a living organism and everyone is valuable (1 Cor. 12:12, 21-25). We must gently try to help them to understand the truth.

Some weaker brothers and sisters may think the Sabbath and Jewish feast days belong to them, but they are Israel's (Lev. 23). The Sabbath was a sign between the LORD and Israel to set them apart from other nations whoever did not keep it was to be killed (Ex. 31:12-15). The Sabbath is a picture of their millennial rest with Christ in the kingdom. Three times a year Israel was to keep a feast to the LORD. These feasts are a picture of God's plan to redeem them. Christ has already fulfilled Passover, Unleavened Bread, and Firstfruits (held in Abib, the first month). The next, Pentecost (50 days later) was fulfilled in Acts 2. The Feast of Trumpets, Day of Atonement, and Feast of Tabernacles (in the 7th month) will be fulfilled when Israel is gathered into their land, the nation is forgiven, and Messiah rules and lives with them. The final feasts have been postponed because of the insertion of the dispensation of grace. Now in our day of Gentile opportunity (Rom. 11:13, 25) we are not under Israel's laws (Rom 6:14, 9:4) and all days are alike (Col. 2:16, 17).

We must be careful not to stumble someone for whom Christ died because of a minor issue which may weaken their faith. As we have opportunity we try "to make all men see what is the fellowship of the mystery, which from the beginning of the world hath been hid in God, who created all things by Jesus Christ" (Eph. 3:9). We should be careful that our liberty and confidence in Christ does not to accidentally harm another. We want to maintain fellowship if we can. Our goal is to build up our brother. We may not agree 100% with everyone. The main thing is that each person is responsible for themselves to God.

Everyone is accountable to God. He is our only Judge. It is between God and ourselves. We are not living to please others, but to please God. They are not living to please us either, but God. The other person is responsible to God. **Knowing this is tremendously freeing.**

What we eat or don't eat does not commend us to God. "But meat commendeth us not to God: for neither, if we eat, are we the better; neither, if we eat not, are we the worse" (1 Cor. 8:8). What we ourselves eat should irrelevant to us.

Our goal in this dispensation is "That ye may be blameless and harmless, the sons of God, without rebuke, in the midst of a crooked and perverse nation, among whom ye shine as lights in the world; Holding forth the word of life [the sound doctrine given by Christ from heaven to Paul]" (Phil. 2:15, 16a.).

14:9 Christ both rose and revived. He was dead (His soul was separated from His body) but then simultaneously His Spirit returned to His body and He rose in His glorified body which was able to go through the grave clothes (linen wrappings). He was the first to put on a glorified immortal body since He can walk through walls and ascend in the air. Have you ever wondered why His disciples did not recognize Him? I believe it was because He looked different in His glorified body, and we will too. People will be able to recognize us but we may not have blood in our special immortal body (1 Cor. 15:50). Let us examine what Paul means by Jesus being the Lord of "both the living and the dead" since believers who have died have souls and spirits that are living (Matt. 22:32). As we know people who are not believers still have eternal souls, but are spiritually dead. Jesus Christ is Lord of ALL "The word which God sent unto the children of Israel, preaching peace by Jesus Christ: (he is Lord of all:)" (Acts 10:36). He is Lord of the saved and the unsaved, justified and unjustified. In Phil. 2:9-11 it says that every knee shall bow to Him and every tongue confess that Jesus Christ is Lord.

14:10 God wants us to have something of value at the judgment seat of Christ, and so should we. The word of God will try everyone's work to see what sort it is. Only gold, silver, and precious stones will not burn (1 Cor. 3:8-15; Prov. 2:1-9; 2 Tim. 2:19-21). None of us are perfect, and so Christ will separate the good things we did (in Christ) form the bad things (done in our flesh). "For we must all appear before the judgment seat of Christ; that every one may receive the things done in his body, according to that he hath done, whether it be good or bad" (2 Cor. 5:10). Rewarding us for the good and destroying the bad, so that we will have just good as we enter into to our eternal heavenly home. He will burn up the fleshly deeds so they cease to exist, and all that will remain is our life lived in Christ. We will not be punished because we are dead and no one can punish a dead man. "**For ye are dead**, and your life is hid with Christ in God (Col. 3:3). We get rewarded for what He did through us! So it is no wonder that we will want to return our reward and give Him all the glory!

Romans 14:1 Him that is weak in the faith [saints who are NOT strong in Pauline doctrine] receive ye, but not to doubtful disputations [we are not to argue about minor issues]. **2** For one believeth that he may eat all things: another, who is weak, eateth herbs [Someone may be fine eating food offered to idols, others may abstain, and some may be a vegetarian. (1 Cor. 8:7-13)]. **3** Let not him that eateth despise him that eateth not; and let not him which eateth not judge him that eateth: for God hath received him [What a person eats or does not eat is not the important thing. If a person has trusted in Christ that is the main thing. God has received us both, 1 Cor. 12:12, 21-25]. **4** Who art thou that judgest another man's servant? to his own master he standeth or falleth. Yea, he shall be holden up: for God is able to make him stand [each person is accountable to God (Psa. 73:22-26; 1 Cor. **4:3**-5; Mat. 7:1-5; Rom. 2:1) God has declared all who are in Christ as NOT guilty (Rom. 4:22, 24, 25; 8:33, 34). We stand 100% righteous in God's sight because we are in Christ (Gal. 3:26-28) not because we have more understanding or are somehow more "spiritual" than anyone else but because of what Christ has done (Rom.3:22-24)]. **5** One man esteemeth one day above another: another esteemeth every day alike. Let every man be **fully persuaded in his own mind** [The Sabbath was a sign between the LORD and Israel to set them apart from other nations whoever did not keep it was to be killed (Ex. 31:12-15). The Sabbath represents the millennium. Now in our day of Gentile opportunity (Rom. 11:13, 25 we are not under Israel's laws (Rom 6:14, 9:4) and all days are alike and important (Col. 2:16, 17). **We cannot force someone to be saved or to come to understand right division.** If they have no interest we should look for those who do, but not to give up on them too soon. We do not want to harden them to the gospel or to turn them off to the message of grace. Perhaps they will listen in the future. Even if the time never comes, so be it. He will learn when he gets to heaven. Since God does not force saved people to read their Bibles and they answer to God, how much more, then, should we not force weaker brethren to learn the truth of God's word. When we do, we are trying to take control over God's Servant, when God knows what is best for them. We should be "fully persuaded" in our minds that we are NOT Israel we have no special days (Gal. 4:10, 11; Col. 2:16, 17; Phil. 2:15, 16)]. **6** He that regardeth the day, regardeth it unto the Lord; and he that regardeth not the day, to the Lord he doth not regard it. He that eateth, eateth to the Lord, for he giveth God thanks; and he that eateth not, to the Lord he eateth not, and giveth God thanks [Some people who are not aware of the dispensation we are living in today may think that they would be more acceptable to God if they shared in Israel's holy days (Gal. 4:9-11). Whatever we do we do it to the Lord who is our only Judge, Col. 3:23-25].

7 For none of us liveth to himself, and no man dieth to himself. **8** For whether we live, we live unto the Lord; and whether we die, we die unto the Lord: whether we live therefore, or die, we are the Lord's [we represent Christ as His ambassadors]. **9** For to this end Christ both died, and rose, and revived, that he might be Lord both of the dead and living [from spiritually dead and alive. Lord of lost and the saved. Notice that Christ both rose and revived. He was dead (His soul was separated from His body) but then simultaneously His Spirit returned to His body and He rose in His glorified body which was able to go through the grave clothes (linen wrappings). He was the first to put on a glorified immortal body since He can walk through walls and ascend in the air. Have you ever wondered why His disciples did not recognize Him? I believe it was because He looked different in

His glorified body, and we will too. People will be able to recognize us but we may not have blood in our special immortal body (1 Cor. 15:50)] **10** But why dost thou judge thy brother? or why dost thou set at nought thy brother? for we shall all stand before **the judgment seat of Christ [1 Cor. 3:8-15; 4:5, God's word is "like a fire" the perfect standard measure by which all things will be judged, Lev. 23:29;** God does the work through us, and we get the reward, so we will then give Him all the glory! We are training here, for reigning there! 2 Cor. 1:14, 5:9, 10; Col. 3:24, 25, 2 Tim. 2:20 our motivation is gratitude and understanding, and God's thinking compels us to allow Him to do good works through us (Gal. 2:20). We are His "purchased possession" (Eph. 1:14), bought with His blood (Acts 20:28; 1 Cor. 6:19, 20) **so living for Him is our reasonable service" (Rom. 12:1) it is our duty, but He still graciously gives us a reward. That is grace! Grace is unearned and undeserved favor. Our operating system is grace, not the Law]**.

11 For it is written, As I live, saith the Lord, **every knee shall bow to me, and every tongue shall confess to God** [Everyone will bow their knee to Christ and confess that He is LORD. Israel shall glory in Him and so shall we. Isa. 45:23; We will bow at His judgment seat. Some may not have confessed Him as Lord in life, but they will, Phil. 2:10, 11]. **12** So then every one of us shall give account of himself to God [We dedicate or consecrate ourselves to God by presenting our bodies a living sacrifice, and living as a Christian should. Not because we have to, but because we want to please God and represent Him well to others. We are personally responsible to God for our actions]. **13** Let us not therefore judge one another any more: but judge this rather, that no man put a stumblingblock or an occasion to fall in his brother's way [we are not to do anything that stumbles another person, but instead be concerned with his spiritual well-being. Rather we are to judge them as weaker and seek to make them stronger. We can use the mind of Christ to judge all things (then we judge righteously)]. **14** I know, and am persuaded by the Lord Jesus, that there is nothing unclean of itself: but to him that esteemeth any thing to be unclean, to him it is unclean [Gal. 5:1; **under grace we have liberty to do all things, but not everything is expedient** 1 Cor. 6:12. We should use our liberty to increase others faith.]. **15** But if thy brother be grieved with thy meat, now walkest thou not charitably. Destroy not him with thy meat, for whom Christ died [1 Cor. 8:7-13, Do not ruin another man's spiritual walk by what you eat or drink "For, brethren, ye have been called unto liberty; only use not liberty for an occasion to the flesh, but by love serve one another" (Gal. 5:13). "For they themselves shew of us what manner of entering in we had unto you, and how ye turned to God from idols to serve the living and true God" (1 Thess. 1:9).] **16** Let not then your good be evil spoken of [**our "good" is the wonderful, liberating sound doctrine found in Paul's epistles (Col. 1:20-26)**]: 17 For the kingdom of God is not meat and drink; but righteousness, and peace, and joy in the Holy Ghost [These are the things that matter to God. Let's focus on the things God is doing, not on petty things such as what man eats or drinks. What we ourselves eat should irrelevant to us. God's will is for people to be saved and to come to the knowledge of the truth (1 Tim. 2:4). When people are saved they receive God's righteousness (3:21, 22) and have peace with God (5:1). When they come to the knowledge of the truth, they "rejoice ever more" (1 Thess. 5:16) over being forgiven of their sin, being seated with Christ in the heavenly places, all the spiritual blessings and Christ living in them. That is why Paul says, "If meat make my brother to offend, I will eat no flesh while the world standees, lest I make my brother to offend" (1 Cor. 8:13). We should concentrate on eternal things.].

18 For he that in these things serveth Christ is **acceptable to God, and approved of men** [In righteousness, peace, and joy there is value to God and men]. **19** Let us therefore follow after the things which make for **peace, and things wherewith one may edify another** [Two things: peace, and edify. Sometimes I have to go along with things I know really do not matter in order to keep peace so I can have a chance to edify. For example, I may not want to serve pork chops to brother or sister who believe they are to follow Israel's dietary laws. So as to not offend them and to have more of a chance to edify the person on eternal matters later, so I may serve them chicken instead. We are adult sons of God and stronger brothers because of the sound doctrine we have learned; we are to operate on a higher spiritual plane, walking by faith not by sight.] **20** For meat destroy not the work of God [God is working in the weak believer to make him stronger]. All things indeed are pure; but it is evil for that man who eateth with offence [we know we can eat whatever we want, but not everyone knows this]. **21** It is good neither to eat flesh, nor to drink wine, nor any thing whereby thy brother stumbleth, or is offended, or is made weak [we should voluntarily abstain from certain practices for the sake of the weaker brother]. **22** Hast thou faith? have it to thyself before God [we should not flaunt our freedom in Christ, but be humble in front to of the weaker brother]. Happy is he that condemneth not himself in that thing which he alloweth [we should follow our conscience Rom. 2:15]. **23** And he that doubteth is damned if he eat, because he eateth not of faith: for whatsoever is not of faith is sin [it is sin to go against your conscience].

Our goal is to help the weaker brother to become a stronger brother so he can join us and set his "affection on things above, not on things on the earth" (Col. 3:2). We follow Christ's heavenly ministry through Paul, not His earthly ministry. **"If we do not rightly divide the Bible, then there is no clear reason to not go back under the law" (a quote from David Reid of Columbus, Ohio).**

Romans Chapter 15 – Paul's Ministry to the Gentiles
15:1-7 We should be patient when teaching the weaker brother or sister Pauline sound doctrine.
15:8-12 Christ was a minister to the circumcision (the Jews) to confirm the promises made to the fathers. Christ's earthly ministry was to the Jews so that they could then save the Gentiles. Gentiles that are saved in Israel's program will not be at the same level as Israel, but below. Today there is no difference between Jews and Gentiles (Gal 3:28). There is a <u>pattern that progresses</u> in these verses quoted by Paul. The Gentiles hear the word (Psa. 18:49); Gentiles rejoice with the Jews (Deut. 32:43); All the Gentiles praise God (Psa. 117:1); The Gentiles trust Christ and enjoy His reign (Isa. 11:10). In Israel's program Gentiles need to believe in the King of the Jews and bless the Jews. Today we are saved by believing the gospel directly without going through Israel and apart from the law. **Notice what Paul says next** "I myself also am persuaded of you, my brethren, that ye also are full of goodness, filled with all knowledge" (15:14) **Paul expects the Romans to understand that he has been talking about Israel's glorious program. Because he explained about Israel's blindness in Ch. 11. Paul treats them as a father does an adult son. He encourages them as to who they are in Christ. <u>We must look at the letter to the Romans as a whole and not narrowly focus our mind on just one passage or chapter</u>.** <u>Under the **law** we obey out of fear of punishment, but under **grace** we obey out of love and gratitude.</u> It is a mistake to think that every time God is speaking about Gentile salvation that He is speaking about us. (Every promise in the book is <u>not</u> mine.) In Time Past and in the Ages to Come Gentiles are saved by believing that Jesus is the Messiah the King of the Jews and blessing Israel. In the Present, Gentiles are saved by believing directly on Christ and what He has done (without going through Israel, apart from Israel) how that Christ died for OUR SINS, was buried, and rose again.
15:13-32 Paul then talks about his plans to go to Jerusalem with a monetary gift before coming to see the Romans and asks them to pray for him.

The biggest mistake made in Christendom is the failure to recognize that the body of Christ began in Acts 9. If people are wrong about when the body of Christ began, they will have everything else in the Bible wrong. If people believe that the body of Christ began in Acts 2 on Pentecost they are going to get everything else wrong in the Bible including the gospel of our salvation. We are not saved by believing John 3:16-18 (this has to do with who the King, the Son of God is), but 1 Cor. 15:3, 4 (what Christ has done for us). Not only is the gospel not correct, but God's instruction for how to live the Christian life is buried and lost, leaving Christians powerless to serve God on earth the way He intends us to. Christians get caught up in man-made denominations and not God's word. They are confused about how to live, how they got saved, and how to share the gospel. This is why the dispensational approach to Bible study is so vitally important. It is impossible to UNDERSTAND God's plan and purpose for our lives TODAY without rightly dividing the KJV Bible and without recognizing who we are in Christ. If we do not know our identity, then we do not know what God would have us think, say, and do for His glory. Without rightly dividing the word of truth it is impossible to have the clarity, peace, and joy that God wants us to have NOW; which results from allowing Christ to live through us while being assured of our glorious hope. We have all spiritual blessings in heavenly places, we have joint inheritance with Christ. Christ has plans for us NOW and in our future positions in the heavenly places. (I was greatly helped by the information given by LeighAnn Mycko's Facebook post about the GREATEST BLUNDER IN CHRISTENDOM (Find her on Facebook, also find it posted on God's Secret Facebook page.)

We must consistently make the division that God makes in the Bible, not invent our own, and not be sub-dispensational (Acts 2), or hyper (Acts 28).

Goals: Study Romans 15. Then learn how to share the right divisions anyplace and anywhere (writing on a paper napkin in a restaurant or drawing in the sand with a stick at the beach). We will also look at four baptisms. Finally, we will examine some of the various gospels (of Jesus and Peter).

We must view the Bible from a Pauline perspective (2 Tim. 2:7). Still I believe that God was killing two birds with one stone, so to speak, when He authored the non-Pauline scriptures (knowing that He would save the body of Christ). God was

109

sharing information and instruction that He knew the body of Christ could also profit from. That is why Paul says, "All scripture . . . is profitable . . . (2 Tim. 3:16). This is also why Paul writes, "For whatsoever things were written aforetime were written for our learning, that we **through patience** and **comfort of the scriptures might have hope**" (Rom. 15:4). **There is often information in Israel's program that we can be learned from.** This is also why in Rom. 16:26, Paul writes ". . . and by the scriptures of the prophets, according to the commandment of the everlasting God, made known to all nations for the obedience of faith."

Here is an example: I was recently comforted by the scriptures as I learned about suffering reproach in Nehemiah. In Neh. 4:1, 4-6 we read that some Gentiles mocked when Nehemiah was building the wall around Jerusalem after their return from the Babylonian captivity. Nehemiah prayed about it and said that they were reproaching God. Reproaches may provoke God to anger if another person's ministry is hindered. In Neh. 6:1-4 the reproach becomes more intense as their work continues, in Neh. 6:7 the Gentiles plan on telling the king lies slandering Nehemiah. The enemies come up with various plots and plans in Neh. 6:8-12 but Nehemiah prays for God to strengthen him (9). Finally, the wall is finished in 52 days (6:15). But now the nobles of Judah (the Jewish brothers) join in with the enemies. We will suffer reproach not only from the weaker brother but also other grace believers. We can have comfort of the scriptures knowing that Nehemiah, our Lord Jesus Christ, and Paul all had to bear reproach from enemies. Sometimes unbelievers, family, and even other believers tried to hinder their work for God. "Yea, and all that will live godly in Christ Jesus shall suffer persecution" (2 Tim. 3:12). I learned that even in the kingdom program the battle with other people who reproach us is similar to what we go through. "There hath no temptation taken you but such as is **common to man**: but God is faithful, who will not suffer you to be tempted above that ye are able; but will with the temptation also make a way to escape, that ye may be able to bear it" (1 Cor. 10:13). So even though Nehemiah is not "my mail" while Paul's letters are, I can learn from it.

So what shall we do when we are persecuted? First we **pray** to God about it, then we examine ourselves to see if they are justified in their criticism. If they are we change. If they are not, we soldier on bearing our reproach knowing we are guaranteed to suffer (2 Tim. 3:12). If we try to step on another person's ministry to exalt our own God will not be pleased. "Who art thou that judgest another man's servant? to his own master he standeth or falleth. Yea, he shall be holden up: for God is able to make him stand" (14:4). God is the one who will judge us. "So then every one of us shall give account of himself to God" (14:12).

110

Our ministry may be hindered by those who should be commending and encouraging us. We should also forgive them as God for Christ's sake has forgiven us (Eph. 4:32). We do not walk by our feelings, but by faith in God's word. Our actions should depend on bravely joining in what God is doing, not whether we feel warm and fuzzy about it. We learned that "no man should put a stumbling block or an occasion to fall in a brother's way" (14:13). We are to continue in the work that God has given us to do even in the face of opposition on every side. Nehemiah and his friends finished building the wall around. Paul also finished his course with much opposition (2 Cor. 7:5). Christ endured the cross alone for all.

We the body of Christ are to have the "mind of Christ" and be **willing to suffer** reproach from the weaker brother in the faith so that he may be able to come to "the knowledge of the truth" (1 Tim. 2:4) because Christ was willing to suffer reproach. Paul also said he was willing to become weak and suffer so that others might be saved and believe sound doctrine see 1 Cor. 9:19-23.

I have been going to a senior living center on Thursday nights for about two months trying to share right division with them. The kind and patient Pastor is teaching on Mark (using various bibles) because he thinks it is the best book for new believers, I told him I believed Romans was. I told him and the group that Israel committed the blasphemy of the Holy Ghost in Acts 7 and he said he disagrees. So I do not insist on being right but wait for another chance to share something that may help him and the others to be edified, saved, and come to come to understand the right Bible rightly divided. I have also given out several copies of early editions of God's Secret to help them. This is how we must gently and patiently "make all men see the fellowship of the mystery" (Eph. 3:9).

There is only one true interpretation of the scriptures, God's. When we get to the Judgement Seat of Christ we are going to be cheering for each other when we allowed Christ to do something through us. With one mind and mouth as a unit will exalt Christ. He will have preeminence in all things because He demonstrated His worthiness. He is LORD God (Jehovah God). We are to be likeminded with one another having the "mind of Christ" (1 Cor. 2:16). We are a team. We should therefore be patient with each other now (Gal. 6:1-5).

We can remain patient (we have all had chances to be patient with people who reproach us) **and have comfort and hope of the scriptures since God has shown His noble, dependable, trustworthy, faithful, loving, just, fair, honorable, and perfect character in His dealings with mankind.**

Four Baptisms – Do you know <u>which baptism</u> is the "one baptism" for today referred to in Eph. 4:5? The answer may surprise you.

Notice how there are **three baptisms mentioned in this verse** (water, Holy Ghost and fire): "I indeed baptize you with **water** unto repentance: but he [Jesus] that cometh after me is mightier than I, whose shoes I am not worthy to bear: he [Jesus] shall BAPTIZE you with the **Holy Ghost**, and *with* **fire**" (Matt. 3:11). *<u>Notice how it is Jesus that does the baptizing with the Holy Ghost</u>.

The Answer is: NONE OF THEM. NO it is NOT the Holy Ghost!!! Today the <u>Holy Spirit has baptized us into Christ</u>. *<u>Notice that now the Holy Spirit does the baptizing into the body of Christ, the roles are reversed from the previous order.

"<u>For by one SPIRIT are we all BAPTIZED into one body</u>, whether *we be* Jews or Gentiles, whether *we be* bond or free; and have been all made to drink into one Spirit" (1 Cor. 12:13).

We are identified with Christ's death, burial, and resurrection. "Know ye not, that so many of us as were BAPTIZED INTO JESUS CHRIST were BAPTIZED into <u>his death</u>? Therefore we are buried with him by <u>BAPTISM into death</u>: that like as Christ was raised up from the dead by the glory of the Father, even so we also should walk in newness of life" (Rom. 6:3, 4).

We are baptized into Christ. "For as many of you as have been <u>BAPTIZED into Christ</u> have put on Christ" (Gal 3:27).

It is important to keep in mind that **baptism means** to be "**placed into**." Looking at the different baptisms is another way of realizing how differently God is dealing with us in this dispensation of grace. God does not change, He is immutable, but His dealings with mankind changes over time. God deals differently with different people at different times.

Today we are living in the <u>But Now</u>, the dispensation of grace. We are NOT living under the law today. Currently, we are saved apart from Israel, and apart from the law, there is no difference between a Gentile and a Jew today. Israel as a nation is not worshiping their Messiah at this time, they do not have preferred nation status at this time. They only occupy a small sliver of all the land promised to them.

Sharing Right Division – It is important to be both Biblical and dispensational.

Dispensationalism is not system of man's theology but God's ordained method for understanding His word. "Rightly dividing" means to cut straight making divisions where God makes them.

"Study to shew thyself approved unto God, a workman that needeth not to be ashamed, rightly dividing the word of truth."   2 Timothy 2:15

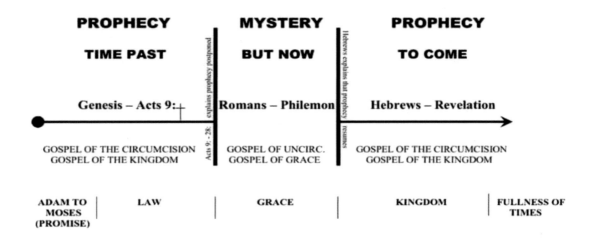

*Notice that the <u>main divisions</u> in the Bible are: **Prophecy – Mystery – Prophecy** The books of the Bible which corresponds to each of the three sections follow the order of the books in the Bible (a divine timeline). TIME PAST, BUT NOW, and AGES to COME are divisions God makes, and the Bible is laid out in that order.

TIME PAST and AGES to COME both have to do with God's "signs and wonders" program with Israel. "For the Jews require a sign . . ." (1 Cor. 1:22).

The present un-prophesied program called BUT NOW has to do with God building the body of Christ. "For we walk by faith, not by sight" (2 Cor. 5:7).

GOD DEALING WITH ...

1) TIME PAST the NATION of ISRAEL under the Law (Genesis to Acts 9);

2) BUT NOW the BODY of CHRIST under Grace (Romans thru Philemon);

3) AGES to COME the NATION of ISRAEL under Law (Hebrews thru Rev.)

Romans 15:1 We then that are strong ought to **bear the infirmities of the weak** [I used to think that "infirmities" were giving into the sin nature. But, Paul calls following religious rules "infirmities" they are weak in Pauline sound doctrine. I used to be a weaker brother, but now I am a stronger brother/sister and so are you if you understand the mystery given to Paul. When we understand Paul's sound doctrine we are more likely to walk in the spirit and put on "the Lord Jesus Christ, and make not provision for the flesh, fulfill the lusts thereof" (13:14)], and **not to please ourselves** [We should not chastise the weaker brothers, but bear with them and **not to please ourselves**. Christ went to Israel in spite of their unbelief because that is what the Father wanted Him to do, and we should be willing to help those who are weak in Pauline truth (immature in sound doctrine) and have become stuck under the law because they follow Peter believing that the body of Christ began in Acts 2, instead of Acts 9 (when Christ saved Paul on the road to Damascus when the dispensation of grace began)]. **2** Let every one of us **please his neighbour** for his good to edification [Every one means all of us brothers and sisters in the faith. We who are strong in the faith should be careful when helping those who are weak in sound doctrine (Gal. 6:1-5). To edify means to "build up." God's word rightly divided is able to build us up (Acts 20:32). Edifying another is not "usurping authority." Priscilla and Aquila edified Apollos. We do our best to please others so they may be edified, "we should minister grace to the hearers" Eph. 4:29; "Let no man seek his own, but every man another's wealth" 1 Cor. 10:24]. **3** For even Christ pleased not himself; but, as it is written, **The reproaches of them that reproached thee fell on me** [This is a quote from Psa. 69:9. Christians are to follow the example of Christ, who did not live to please Himself, Phil 2:5-8. He bore the reproach of those who crucified Him. So we should be able to bear a little reproach from a weaker brother who may be resistant to sound doctrine because they don't understand it or those who criticize us. Notice how Paul points us to Jesus as our example when we know that Paul suffered a lot of reproach from the Jews and also from the Corinthian brethren].

4 For whatsoever things were written aforetime were written for our learning, that we through patience and comfort of the scriptures might have hope [What Paul just quoted in Psa. 69:9 is for our learning. We can learn from what Christ did. He bore the reproach of those who crucified Him even begging the Father to forgive their ignorance, "for they know not what they do" (Luke 23:34). Paul also suffered reproach (1 Cor. 9:19-23). All of us have had to suffer reproach at some time, and we should be willing to do it for the lost so they may be saved, and those weak in Pauline sound doctrine. We gain spiritual comfort of the scriptures by experience. The Bible is spiritual nourishment from our Head "in whom are hid all treasures of wisdom and knowledge" (Col. 2:2-3). We must view the Bible from a

Pauline perspective. All the Bible is for us, but not all of the Bible is "to" or "about us." Even so, I still believe that God was killing two birds with one stone so to speak, and that He was sharing information with Israel that He knew the body of Christ could profit from. That is why Paul says that "All scripture . . . is profitable . . . (2 Tim. 3:16, 17). We will only get the profit out of the Bible that God has for us if we study it diligently.]. **5** Now the God of patience and consolation grant you to be **likeminded** one toward another according to Christ Jesus. [We should think **like Christ** who was willing to bare reproach]: **6** That ye may with one mind and one mouth glorify God, even the Father of our Lord Jesus Christ [Phil. 1:27 when we have the humble "mind of Christ" (Phil. 2:5-8; 1 Cor. 2:16) that brings glory to God]. **7** Wherefore receive ye one another, as Christ also received us to the glory of God [receive each other and those weak in the faith, those who are saved but unlearned in Pauline truth because God received us "while we were yet sinners" (Rom. 5:8)].

8 Now I say that **Jesus Christ was a minister of the circumcision** for the truth of God, **to confirm the promises made unto the fathers** [Christ came to minister to the circumcision (the Jews) which is Israel see Matt. 10:5, 6, 15:24. Why? Because God started the nation with Abraham, Isaac, and Jacob, and their descendants. How does this verse end? With a colon! So the sentence continues because Paul is demonstrating that Christ came to Israel so that the nation of Israel could be saved and then be a kingdom of priest **to save the Gentiles**, Isa. 61:6, Ex. 19:5, 6. **God intended to use His nation to bless all nations with the opportunity of salvation.** Christ lets the woman of Canaan know that the Gentiles will be blessed after the overflow of Israel's fullness, their table with the crumbs (Matt. 15:24-28). There is a parallel in the two programs because **Gentiles can be saved in both**, but the Gentiles in Israel's program will not be on the same level with Israel because the middle wall of partition will be up]: **9** And that the **Gentiles might glorify God for his mercy**; as it is written, For this cause I will confess to thee among the Gentiles, and sing unto thy name. [Notice the "And" Christ wants Gentiles to be saved through Israel. Then Paul quotes, Psa. 18:49] **10** And again he saith, Rejoice, ye Gentiles, with his people [Israel, Deut. 32:43]. **11** And again, Praise the Lord, all ye Gentiles; and laud him, all ye people [Psa. 117:1]. **12** And again, Esaias saith, There shall be a root of Jesse [Jesus Christ], and he that shall rise to reign over the Gentiles; in him shall the Gentiles trust. [Isa. 11:10. There is a pattern that progresses the Gentiles hear the word (Psa. 18:49); Gentiles rejoice with the Jews (Deut. 32:43); All the Gentiles praise God (Psa. 117:1); The Gentiles trust Christ and enjoy His reign (Isa. 11:10)] **13** Now the God of hope fill you with all joy and peace in believing, that ye may abound in hope, through the power of the Holy Ghost [believe that God has always wanted to save the Gentiles in every dispensation. The wonderful thing is that today Jews can be saved into the body of Christ in God's time of opportunity for the Gentiles by joining them. But in the kingdom God will give the Gentiles 1,000-year opportunity to be saved in Israel's program]. **14 And I myself also am persuaded of you, my brethren, that ye also are full of goodness, filled with all knowledge**, able also to admonish [Paul knows that the saints in Rome already knew that Christ wanted to save Gentiles in Israel's program and in His program to the body of Christ. The Daniel Webster 1828 dictionary definition of "admonish" is "To warn, notify of a fault; to reprove with mildness." If I notice someone to has a wrong understanding I may tell them what I know privately when I have a chance] one another [Paul knew that the believers in Rome were mature knowledgeable saints, but he still wanted them to have all this fundamental knowledge which he lays out in Romans. They know that Paul has a special commission to reach the Gentiles with the gospel and to share the mystery will all believers.]. **15 Nevertheless, brethren, I have written the more boldly unto you in some sort**, as putting you in mind, because of the grace that is given to me of God [Paul reminds the saints in Rome of some things that they already knew and tells them some things that they had not heard yet, see 12:3], **16 That I should be the minister of Jesus Christ to the Gentiles, ministering the gospel of God, that the offering up of the Gentiles might be acceptable, being sanctified by the Holy Ghost** [Christ appointed Paul to be His minister (Acts 26:16). Paul wanted the Gentile believers to be acceptable to God, the best they can be, what an Apostle's heart he had, it will be a privilege for all of us to meet him. The "gospel of God" appears 7 times in the KJB 6 in Paul's writings and once in Peter's (1 Peter 4:17). The gospel of God is the basic prophesied information of Christs death, burial and resurrection for sins. Both Peter and Paul preached the basic gospel of the Redeemer for both groups. But Peter emphasized the gospel of the kingdom and Paul the gospel of Christ. Peter said that Christ was the King of the Jews to sit on the throne in the coming kingdom and Paul the gospel of Christ. So what is the difference between Paul's gospel and Peter's. Paul said Christ died for OUR SINS (the Gentiles) apart from Israel. Paul never said that the body of Christ would live in a kingdom on earth but in heavenly places (Eph. 2:6, 2 Cor. 5:1). Gospel means "good news." There is more than one gospel in the Bible but there is only one that saves today, Paul's].

17 I have therefore whereof I may glory through Jesus Christ in those things which pertain to God [He can glory in those things that he is doing in Christ, that Christ gave Him to do as His minister]. **18 For I will not dare to speak of any of those things which Christ hath not wrought by me, to make the Gentiles obedient, by word and deed** [Obedient means to have faith (Rom. 1:5) in what Christ gives Paul to write and do, so that after salvation we can also do and serve God. "Those things, which ye have both <u>learned,</u> and <u>received,</u> and <u>heard,</u> and <u>seen in me, do</u> (Paul is our pattern, so **we should copy what he does**): and <u>the God of peace shall be with you</u>" (Phil 4:9). In order to live a godly life, we must have the sound doctrine found in Paul's epistles built up in our inner man. When we do that we have peace and are in God's will.], **19** Through mighty **signs and wonders** [Acts 19:11; 15:12], **by the power of the Spirit of God** [the Spirit of God worked in Paul and He works in us]; so that **from Jerusalem, and round about unto Illyricum, I have fully preached the gospel of Christ** [the gospel of Christ is found in 1 Cor. 15:3, 4. After the **uproar in Ephesus** which was a mob that chanted for two hours and basically wanted to tear Paul apart (Acts 19:29-32, 40), Paul went to Macedonia, then to Illyricum, then down to Corinth. Most maps miss this but the map in God's Secret includes it.]. **20** Yea, so have **I strived to preach the gospel, not where Christ was named, lest I should build upon another man's foundation** [Christ is the foundation for both prophecy and according to the revelation of the mystery (16:25). Paul was commissioned to preach to those heathen (unsaved Jews and Gentiles) who had <u>not heard about a chance for salvation,</u> while Peter and his group went to the saved Jews, the circumcision. So any heathen was Paul's territory and saved Jews was not (Gal. 2:9). This is the way Paul did not build on Peter's foundation. The Jews would not go to the Gentiles so Jesus sent Paul (Acts 11:19)]: **21** But as it is written, **To whom he was not spoken of, they shall see: and they that have not heard shall understand** [Isa. 52:15, Christ spoke to Paul by revelation, and the Holy Spirit also used the Old Testament scriptures]. **22** For which **cause** [preaching to those who had not heard] also I have been much hindered from coming to you [Paul had been busy preaching to the heathen]. **23** But now **having no more place in these parts** [having been forced to leave Ephesus because of the uproar caused by the silversmiths (Acts 19:29-32, 40), and having covered the other ground preaching the gospel (so that in Col. 1:5, 6, 23 he says everyone had heard], and having a great desire these many years to come unto you; **24** Whensoever I take my journey into Spain, I will **come** to you [they are next on his list]: for I trust to see you in my journey, and to be brought on my way thitherward by you, if first I be somewhat filled with your company. **25** But now I go unto Jerusalem to minister unto the saints [Paul arrived in Jerusalem in Acts 21:17 so this is another clue that the book of Romans was written in Acts 20:1-3]. **26** For it hath pleased them of Macedonia and Achaia to make a certain contribution for the poor saints which are at Jerusalem [in 2 Cor. 8-9:15 Paul speaks about the collection that was being taken for the saints in Jerusalem which helps us to know that Romans was written after that. He is rather funny the way He used the Macedonian giving to encourage the Corinthians to give and visa-versa]. **27** It hath pleased them verily; and their [saints at Jerusalem] **debtors they are**. For if the Gentiles have been made partakers of their spiritual things [How are we partakers of Israel's spiritual things? Because spiritually the little flock saints are "in Christ" and "Christ is in them." Now Christ is in us and we are in Him. Peter and the remnant have been placed on hold, their program has been postponed because of the unbelief of their nation.], their duty is also **to minister unto them in carnal things** [material things, since God has postponed Israel's program and is giving Gentiles an opportunity to believe directly on what Christ has done apart from going through Israel. The saints in Jerusalem had bravely stood up for God, not man, but now they were poor since they had obeyed Christ command to sell all that they had (Luke 12:33, Acts 2:45, 4:34, 35). They were anticipating going into the Tribulation and would not be able to buy or sell because they would not have the mark of the beast. Also for the purpose of having the little flock's good will and blessing so that there would be no strife or hindrance between the two groups of believers. The Christians would be edified, being able to do their duty and give, and the saints in Jerusalem would experience Christian love in action]. **28** When therefore I have performed this, and have sealed to them **this fruit** [gift of money], I will come by you into Spain. **29** And I am sure that, when I come unto you, I shall come **in the fulness of the blessing of the gospel of Christ** [Paul may have received revelation from Christ that he would have the full revelation of the mystery when he came to Rome, even if he had not written everything down yet. Paul would be able to share this with the saints at Rome when he arrived.].

30 Now I beseech you, brethren, for the Lord Jesus Christ's sake, and for the love of the Spirit, that ye **strive together with me in your prayers to God for me** [prayer is work because the flesh does not want to do it. Paul believed in the power of prayer, and asked for specific prayer regarding **three things: him to be delivered, gift accepted, and to come to them in Rome with joy by the will of God, and be refreshed with them**]; **31** That I may be delivered from them that do not believe in Judaea **[1]**; and that my service which I have for Jerusalem may be accepted of the saints **[2]**; **32** That I may come unto you with joy by the will of God, and may with you be refreshed **[3]**. **33** Now the God of peace be with you all [Was Paul's prayers answered? Yes! God's peace is with those who present their bodies a living sacrifice so that God can live through them (Gal. 2:20). We can have peace even as aliens in a foreign country, this evil world (Gal. 1:4), being so to speak in the "eye of the storm" by the grace of God, and truth of His word. God saves us, lives in us, and keeps us]. Amen.

Did Peter and Paul preach the same gospel?

Several gospels are mentioned in the Bible we will review several including the everlasting gospel. Jesus Christ is the Redeemer (Saviour) for all mankind but His instruction by which people are saved has changed over time.

What gospel did Peter preach? Peter preached the gospel of the kingdom on Pentecost. Peter preached to the Jews that Jesus proved by miracles and signs that He was their Messiah and the King to sit on the throne of David. The BAD NEWS was that they had killed Him. But God had raised Jesus up again "Ye men of Israel, . . . Jesus of Nazareth . . . by miracles and wonders and signs . . . Him, ye have taken, and by wicked hands have crucified and slain: Whom God hath raised up, having loosed the pains of death: because it was not possible that he should be holden of it" (Acts 2:22-24). Peter said that David, being a prophet, had told them that God would raise up their King ". . . raise up Christ to sit on his [David's] throne" (Acts 2:30). The men of Israel, devastated with grief, asked what they should do. "Now when they heard this, they were PRICKED IN THEIR HEART, and said unto Peter and to the rest of the apostles . . . WHAT SHALL WE DO?" (Acts 2:37). Peter answered ". . . **Repent** [change your mind and believe God that Jesus of Nazareth is the prophesied King of the Jews, the Messiah], and be **baptized** [in water to demonstrate your faith and be priests] every one of you in the name of Jesus Christ for the remission of sins [forgiveness], and ye shall receive the gift of the Holy Ghost [the power to witness and receive sign gifts]" (Acts 2:38). It is important to notice that Peter continued to preach repent, and be baptized just like John the Baptist (Matt. 3:2, 6, 11). God's spokesman Moses had said, "ye shall be a kingdom of priest, and a holy nation" (Ex. 19:6). Peter called the Jews "a royal priesthood, an holy nation" (1 Peter 2:9).

What gospel did Jesus preach?
Jesus preached the "gospel of the kingdom" (the 12 preached this gospel for a few years before the cross which they did not understand Luke 9:1-6, 18:31-34; Matt. 16:21, 22). Those that believed the "gospel of the kingdom" became part of the Lord's generation and were no longer identified with apostate Israel.

"Now after that John was put in prison, Jesus came into Galilee, preaching the **GOSPEL OF THE KINGDOM** of God, and saying The time [of Daniel's timeline] is fulfilled, and the kingdom of God is at hand . . ." (Mark 1:14, 15).

"And Jesus went about all Galilee, teaching in their synagogues, and preaching the **GOSPEL OF THE KINGDOM**, and healing all manner of sickness and all manner of disease among the people [Christ healed the Jews perfectly, so that these Jews could be part of the perfect unblemished kingdom of priests]" (Matt. 4:23).

"And Jesus went about all the cities and villages, teaching in their synagogues, and preaching the **GOSPEL OF THE KINGDOM**, and healing every sickness and every disease among the people" (Matt. 9:35).

The "gospel of God" appears seven times in the King James Bible. Six times in Paul's writings and once in Peter's (1 Peter 4:17).

So did Peter preach the same gospel as Paul? The "gospel of God" is the basic prophesied redemptive information of Christs death, burial, and resurrection for sins. Both Peter and Paul preached this basic gospel because the Lord Jesus Christ is the prophesied Redeemer (Gen. 3:15) for both groups. But Peter emphasized the "gospel of the kingdom" and Paul the "gospel of Christ." Peter said that Christ was the King of the Jews to sit on the throne in the coming kingdom on earth and Paul preached the "gospel of Christ" (salvation for all). Paul said that today Gentiles can be saved apart from the law and apart from going through Israel and become part of the body of Christ. The destiny for the body of Christ is the heavenly places. (2 Cor. 5:1; Eph. 2:6). **So what is the difference between Paul's gospel and Peter's?** Paul said Christ died for OUR SINS (the Gentiles). Paul never said that the body of Christ would live in a kingdom on earth but in heavenly places. Gospel means "good news." There is more than one gospel in the Bible but there is only one that saves today, Paul's.

What gospel did Paul preach?
Paul said "I thank God that I baptized none of you . . . For Christ sent me not to baptize . . ." (1 Cor. 1:14, 17). Paul preached the gospel of the grace of God (Acts 20:24) which is also called the gospel of Christ (1 Cor. 15:1-4). Paul said Christ died for OUR SINS (the Gentiles) apart from Israel.

Some have described the "gospel of God" like a pie crust.
The crust is the basic gospel message of the Redeemer sacrificing His blood to save man. But, the filing of the crust can be: apples = the gospel of the kingdom; or cherries = the gospel of Christ.

What is the everlasting gospel?
It is a gospel that says to worship God because He is the Creator.
"And I saw another angel fly in the midst of heaven, having the everlasting gospel to preach unto them that dwell on the earth, and to every nation, and kindred, and tongue, and people, Saying with a loud voice, Fear God, and give glory to him; for the hour of his judgment is come: and worship him that made heaven, and earth, and the sea, and the fountains of waters" (Rev. 14:6, 7).

Christ is the redeemer for both the earthly kingdom believers and the believers destined for the heavenly places. The people of Israel were waiting for the "King of the Jews" to save them from their enemies and many did not know that they also needed to be saved from their sins and the power of Satan. Peter said, "Forasmuch as ye know that ye were not redeemed with corruptible things, as silver and gold, from your vain conversation received by tradition from your fathers; But with the <u>precious blood of Christ, as of a lamb without blemish and without spot</u>" (1 Peter 1:18, 19).

Paul also said we are redeemed by His blood. "Being justified freely by his grace through the redemption that is in Christ Jesus: Whom God hath set forth to be a propitiation through **faith in his blood**, to declare his righteousness for the remission of sins that are past, through the forbearance of God; To declare, I say, at this time his righteousness: that he might be just, and the justifier of him which believeth in Jesus" (Rom. 3:24-26).

Christ is the Redeemer for both groups. There are more than one gospel, but He is the only Saviour. He is King, and His kingdom includes both heaven and earth. Gentiles are saved in both programs, but in the kingdom Gentiles will not be on equal footing with God's special people Israel. On the other hand, in the body of Christ there is no difference because there is neither Jews and Gentile because they are all one in Christ. In the body of Christ there is neither Jew nor Gentile. "There is neither Jew nor Greek, there is neither bond nor free, there is neither male nor female: for ye are all one in Christ Jesus" (Gal. 3:28).

From heaven Christ through Paul began the Church the body of Christ. Christ had already begun another church during His earthly ministry through Peter and the eleven (Matt. 16:18). We need to understand that Christ is the head of both Churches, but they are different from one another and contain a different group of people saved by believing two different gospels and by two different preachers.

The **twelve disciples** preached the "gospel of the kingdom" this gospel is not in effect today. It has been temporarily set aside and does not have the power to save anyone today (not even the Jews). However, the Apostle Paul was given the gospel of the grace of God and it is to Jew and Gentile alike (1 Cor. 15:1-4). Both Gentiles and Jews are saved by the same gospel and in this age, there is no difference. Anyone that is in the Church, the body of Christ, are saved by the gospel that Paul preached. If Paul did not preach it, then it does not have the power to save you in this dispensation. Preaching anything other than the grace of God is preaching another gospel. Paul said, "But though we, or an angel from heaven, preach any other gospel unto you than that which we have preached unto you, **let him be accursed**" (Gal. 1:8). *** **Satan's current policy of evil is for Christendom to follow Peter instead of Paul, or to mix Peter and Paul.**

Romans Chapter 16 – Benediction about the revelation of the mystery

Goal: Finish the book of Romans by completing chapter 16. Elaborate on what Paul means when he says, "Adronicus and Junia . . . were <u>in Christ</u> before me" (16:7); discuss "labour in the Lord" as it pertains to both men and women (16:12); what is meant by "the God of peace shall bruise Satan under your feet shortly" (16:20), more clues that Romans was written in Acts 20:2,3 (16:23), examine in detail verses 16:25-27 and what the mystery is.

We must realize that all the books of the Bible were written before Paul wrote 2 Timothy (Col. 1:25). With his letters Paul puts the capstone (the final piece of the puzzle) on God's information to mankind finishing the Bible. Paul is the due time testifier who tells us all that Christ accomplished at the cross. He is God's spokesman in this dispensation of grace. <u>Not until Paul do we learn that it was checkmate at the cross for Satan. Satan lost both heaven and earth.</u>

<u>Paul has given the Romans the foundational doctrine for living the Christian life.</u> He has shown them that a dispensational change has taken place in the "But Now" of Romans 3:21 and the dispensational information given in Romans 9-11 which declare that Israel as a nation has been blinded temporarily. The nation of Israel is a vessel of dishonor at present but after the fullness of the Gentiles God will make them a vessel of honor again. In the future, God will use the nation Israel that He created to save souls, rule, and reclaim the earth. But for now we are living in the time of Gentile opportunity for salvation apart from having to go through Israel, and apart from the law. We must be both biblical and dispensational. We must also study God's word His way by applying 2 Tim. 2:15.

In the meantime, <u>God in His mercy, has declared all people in unbelief so that He may have mercy on all who believe the gospel that Paul told us to preach.</u>

The cross, burial, and resurrection of the Lord Jesus Christ is the greatest event in history! Christ bore our sins, conquered Satan, and when He rose He conquered death. His resurrection proves that our sins are paid for.

Israel was looking for the king promised to them through David (2 Sam. 7:16) and by Daniel (Dan. 2:44) they had forgotten that they needed a Redeemer for their sins (Gen. 3:15). Jesus came to "save his people from their sins" (Matt. 1:21) when He came the first time (Isa. 53:4-8) notice it says "my people" Jesus only came to save His people (Matt. 20:28, 26:28).

If we do not rightly divide the word of God, we could be guilty of saying that Christ's atonement was limited to the Jews only. But then to include themselves many pretend that they are "spiritual Israel." This is called **Calvinism**. But the truth is that Israel is Israel and we are the body of Christ.

Paul explained in Romans 11:11 that because of Israel's fall "salvation has come to the Gentiles." Paul, the one apostle of the Gentiles (11:13), says that Christ came to be a "ransom for all" (1 Tim. 2:4-6). We are living in the "But now" period of Gentile opportunity to be saved and to have eternal life as a member of the one new man, the body of Christ (Eph. 2:11-16) by believing the gospel (Rom. 3:21-28). It is sad that so many Gentiles (which includes Jews today since there is no difference and all have sinned and must believe the same thing) do not take the opportunity to believe.

Besides triumphing over Satan, sin, and death, the cross also helped us to win over **our other worst enemy, ourselves**. We no longer have to be ruled by our flesh (the old sin nature) we now live by the "law of the Spirit of life in Christ Jesus" which has made us free from the "law of sin and death" (Rom. 8:2).

The sinner needs the imputed righteousness of God in order to stand before the Holy Father. When we trust in what Christ has done by believing the gospel we receive Christ's righteousness (Rom. 4:22-25; 2 Cor. 5:21).

God's will: is for "all men to be saved, <u>and</u> to come unto the knowledge of the truth" (1 Tim. 2:4). Often there are many years between being saved and coming to the knowledge of the truth. In my case 25 years, in my friend's case 40, and in another friend's case 9. <u>Until a person understands the difference between Israel and the body of Christ they will never understand the Bible.</u>

It is best for all to listen to the word of God being taught in person, because it takes more discipline to listen on line. But I guarantee that this teaching today will be a great blessing to everyone who does.

Very few grace preachers are teaching an intermediate level class which covers a whole chapter in Paul's Epistles in two hours. Most grace pastors are more detailed covering one or two verses in depth.

16:7 When Paul talks about **Andronicus and Junia** he makes it clear that they were "in Christ" before him. We learn from Paul that all saved are "in Christ." They were saved by the preaching of the little flock; this is how they are "in

Christ" before Paul. Since we know that Paul is the first one in the body of Christ (1 Tim. 1:16). What was the gospel that they had trusted? The gospel of the kingdom. They repented (changed their minds) and believed that Jesus Christ was the King of the Jews and were baptized with water and the Holy Ghost. They met Paul in prison (perhaps in Philippi, Acts 16:25). They were respected by the 12 apostles. Christ told Peter and the little flock that they will be in Him and He will be in them (John 14:20, 17:23). However, those saints realized that God had changed dispensations and had begun working through a new apostle, Paul. They wanted to be part of what God is now doing so they joined Paul. Barnabas and Silas are examples of other "little flock" saints who also helped Paul. Paul mentions that his face for a while was unknown to the "churches of Judae which were in Christ" (Gal. 1:22). Everyone who is saved is "in Christ" and not in Adam. This is how we have so "much more" in Christ because we have the gift of his righteousness (Rom. 5:17). In the fullness of times God will gather everyone who is "in Christ" into the new heaven and the new earth (Eph. 1:10).

Romans 16:1 I commend unto you Phebe our sister [a saint that carried the letter to Rome], which is a servant of the church which is at Cenchrea [a seaport near Corinth]: **2** That ye receive her in the Lord, as becometh saints [in the gracious manner that becomes saints, Phil. 1:27], and that ye assist her in whatsoever business she hath need of you [help her in every possible way]: for she hath been a succourer [helper] of many, and of myself also. **3** Greet Priscilla and Aquila my helpers in Christ Jesus [This couple had met Paul in Corinth after being told to leave Rome and after helping Paul in Ephesus had moved back to Rome. Acts 18:2, 18, 26; 2 Tim. 4:19]: **4** Who have for my life laid down their own necks [Why does Paul begin to mentions Priscilla first? Perhaps in the uproar (Acts 19:40) Priscilla may have been braver or she may have been stronger in the doctrine]: unto whom not only I give thanks, but also all the churches of the Gentiles [without Paul the Gentile churches would have no further revelation from Christ's heavenly ministry]. **5** Likewise greet the church that is in their house [they had a house church, I believe Paul mentions three or more in this letter]. Salute my wellbeloved Epaenetus, who is the firstfruits of Achaia unto Christ [among the first to believe, probably a member of the household of Stephanas, 1 Cor. 16:15]. **6** Greet Mary, **who bestowed much labour on us** [She worked hard to serve Paul and his friends, possibly the mother of John Mark, Acts 12:12].

7 Salute Andronicus and Junia, my kinsmen, and my fellowprisoners, who are of note among the apostles, who also were in Christ before me [When Paul talks about **Andronicus and Junia** he makes it clear that they were "in Christ" before him. We learn from Paul that all saved are "in Christ." They were saved by the preaching of the little flock; this is how they are "in Christ" before Paul. Since we know that Paul is the first one in the body of Christ (1 Tim. 1:16). What was the gospel that they had trusted? The gospel of the kingdom. They repented (changed their minds) and believed that Jesus Christ was the King of the Jews and were baptized with water and the Holy Ghost. They met Paul in prison (perhaps in Philippi, Acts 16:25). They were respected by the 12 apostles. Christ told Peter and the little flock that they will be in Him and He will be in them (John 14:20, 17:23). However, those saints realized that God had changed dispensations and had begun working through a new apostle, Paul. They wanted to be part of what God is now doing so they joined Paul. Barnabas and Silas are examples of other "little flock" saints who also helped Paul. Paul mentions that his face for a while was unknown to the "churches of Judae which were <u>in Christ</u>" (Gal. 1:22). Everyone who is saved is "in Christ" and not in Adam. This is how we have so "much more" in Christ because we have the gift of his righteousness (Rom. 5:17). In the fullness of times God will gather everyone who is "in Christ" into the new heaven and the new earth (Eph. 1:10).] **8** Greet Amplias my beloved in the Lord. **9** Salute Urbane, our helper in Christ, and Stachys my beloved. **10** Salute Apelles approved in Christ. Salute them which are of Aristobulus' household [possibly another house church]. **11** Salute Herodion my kinsman [a Jew]. Greet them that be of the household of Narcissus, which are in the Lord [possibly another house church].

12 Salute Tryphena and Tryphosa [probably twins women,], <u>who labour in the Lord</u> [These women helped others to be saved and to come to the knowledge of the truth of sound doctrine getting the gospel out. Women are to be faithful to share what they have learned about Pauline truth just like men are. Many women helped in the ministry, Phil 4:3. Notice who is sanctifying believers and cleansing us by His word in these verses: "Husbands, love your wives, even as Christ also loved the church, and gave himself for it; That he [Christ] might sanctify and cleanse it with the washing of water by the word, That he might present it [the Church] to himself a glorious church, not having spot, or wrinkle, or any such thing; but that it should be holy and without blemish" (Eph. 5:25-27). The Bible is clear (especially in the pastoral epistles) that women should not be pastors and we all agree with that. The KJB is our final authority. When Paul said teach other faithful men who in turn would teach other faithful men, he did not mean that women should not also be faithful to teach others so they may be saved, come to the knowledge of Pauline sound doctrine, and understand all of the Bible. Both men and women can be beguiled by false doctrine (2 Cor. 11:3). We all constantly have to be on our guard to remain both Biblical and dispensational correct. Paul does not discount 50% of the human race. He says that we "are all one in Christ" (Gal.

3:28). Each person is important to God. He wants all to be saved. Even the North Koreans.]. Salute the beloved Persis [a woman], which **laboured much in the Lord**. **13** Salute Rufus chosen in the Lord, and his mother and mine [Mark 15:21, this mother mothered Paul]. **14** Salute Asyncritus, Phlegon, Hermas, Patrobas, Hermes, **and the brethren which are with them** [possibly another house church]. **15** Salute Philologus, and Julia, Nereus, and his sister, and Olympas, and **all the saints which are with them** [possibly another house church]. **16** Salute one another with an holy kiss [affectionately on the cheek]. **The churches of Christ salute you.**

17 ¶ Now I beseech you, brethren, mark them which cause divisions and offences contrary to the doctrine which ye have learned [Phil. 3:17-19. **Paul warns them not to let anyone take them away from following the sound doctrine they have learned from him**]; **and avoid** them [those false doctrine teachers should be avoided (**those who believe that the body of Christ began in Acts 2**). Most of these pastors preach Acts 2 out of ignorance, they just don't know any better. We must remember that we were like them.]. **18** For they that are such serve not our Lord Jesus Christ [unless the ministry is Pauline they are NOT serving Christ, **2 Cor. 6:15-17**], but their own belly [they just want to promote themselves and their mixed up beliefs they do not know the truth and they care more about money to feed themselves than feeding others spiritual truth]; and by good words and fair speeches deceive the hearts of the simple [they may sound eloquent and their spiritualizing of God's word and cute stories may sound like they are saying something of value, but they are not]. **19** For your obedience is come abroad unto all men [your faithful following of Paul's sound doctrine]. I am glad therefore on your behalf [Paul is happy to hear that]: but yet I would have you wise unto that which is good [**"good" means Paul's sound doctrine stored up in the inner man. Just like Christ we can have faith in God's plan. God has told us to live by allowing Christ to live through us. "Christ liveth in me" (Gal. 2:20). So now we live by the faith of the Son of God, offering our bodies as living sacrifice**], and simple concerning evil [false doctrine]. **20** And the God of peace [not war] shall bruise Satan under your feet shortly [Christ can live through us and bruise Satan under our feet by His faith working through us. God can use all that we have learned in Romans chapters 1-16. Satan cannot stand Paul's powerful truth. It is in Paul's epistles that Christ triumph over him is made known (Col. 2:15). But Satan does what he can **to conceal Pauline truth**. When a group of believers are strong together in the truth with Christ working through them laboring to get the message out (1 Tim. 2:4) Satan is bruised. Satan hates the final authority of the King James Bible because his lies cannot prevail against it. What does Paul mean by shortly? I believe that in 15:29, Christ had revealed to Paul that he would have the full revelation of the gospel by the time he came to Rome (even if it was not written down yet) so Paul says that <u>the truth will do damage to Satan.</u> God's knowledge is power.]. The grace of our Lord Jesus Christ be with you Amen. [Paul often says "Amen" which means "so be it" it does not mean that it is necessarily the end of his letter. Each of Paul's letters begin with his name and end with grace, 2 Thess. 3:17, 18.] **21** Timotheus my workfellow, and Lucius, and Jason, and Sosipater, my kinsmen [Possibly Luke, or the Lucius in Acts 13:1], salute you. **22** I Tertius, who wrote this epistle, salute you in the Lord [the secretary or amanuensis who wrote down the dictated letter. Paul only wrote Galatians with his own hand Gal. 6:11]. **23** Gaius mine host, and of the whole church, saluteth you. Erastus the chamberlain of the city saluteth you [probably the Gaius in 1 Cor. 1:14. Perhaps it is the Gaius of Derbe that traveled with him in Acts 20:4 and or the Gaius of Acts 19:29: Erastus held an office in that city he is mentioned as being in Corinth 2 Tim. 4:20. So that is another clue that the letter was probably written in Acts 20:2, 3], and Quartus a brother. **24** The grace of our Lord Jesus Christ be with you all. Amen.

25 ¶ Now to **him that is of power [Christ's living Spirit in us has the power to use His living word in us because we are His workmanship (Eph. 2:10)]** to **stablish** [To "establish" is to begin a work, to "stablish" is to make stable] you according to **my** gospel [<u>Paul calls the body of sound doctrine that he received by revelation from the ascended, glorified Lord Jesus Christ "my gospel" to distinguish it from the gospel of the kingdom given to the twelve.</u> "My gospel" is the "gospel of Christ" and the "gospel of grace," and the audience Paul preached to is the uncircumcision. Paul's gospel is the only gospel that saves today. Paul is the only apostle of the Gentiles who says that Christ died for OUR SINS. Paul makes it clear Christ died to be a "ransom for all" (1 Tim. 2:6). In this age anyone can be saved by believing what Christ has accomplished for him], and the preaching of Jesus Christ [Christ's death, burial and resurrection for our sins], according to the revelation of the mystery, which was kept secret since the world began [**Paul calls his doctrine the "mystery" because it was kept secret until it was revealed to him. Jesus Christ Himself revealed the mystery to Paul. He did not receive it from another man such as Peter, and he didn't need another man to teach him (Gal. 1:1, 11, 12). The mystery revelation was not known until Christ first revealed it to Paul in Acts 9. The mystery was unsearchable [Eph. 3:8, read Eph. 3:1-9]. <u>No creature was as surprised as Satan when Christ returned after a year in heaven and saved His worst enemy on the road to Damascus.</u> "What?" Satan said, "that is not what the scriptures say? That is un-prophesied! That was not what was supposed to happen next! Where is God's wrath on His people?" God defeated Satan by keeping a secret: the formation**

of the body of Christ in the dispensation of grace. Compare this to what Peter says in Acts 3:19-21], 26 But now is made manifest [God has now revealed it through Paul, Eph. 3:1-9], and by the scriptures of the prophets (the scriptures outside of Paul's writings) both the Old Testament and New Testament scriptures. Further and more advanced knowledge was given to Paul. Paul often quotes the Old Testament and by the inspiration of the Holy Spirit he sometimes changes words to give more revelation. (Paul could do that but we cannot we are to believe what is written. God is the author of the Bible so all of the Bible could be in red letters.], according to the commandment of the everlasting God, made known to all nations for the obedience of faith [**God has commanded that the revelation that God is now forming the body of Christ, (the one new man, Eph. 2:15) during the dispensation of grace, to reign with Christ in the heavenly places, should be made known to all nations. So all can believe what God says in Romans to Philemon, the sound doctrine Christ gave us through Paul. God can stablish the believer by three things: 1) "My gospel," 2) "The preaching of Jesus Christ, according to the revelation of the mystery," and 3) "By the scriptures and the prophets" meaning all scripture, both the Old and New Testament, outside Paul's epistles. As the scriptures relate according to Pauline sound doctrine.**]: 27 To God only wise, be glory through Jesus Christ for ever. Amen [**God alone is wise. Paul constantly exalts our Saviour the Lord Jesus Christ and gives Him the glory and so should we** because He has done everything that was necessary to save us. Therefore, **God's will is first, for "all men to be saved" (1 Tim. 2:4) by believing the gospel (1 Cor. 15:3, 4). Second, "to come to the knowledge of the truth" (1 Tim. 2:4) by learning the sound doctrine that is found in Paul's 13 letters (2 Thess. 2:15; 1 Tim. 1:3; 2 Tim. 2:7). Then third, learn the rest of the truth in the Bible found outside Paul's epistles, because "all scripture . . . is profitable" (2 Tim. 3:16)**].

How can the God of Peace bruise Satan under our feet shortly?

God can bruise Satan under our feet because of the mystery doctrine learned in Paul's letter to the saints in Rome.

A Review of the 16 chapters of Romans:

1. Gentiles are under sin.

2. Jews are under sin.

3. God has made a dispensational shift and revealed all that Christ accomplished at the cross to us through Paul. "**But now** the righteousness of God without the law is manifested [God revealed how He solved the sin problem. He remains righteous, while allowing all to have free will, justifying believers in Christ apart from the law] . . . Even the righteousness of God which is by faith of Jesus Christ [Christ had the faith] unto all and upon all them that believe [we put our faith in what Christ has done]: for there is no difference [between Jew and Gentile]: For all have sinned, and come short of the glory of God; Being justified freely by his grace through the redemption that is in Christ Jesus: Whom God hath set forth to be a propitiation through **faith in his blood** [faith that His blood paid the redemption price], to declare his righteousness for the remission of sins that are past [Christ's righteousness is credited to those who died before the cross], through the forbearance of God [the Father held back His wrath]; To declare, I say [Paul is the due time testifier 1 Tim. 2:4-6], **at this time** his righteousness [in this dispensation believers are also declared righteous]: that he might **be just, and the justifier of him which believeth in Jesus [God can remain just]**. . . . Therefore we conclude that **a man is justified by faith without the deeds of the law**" (3:21-28).

4. We receive Christ's **imputed** righteousness when we believe what He has done.

5. We are justified – **Christ died for us** while we were yet sinners. We have much more in Christ than we lost in Adam (He gave us the gift of His righteousness).

6. We died with Christ. We are dead to sin, but alive unto God. We believe God's word as we **know, reckon,** and **yield** to the truth that "Being then made free from sin, ye became the **servants of righteousness**" (6:18). The power of sin has been broken, and we **walk in newness of life**. We are under grace, not the law.

7. We are dead to the law (a dead man cannot be brought to trial). But we still have the no good flesh in our body. Which is very useful information to know.

8. Because of **Christ's Spirit and life in us** we can live on a higher plane above sin and self. "There is therefore now no condemnation to them which are in Christ Jesus, who walk not after the flesh, but after the Spirit. For the law of the Spirit of life in Christ Jesus hath made me free from the law of sin and death" (8:1, 2).

9-11. What has happened to the promises God gave to Israel? We are living in the time of Gentile opportunity because of the nation of Israel's temporary blindness (for nearly 2,000 years). God will still keep His promises to the nation of Israel after Gentile believers are raptured. In the meantime, individual Jews can be saved by believing the gospel that Paul preached.

12. We are to **present our bodies a living sacrifice for Christ to live through,** and to be transformed by the renewing of our minds by His word.

13. We can be **model citizens** because "love worketh no ill to his neighbour" (13:10) and God has set up the governmental structures to protect us.

14. Be **patient with people who are weak in the faith (Pauline sound doctrine)** and try to help them learn and be strong. We should not do things that may upset them such as eat certain foods or argue. What we eat doesn't matter to God but it may to the weaker brother or sister, so we should be careful not to offend them. God cares about "righteousness, and peace, and joy in the Holy Ghost" (14:17).

15. Be **willing to suffer reproach** to help others who are weak in the faith (sound doctrine) they may be saved but have not "come to the knowledge of the truth" (1 Tim. 2:4) since there can be many years between these two events. Christ has sent Paul directly to the Gentiles, so they may believe without going through Israel. "That I should be the minister of Jesus Christ to the Gentiles . . ." (15:16).

16. If we separate the sentences in Romans 16:25, 26 by "and" it is often easier to understand the three things Paul tells us, he writes:
"Now to him that is of **power to stablish** you according to **my gospel**,
and the preaching of Jesus **Christ** [His death, burial, and resurrection for our sins], **according** to **the revelation of the mystery**, which was kept secret since the world began, But now is made manifest,
and by the **scriptures** of the prophets, according to the commandment of the everlasting God, made known to all nations for the obedience of faith" (16:25, 26).

The theme of Romans is "the righteousness of God" and the key verses are Rom. 1:16, 17. Paul began the letter to the saints in Rome talking about the power of the gospel of Christ to save all who believe so that they may receive the righteousness of God, be justified, and live by faith.

"For I am not ashamed of the gospel of Christ: for it is the **power of God** unto salvation to every one that believeth [**every time a person is saved it is a miracle of God**. They are miraculously made alive spiritually and translated out of Adam and into Christ, Col. 1:13. "Salvation" means more than rescued from eternal hell. We are saved to allow Christ's Spirit to live through us (Gal. 2:20) so we can understand all the truth that is in Paul's thirteen letters, Romans to Philemon]; to the Jew first, and also to the Greek. <u>For therein is the righteousness of God revealed from **faith to faith**</u> [God's righteousness is revealed from Christ's faith to our faith]: as it is written, The just shall live by faith [we live (walk) by our little faith in His perfect faith] (Rom. 1:16, 17).

We have a living God living in us, who uses His living word to transform us. Let us renew the spirit of our mind with His word daily, and walk not after the flesh, but after the Spirit.

What Does It Mean to be "In Christ"? There are only two kinds of people in the world those who are in Adam and those who are in Christ. Even Adam has to be in Christ. Adam was innocent in the Garden but he did not have the imputed righteousness of Christ. Therefore, after the fall even Adam needed to be "in Christ." When Adam believed what God said, that God would send a Redeemer (Gen. 3:15) as evidenced by him calling his wife Eve, the mother of all living, he demonstrated his faith. Adam was created to live forever, and so are we. **This life is about laying hold of eternal life**. When Adam died his soul went to paradise (also called "Abraham's bosom" in Luke 16:22). After Christ died on the cross He went and preached that He had paid their ransom with His blood to everyone there and took them to the third heaven (2 Cor. 12:4; **Heb. 12:23**).

Paul described the differences between being "in Adam" and being "in Christ" in Romans chapter 5. Through Paul's writings we learn that everyone needs to be "in Christ." In Gal. 1:22, Paul says that "the churches of Judaea which were in Christ." In the end, God will "gather together all things in Christ, both which are in heaven, and which are in earth; even in him" (Eph. 1:10).

Comparing and contrasting Adam with .... Christ (from Romans 5:15-21):
sin ..... righteousness
death .... life
offence ..... free gift
transgression .... abounding grace
condemnation ..... justification
death reigned ...... reign in life by Jesus
inherited sin nature .... gift of righteousness
judgement on all men .... all men unto justification
disobedience many made sinners .... obedience many made righteous
then the law entered . . .
that offences might abound to sin .... but grace abounded much more
sin reigned to death. But ... grace reigned unto eternal life by Jesus Christ our Lord.

Everyone needs to be translated out of Adam and into Christ (Col. 1:13). Have you trusted that God died for you in your place? If so, then you are in Him.

The words "in Christ" appears 77 times in the Bible, in Acts 24:24, 1 Peter 3:16 and 5:14, and the rest are in Paul's letters.

But Christ said "in me." "At that day ye shall know that I am in my Father, and ye **in me, and I in you"** (John 14:20).

John 15:4 Abide **in me, and I in you**. As the branch cannot bear fruit of itself, except it abide in the vine; no more can ye, except ye **abide in me**.

John 17:23 **I in them, and thou in me, that they may be made perfect in one**; and that the world may know that thou hast sent me, and hast loved them, as thou hast loved me.

Peter understood about the value of Christ's blood. "Forasmuch as ye know that ye were not redeemed with corruptible things, as silver and gold, from your vain conversation received by tradition from your fathers; But with the <u>precious blood of Christ, as of a lamb without blemish and without spot</u>" (1 Peter 1:18, 19). Peter was born again by faith in the word of God (the gospel of the kingdom) (1 Peter 1:23). The nation of Israel will be "born again" at Christ' return to earth. The Kingdom on earth believers will receive their eternal bodies at His Second Coming (Isa. 66:8, 45:17, 59:20; Ezek. 37:12, 13). They will receive God's Spirit in them then (the New Covenant, Zech. 12:10; Jer. 31:31; Ezek. 36:24-28).

We have Christ in us now (Col. 1:27). **The Father loves His Son more than anything, and we are "in Him."** The Lord Jesus Christ is manifesting Himself to the world through us. Paul also said that faith comes by the hearing of the word of God (the gospel of Christ) (Rom.10:17). The members of the body of Christ will receive their glorified immortal bodies at the Rapture (1 Cor. 15:51-53).

Why is OUR gospel called "the mystery"?

1. It was kept secret (Rom. 16:25)
2. It was hid in God (Eph. 3:9)
3. Hid from ages and generations (Col. 1:26)
4. In other ages not made known (Eph. 3:5)
5. Hidden wisdom ordained by God before the world (1 Cor. 2:7, 8)
6. Could NOT be searched out in the Bible before Paul (Eph. 3:8)
7. Paul does not want us to be ignorant of the mystery of Israel's blindness until the Rapture (Rom. 11:25)

1. Because it was KEPT SECRET
Romans 16:25 ". . . the revelation of the MYSTERY, which was KEPT SECRET since the world began."

2. Because it was Hid in GOD

Ephesians 3:9 ". . . the MYSTERY which from the beginning of the world hath been HID in GOD"

3. Because it was HID FROM AGES AND GENERATIONS

Colossians 1:26 "Even the MYSTERY which hath been HID FROM AGES AND AGES GENERATIONS . . ."

4. Because in other AGES was NOT MADE KNOWN unto the sons of men

Ephesians 3:5 "Which in other AGES was NOT MADE KNOWN unto the sons of men . . ."

5. Because it was HIDDEN WISDOM ORDAINED OF GOD BEFORE THE WORLD kept from Satan so Christ could pay the ransom.

1 Corinthians 2:7, 8 "But we speak the wisdom of God in a MYSTERY, even the HIDDEN WISDOM, which GOD ORDAINED BEFORE THE WORLD unto our glory: Which none of the princes of this world knew: for had they known it, they would not have crucified the Lord of glory."

6. Because it was riches that COULD NOT BE SEARCHED OUT in the scriptures before Paul.

Ephesians 3:8 Unto me, who am less than the least of all saints, is this grace given, that I should preach among the Gentiles the UNSEARCHABLE riches of Christ.

7. Because Paul does not want us to be IGNORANT that the reason Christ has NOT come back yet is that we are living in the time of Israel's BLINDNESS and has postponed His dealings with them UNTIL after the Rapture.

Romans 11:25 For I would not, brethren, that ye should be IGNORANT of this MYSTERY, lest ye should be wise in your own conceits; that BLINDNESS in part is happened to Israel, UNTIL the fulness of the Gentiles be come in.

In the "revelation of the mystery" given to Paul, God reveals the end of the law and salvation by grace alone, through faith alone, in the blood of Christ alone. He also reveals His plan to form the body of Christ, the one new man, composed of both Jews and Gentiles to rule with Christ in the heavenly places. **The mystery is all that Jesus Christ accomplished for us through the cross explained through Paul, and the wisdom given us in his letters.** It was God's wise plan to keep it a secret from Satan. Satan thought that, if he could inspire to leaders of Israel to crucify their king, that he would win the earth. However, because of God's secret (the mystery) Satan lost not only the earth, but heaven as well!

The Key Verse in the Bible: The only verse in the Bible that tells us how to study the Bible is <u>2 Tim. 2:15</u>: "<u>Study</u> to shew thyself approved unto God, a workman that needeth not to be ashamed, <u>RIGHTLY DIVIDING THE WORD OF TRUTH</u>."

The instruction is to divide truth. Not error from truth, but truth from truth. All the Bible is truth, but it needs to be divided up so we know which part is our truth. It makes sense that Paul who told us to divide truth, would also tell us how to divide truth, and he does in Ephesians chapter two. The main division in the Bible is between prophecy and mystery.

In Ephesians chapter two Paul gives us three time divisions: <u>Time Past, But Now, Ages to Come</u>

<u>Time Past:</u> Eph. 2:11, 12 Wherefore remember, that ye *being* in TIME PAST Gentiles in the flesh, who are called Uncircumcision by that which is called the Circumcision in the flesh made by hands; That at that time ye were without Christ, being aliens from the commonwealth of Israel, and strangers from the covenants of promise, having no hope, and without God in the world.

<u>But Now:</u> Eph. 2:13 BUT NOW in Christ Jesus ye who sometimes were far off are made nigh by the blood of Christ.

<u>Ages to Come:</u> Eph. 2:7 That in the AGES TO COME he might shew the exceeding riches of his grace in *his* kindness toward us through Christ Jesus.

A distinctive feature indicating that <u>Time Past</u> is in effect is whenever God makes a **distinction** between the Jews and all other nations. **This distinction is called "the middle wall of partition"** (Eph. 2:14). God gave Israel the covenant of **circumcision** (Gen. 17) making them **unlike all other nations**. When God added the law by Moses He solidified the difference between the Jews and Gentiles even more through dietary, and other laws. God set the nation of Israel (the circumcision) above the rest of the nations. Whenever the word of God distinguishes between Jews and Gentiles we know that "prophecy" not "mystery" is in effect. (In the <u>Ages to Come</u> (prophecy) the law, and Israel's preferred nation status will again be in effect.)

How do we know that Paul's ministry began in Acts 9? His unique dramatic salvation is rehearsed in Acts 9, 22, and 26. When Jesus of Nazareth appears to Paul on the road to Damascus He says NOW I SEND THEE "Delivering thee from the people, and from the Gentiles, unto whom now I send thee . . ." (Acts 26:16). Paul himself says that he was the first one in the body of Christ. "Howbeit for this

134

cause I obtained mercy, **that <u>in me first</u> Jesus Christ** might shew forth all longsuffering, **for a pattern to them which should hereafter believe on him to life everlasting**" (1 Tim. 1:16).

After Adam and Eve disobeyed God, God had made a promise to Adam and Eve (Gen. 3:15). Then after the flood, God gave up the Gentiles at the Tower of Babel because they did not obey Him and tried to set up their own evil one world government and religion. (In the kingdom Christ will set up His righteous one world religion and government). Next God made a nation out of one man who did obey Him, Abram. God made promises to Abram Gen. 12:1-3. God instituted circumcision in Gen. 17:10, 11 after changing Abram's name to Abraham saying he would be a father of many nations. The removal of a piece of flesh was something each Hebrew man carried with him. It was a token between God and His people. Circumcision represented <u>death to the flesh</u>. Abram had tried to have a son by the bond woman in his flesh. God did not accept them. "Nevertheless what saith the scripture? Cast out the bondwoman and her son: for the son of the bondwoman shall not be heir with the son of the freewoman" (Gal. 4:30). God caused barren Sarah to miraculously have a son so that the formation of His nation from Abraham would be God's doing. God changed Sarai name to Sarah saying, "And I will bless her, and give thee a son also of her: yea, I will bless her, and she shall be a mother of nations; kings of people shall be of her" (Gen. 17:16).

God made a difference between His people and all other nations. He separated them and put them above all other people (Deut. 7:5) intending to save the Gentiles by their good example (Deut. 4:5-7). By doing this God created a middle wall of partition. When God added the law He further strengthend the wall (Gal. 3:19).

After the cross, God gave the nation of Israel an additional opportunity to believe in Jesus. However, they rejected the renewed offer given through the Holy Ghost filled Stephen and committed the unpardonable blasphemy of the Holy Ghost. When Israel fell in Acts 7:51-60, because of their uncircumcised heart and ears, they fell down to the level of the Gentiles.

Then God saved Paul making him His minister to the Gentiles, inserting the dispensation of the grace of God in which we now live (Eph. 3:1-10). Today people are saved apart from going through Israel and apart from the law by faith in what Christ had done (1 Cor. 15:3, 4).

IN THE BIBLE GOD IS OFTEN <u>NOT</u> SPEAKING TO US, BUT ABOUT THE KING AND HIS KINGDOM.

Appendix

The 3 Time Periods and 5 Dispensations* Described in the KJV Bible

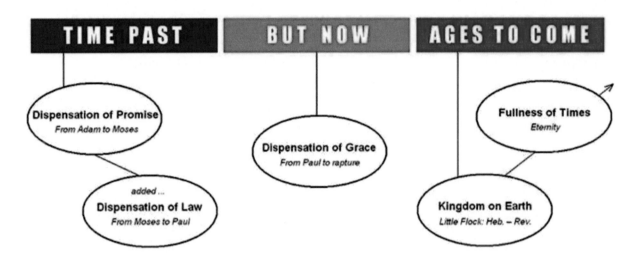

*Explained in greater detail in Grace School of the Bible's course: Fundamentals of Dispensationalism 101

Three Time Periods & Five Dispensations - by Pastor Richard Jordan

HOW MANY DISPENSATIONS DOES APOSTLE PAUL SAY THERE ARE IN THE BIBLE? (a major study for beginners)

We recall that the Bible is its final authority and we let the Word of God be our teacher. We also call to mind that the Apostle Paul, in Ephesians two, divides the Bible into three basic divisions or periods of time. We saw that as you can actually place the books of the Bible in that THREE FOLD DIVISION and that it is the key to understanding what program you are reading about in each book.

The three-fold division summary:

TIME PAST - Genesis to Malachi, Matthew – John, Early Acts – (Includes earthly ministry of Christ, to the nation of Israel only)

BUT NOW - Romans – Philemon (The Church, which is His Body is raptured to heaven)

AGES TO COME - Hebrews - Revelation (the tribulation and then Christ's second coming to earth)

Christ comes to earth, is crucified and ascends back to heaven and sends the Holy Spirit on the apostles of the Little Flock. Then comes the fall of Israel when salvation goes to the Gentiles. Jesus Christ, from heaven's glory, saves Saul of Tarsus, renames him the Apostle Paul and gives him the Dispensation of the Grace of God which has to do with the church, the Body of Christ.

Paul said: Rom. 11:13 For I speak to you Gentiles, inasmuch as I am the apostle of the Gentiles, I magnify mine office: In Romans through Philemon, Paul speaks to the Gentiles of the Body of Christ. Then there is the Rapture of the church when Christ comes and takes the church back to heaven to be with him and the world goes back into a time when there is a distinction between the circumcision and the uncircumcision. The Great Tribulation period takes place; then the second coming of Christ when he will set up the kingdom of heaven spoken of in the books of Hebrews through the book of the Revelation.

All of the Bible is for you but it is not all written to you nor all written about you. You need to understand that God has other people in his program besides you and me. We should not be so self–centered to think that all that is in Scripture is just about us. We cannot "claim" the whole Bible "to" you. That is handling the Word of God dishonestly.

When the Apostle Paul rightly divides it, he does not give you the "Scofield System" or the "Larkin System" or the "Jordan System"; it is the "Paul System". The Pauline system is the one we want to use.

The thing to remember is when you find God is dealing with man based on the circumcision or the uncircumcision division, you will know you are in Time Past. When you find Scripture dealing with the equality among people: no difference between the Jew and the Greek, for the same Lord is over all; is rich upon all, etc., you will know you are in the But Now. Then in Hebrews through Revelation you go back to the distinction between circumcision and uncircumcision where God brings to fruition the purpose he started back in Genesis, in the Ages To Come.

In the next lesson we will study in some detail the issues back in Time Past. What we want to do now is learn how to do that. Let that be the framework out of which you operate when you study the Scripture. Then you can be free to let the Bible teach you.

This three-fold division in Paul's epistles is filled up with five dispensations. Again, A DISPENSATION IS A PARTICULAR SET OF INSTRUCTIONS GIVEN BY GOD FOR MAN'S OBEDIENCE.

A dispensation WILL COVER a period of time because the instructions are given for obedience at different times. However, THE TIME ELEMENT IS NOT THE ISSUE; rather the instructions and the program that God is executing during that time period.

In Romans 5 Paul gives us three very important divisions.

Rom. 5:12 Wherefore, as by one man sin entered into the world, and death by sin; and so death passed upon all men, for that all have sinned: 13 (For until the law sin was in the world: but sin is not imputed when there is no law. 14 Nevertheless death reigned from Adam to Moses, even over them that had not sinned after the similitude of Adam's transgression, who is the figure of him that was to come.

There is a situation here that starts with Adam and goes to Moses: "From Adam to Moses" as a time period, a particular dispensation. From studying Genesis you see you move from Adam to Abraham; then God separates Abraham from the world and that begins the middle wall of partition. From there you wind up with Moses. That time or era was a dispensation in Paul's thinking. Often in Scofield, Larkin and the standard dispensational scheme you will find three dispensations back there:

1. Conscience – from the fall of man (Adam) to Noah.
2. Human Government – Between Noah and Abraham.
3. Promise – From Abraham to Moses.

In my teaching, I don't deal with it that way because of Romans 5:14. Paul "lumps" it all together when he said, "death reigned from Adam to Moses". Paul doesn't divide it into Conscience and Human Government. Conscience is not identified in Scripture as a dispensation. Conscience is a mode of revelation; a means of knowing things – not a dispensation. Human government is not a dispensation, but rather one of the four divine establishment institutions. God Almighty authored four institutions for the establishment of the human race so that man could operate and function properly. No matter what the instructions that he gave, no matter what the dispensation was, these four institutions were a framework in which God's word and God's program would successfully operate among mankind. So Human Government, in Genesis 9, is the fourth of those divine institutions for the establishment of the human race.

So then, Adam to Moses is a dispensation, which was called by Paul, the dispensation of Promise. The issue between Adam and Moses, between God and man, was that God had made man a promise.

Gal. 3:17 And this I say, that the covenant, that was confirmed before of God in Christ, the law, which was four hundred and thirty years after, cannot disannul, that it should make the promise of none effect.

What comes in with Moses, is the LAW. So the next dispensation we know will be The Law. It comes in with Moses and goes on to Jesus Christ. What was there before the law? The promise.

Gal. 3:18 For if the inheritance be of the law, it is no more of promise: but God gave it to Abraham by promise. 19 Wherefore then serveth the law? It was added because of transgressions, till the seed should come to whom the promise was made; and it was ordained by angels in the hand of a mediator.

Therefore, if you want to put a name on that dispensation between Adam and Moses, the name would be PROMISE and that promise starts in Genesis 3:15 with the promise of the seed of the woman; God's first promise of a Redeemer.

Then that seed line comes over to Abraham and then, God said to Abraham, "In thy seed . . ."

From Adam to Abraham, it is just the seed of the woman – mankind. That is why, when we study Genesis, you will see that the whole issue at the flood is the Satanic Policy of Evil trying to corrupt mankind in order to destroy the seed line. He does that with Adam and Eve and their boys and with Noah, etc. But then God, at the Tower of Babel, sets aside all the nations of the earth. He calls out one man and gives him the promise. He narrows the seed line down from the seed of the woman to the seed of Abraham. It is not just any seed of Abraham. He had two boys: Ishmael and Isaac. Which one is it? Genesis 22:18 – It is Isaac. In verses 15 to 18 we read the account of Abraham offering Isaac in type there on the mountain:

Gen. 22:15 And the angel of the LORD called unto Abraham out of heaven the second time, 16 And said, By myself have I sworn, saith the LORD, for because thou hast done this thing, and hast not withheld thy son, thine only son: 17 That in blessing I will bless thee, and in multiplying I will multiply thy seed as the stars of the heaven, and as the sand which is upon the sea shore; and thy seed shall possess the gate of his enemies;

Notice that God is talking about the multiplied seed of Abraham. . . not just one son, but a multiplied nation.

Gen. 22:18 And in thy seed (Abraham's multiplied seed) shall all the nations of the earth be blessed; because thou hast obeyed my voice.

That seed in the first instance is Isaac.
So far we have a seed line as:
Seed of the woman
Seed of Abraham
Seed of Isaac

Gen. 26:1 And there was a famine in the land, beside the first famine that was in the days of Abraham. And Isaac went unto Abimelech king of the Philistines unto Gerar. 2 And the LORD appeared unto him, and said, Go not down into Egypt; dwell in the land which I shall tell thee of: 3 Sojourn in this land, and I will be with thee, and will bless thee; for unto thee, and unto thy seed, I will give all these countries, and I will perform the oath which I sware unto Abraham thy father; 4 And I will make thy seed to multiply as the stars of heaven, and will give unto thy seed all these countries; and in thy seed shall all the nations of the earth be blessed;

You see God confirm to Isaac what he promised to Abraham. However, he does not just confirm it to Isaac. . . Isaac has two boys: Esau and Jacob. God chooses Jacob; not Esau. Jacob is out under the stars at Bethel and the Lord speaks to him:

Gen. 28:13 And, behold, the LORD stood above it, and said, I am the LORD God of Abraham thy father, and the God of Isaac: the land whereon thou liest, to thee will I give it, and to thy seed; 14 And thy seed shall be as the dust of the earth, and thou shalt spread abroad to the west, and to the east, and to the north, and to the south: and in thee and in thy seed shall all the families of the earth be blessed.

That Abrahamic Covenant is confirmed and handed down to Jacob. Notice that Israel as a nation comes out of Egypt and prepares to go into the Promised Land. God confirms that Abrahamic blessing, that seed line, to the whole nation.

Deut. 1:8 Behold, I have set the land before you: go in and possess the land which the LORD sware unto your fathers, Abraham, Isaac, and Jacob, to give unto them and to their seed after them.

For me personally, this passage we will look at now is the one that helped me understand what was going on in Genesis between Adam, Moses and the promise.

You could say, the kingdom is promised to Abraham, but really this promise in Genesis looks forward to the kingdom presented in Matthew and to the nation Israel dwelling in the land and God's blessing going to the nations through Israel. That promised kingdom is the issue with God starting with Adam, not just with Abraham. That's why it says, Adam to Moses. Abraham is where the middle wall of partition is built and where the separation of the seed line is made; but the purpose begins with Adam.

Mat. 25:31 When the Son of man shall come in his glory, and all the holy angels with him, then shall he sit upon the throne of his glory: (32) And before him shall be gathered all nations, Mat. 25:34. Then shall the King say unto them on his right hand, Come, ye blessed of my Father, . . .

Do you remember what God told Abraham? "Them that bless thee, I will bless. Them that curse thee, I will curse." Here are the nations of the earth coming out of the great Tribulation; going into the kingdom to inherit the Abrahamic blessing. Come, ye blessed of my Father.

Verse 41: Then shall he say also unto them on the left hand, Depart from me, ye cursed. (curse them that curse thee. . . bless them that bless thee.) The verses say that the way the nations get the blessing is by blessing Israel. "If you have done it to the least of these, my brethren." Likewise, they get the curse by cursing Israel. "When you did not do it to the least of these, my brethren." What is the blessing?

The rest of verse 34: INHERIT THE KINGDOM prepared for you FROM THE FOUNDATION OF THE WORLD: Not since the promise was made to Abraham.

The issue with God, from the time he put man on the earth (Adam), has been God's authority being executed over this planet through the instrumentality of a kingdom that was vested in the nation Israel. Israel was set apart as God's people. First it was given to man, then Abraham was called out and set apart and it was given to Abraham's seed but since Abraham's seed is still the seed of Adam, Jesus Christ, the true seed of Abraham came and redeemed the seed of Abraham. He saved Abraham's seed, blessed that seed and through Abraham's seed sent salvation to everybody else. That is the Promise Program--a program of Promise.

Genesis 1:26 – And God said, Let us make man in our image, after our likeness: and let them have dominion over the fish of the sea, and over the fowl of the air, and over the cattle, and over all the earth, and over every creeping thing that creepeth upon the earth. 27 So God created man in his own image, in the image of God created he him; male and female created he them. 28 And God blessed them, and God said unto them, Be fruitful and multiply, and replenish the earth, and subdue it: and have dominion over the fish of the sea, etc.

You see, God set man on the earth to be a king; to be the ruler in the earth. Man failed, so God promised man a redeemer who would come and do for man what man could not do for himself. He separated out a seed line; the Lord Jesus Christ showed up as Redeemer who then is rejected, goes away and comes back with salvation, etc. So you start out with the Dispensation of Promise.

The next period is called LAW – Moses to Christ.

Rom. 5:20 - Moreover the law entered, . . . You start out Adam to Moses and then the law enters – or as Galatians 3:19 says – it was added. The law was added to the Promise. Notice that this verse says that the law was added till the seed should come. The law was not there to disannul the promise. It is not there to cancel the promise. The promise is still there. The law comes in to make Israel know they need the Redeemer.

John 1:17 says that the law came by Moses, but grace and truth came by Jesus Christ. If you go back to Romans 5:20: Moreover the law entered, that the offence might abound. But where sin abounded, grace (the next Dispensation) did much more abound.

Perhaps you are saying, "Wait a minute, then Grace came in with the Apostle Paul, but I thought it said from Moses it brought you to Christ?" It did. But understand that Moses gave Israel the Law but he did not give Israel the law at his birth. Israel rejected him the first time he sought to be their deliverer and he came the second time as the law giver. So it is, with the Lord Jesus Christ. It was not in his earthly ministry that he took away the Law, nor is it even in his resurrection ministry, it was in the Ages To Come, when the New Covenant is established. They move from the Old Testament, the Mosaic Law, to the New Covenant in the Ages To Come. Whether, as in the Acts period, it is the Old Covenant or in the Ages To Come, the New Covenant, it is still the LAW program. We moved to GRACE (where sin abounded, grace did much more abound) as a dispensation when you come to the ministry of the Apostle Paul.

Rom. 3:19, 21 Now we know that what things soever the law saith, it saith to them who are under the law: [Moses to Adam] that every mouth may be stopped, and all the world may become guilty before God. 21 But now the righteousness of God without the law is manifested, being witnessed by the law and the prophets;

When we move into the BUT NOW section, there is a new way of making righteousness known. Back in Time Past, God's righteousness was made known through the law. But now there is a new way of God's righteousness being made known through this program of Grace.

19 Now we know that what things soever the law saith, it saith to them who are under the law: that every mouth may be stopped, and all the world may become guilty before God. Gal. 3:20 Therefore by the deeds of the law there shall no flesh be justified in his sight:

Back there from Adam to Moses, death reigned.
Moses to Christ, under the law, sin reigned.
With Adam came the entrance of sin.
With Moses came the knowledge of sin.
With Christ came the forgiveness of sin.

In Romans 5 – the law entered (vs 20); grace did much more abound (vs 20) and in verse 21 we see why grace abounded:

That as sin hath reigned unto death, even so might grace reign through righteousness unto eternal life by Jesus Christ our Lord.

TIME PAST - BUT NOW - AGES TO COME

TIME PAST
The issue is: SIN

BUT NOW
The issue is: GRACE

Now we have moved to another Dispensation.
1. Promise (Adam to Moses)
2. The Law (Moses)
3. Grace (Paul)

Eph. 3:1 For this cause I Paul, the prisoner of Jesus Christ for you Gentiles, 2 If ye have heard of the dispensation of the grace of God which is given me to you-ward: 3 How that by revelation he made known unto me the mystery; (as I wrote afore in few words,

That dispensation of the grace of God in the "But Now" was called "the mystery".

143

Verse 5 - Which in other ages was not made known unto the sons of men, as it is now revealed unto his holy apostles and prophets by the Spirit;

It was "hid in God" . . . Not revealed back in Time Past. Christ gave that to Paul. So when you come to that point you have the Dispensation of Grace.

The program of God in the Dispensation of Grace does not cancel the Law Program; it just postpones it. The way it is described in Acts 15 is how they have come to understand that God is currently visiting the Gentiles to call out a people for his name. God is out among the Gentiles forming a new agency, The Body of Christ. It is described as a visit It does not say that God has left home and moved from one place to another and abandoned his former place or done away with the house of Israel. It says God has left the house of Israel to visit the Gentiles to form the Body of Christ. When you visit someone, do you not return home? You have left temporarily with the intention of returning. That is what God has done.

Then . . .

After this I will return, and will build again the tabernacle of David, which is fallen down; and I will build again the ruins thereof, and I will set it up: Acts 15:16

In other words, in the Ages to Come, Christ is going to come and set up the kingdom.

The preaching of the kingdom is actually in two phases. In the earthly ministry of Christ, the kingdom is preached as being at hand. (John the Baptist preached, "Repent, for the kingdom of heaven is at hand." – the opportunity is in front of you, or as close as your hand.) In the Ages To Come Christ will actually return and set it up. So in Acts, what James is saying there is not that the kingdom has been thrown out, but that Christ will come back after the interruption is finished and actually set up that kingdom.

Daniel 2:44 – … shall the "God of heaven set up a kingdom, which shall never be destroyed;"

If the God of heaven sets up a kingdom, what do you call that kingdom? The kingdom of God or the kingdom of heaven?

Deut. 11:21 – Moses tells Israel that kingdom is going to be "as the days of heaven upon the earth."

Now we have moved to another Dispensation.
1. Promise (Adam to Moses)
2. The Law (Moses)
3. Grace (Paul)
4. The Kingdom

At the end of the Kingdom, Satan having been bound in the bottomless pit for 1,000 years, will be released. Then there is the Great White Throne Judgment. The heaven and the earth are melted and burned up and the judgment set. After the Great White Throne Judgment, there is one more Dispensation in the Ages To Come. It is called the Dispensation of the fullness of times.

Eph. 1:9-11 Having made known unto us the mystery of his will, according to his good pleasure which he hath purposed in himself: 10 That in the dispensation of the fulness of times he might gather together in one all things in Christ, both which are in heaven, and which are on earth; even in him: 11 In whom also we have obtained an inheritance, being predestinated according to the purpose of him who worketh all things after the counsel of his own will:

Think about the expression, "fullness of times". That is when time will be brought to its fullness: when the purpose for which God created time will have been accomplished. That will occur in the Ages To Come.

From Adam to the end of the millennium is a period of seven-thousand (7,000) years. The Dispensation of the Fulness of Times will be a period of thirty-three thousand years. That adds up to a period of 40,000 years to fulfill time. The number 40 in your Bible is the number of testing. The purpose for which time was created was to fill the universe with a perfect creation that willingly chose, (voluntarily of its own free will), to serve, worship, love and honor God Almighty because of who He is – to look at Him and say, I love you because you love me. That is the purpose for which creation was established. There is a period of probation (testing) in which that purpose is brought to fruition. At the end of that dispensation of the fullness of times in the Ages To Come, ETERNITY will begin.

In Deuteronomy 7, Israel is promised 1,000 generations of possession and rule of their land. A perfect generation in the Bible would be the age of the Lord Jesus Christ: thirty-three (33) years.

Leviticus 12 speaks of a woman having a man-child after which she will be unclean for forty (40) days. Seven days; a division; then 33 more days. This is based on using "types" and I don't demand that you understand that or believe it. I just tell you what I think about it. You don't have to get into that if you don't want to. However, the key to the dispensation of the fullness of times is that that is when God is going to establish his authority in the government of the universe.

Col. 1:16 For by him were all things created, that are in heaven, and that are in earth, visible and invisible, whether they be thrones, or dominions, or principalities, or powers: all things were created by him, and for him:

One man at a Bible conference said to me, "That verse proves that God created sin." When I asked how he came to that conclusion, he replied, "Well, it says all things are created by him." I suggested he read the verse again. The verse is not talking about God creating houses, trees, blackboards, etc. The verse spells out the "all things" Paul is talking about and sin is not mentioned in there at all. "…Whether they be thrones, dominions, principalities or powers. Those things are positions of government that God created in the earth and in the heavenly places. Jesus Christ created them all and…

Col. 1:17 And he is before all things, and by him all things consist. 18 And he is the head of the body, the church: who is the beginning, the firstborn from the dead; that in all things he might have the preeminence. 19 For it pleased the Father that in him should all fulness dwell; 20 And, having made peace through the blood of his cross, by him to reconcile all things unto himself; by him, I say, whether they be things in earth, or things in heaven.

God's purpose is to reconcile all those positions in the government unto himself and that will be accomplished in the fulness of times. What God is doing in Time Past, But Now and in the Ages To Come is forming the two agencies that he will use in the dispensation of the fullness of times to bring all those things under the headship of the Lord Jesus Christ.

1. He forms the nation Israel to bring the earth under his authority.
2. He forms the Body of Christ to bring the heavenly places under his authority.
In the dispensation of the fullness of times, the eternal purpose that God the Father purposed in His Son, will be brought to pass.

1. Adam to Moses - Dispensation of Promise
2. Moses - Dispensation of The Law
3. Paul - Dispensation of Grace
4. After Rapture - Dispensation of the Kingdom
5. After Kingdom - Dispensation of the Fullness of Times – Eternity.

Each one of these dispensations is introduced BY AN INTRODUCTORY PERIOD IN WHICH THERE IS A TRANSITION.

FOR EXAMPLE:
Before Adam gets the promise (before the fall), he was in the Garden of Eden. Before the Dispensation of Promise starts there is a transition into it – an introductory period. Promise is introduced by the time man was in the garden fellowshipping with God. At the fall, man acquired an old sin nature which is the source of man's desire to be independent from God. That sin nature was imputed to man when he fell. That is the imputation being discussed in Romans 5:12, 13, 14.

Where in verse 14 it says: "Nevertheless death reigned from Adam to Moses, even over them who have not sinned after the similtude of Adam's transgression, . . ." They did not go out and actively violate a mandate. Yet it says they sinned and death reigned. Why? Because they had been given that sin nature. So Promise is introduced by a period in the garden, where man was in a state of innocence but then sins and has imputed to him an "old sin nature", after which Promise begins.

The Law is introduced by a period of wandering in the wilderness for Israel. If you want to see the life of Israel under the Law, look in Numbers 14 where you will find the illustration of the breaking of the law and rebellion against God and the penalty for it, in verses 26 to 33. Israel is told they are going to wander in the wilderness for violating the commandment of God to go into the land. They wander in the wilderness and everybody twenty and over dies there. So at the beginning of Israel's sojourn as a nation there is that introductory period that illustrates what is to happen to them under the Law. In 1 Corinthians 10, Paul uses that very experience in the wilderness as an introduction.

Grace is also introduced by a transition period. Every dispensation has an introductory period wherein things are set in motion for the operation of the new dispensation.

1 Cor. 13:8-10 Charity never faileth: but whether there be prophecies, (the gift of prophecy) they shall fail; (this is not speaking of a prophecy not coming to pass; it is speaking only of the gift of prophecy; that it is not going to work any more). … whether there be tongues, (the gift of tongues) they shall cease; (People can still talk so it is not addressing whether they will be able to speak but that the gift shall cease). …whether there be knowledge, it shall vanish away. This is not talking about knowing things. In John 17, Jesus Christ said, "This is eternal life; that they may know thee." So if this Scripture were talking about knowing things, eternal

life would be over but rather this verse refers to the gift of knowledge. The Corinthians were being told that these gifts mentioned are going to vanish; they will cease; they will fail. When was that to happen?

Verse 13:9: - For we know in part, and we prophesy in part. 10 But when that which is perfect is come, then that which is in part shall be done away.

Paul told them they were in a transition period where they only had partial knowledge. When the completion of the Mystery revelation is given, then that which is "in part", the transition period would be done away with. Verse 11 is an illustration:

13:11 When I was a child, I spake as a child, I understood as a child, I thought as a child: but when I became a man, I put away childish things. When we grow up, we put away the toys, diapers, etc. We act grown up. (Interpretation)

13:12 For now we see through a glass, darkly; We don't have full understanding. (Transition period) 13 but then face to face: now I know in part; but then shall I know even as also I am known.

Right now (in 1 Corinthians) we know in part. When that which is perfect is come, that "in part" will be done away with and we will know. We will be able to see plainly. He said when they could not see plainly, as looking through a glass, it was fuzzy and they did not understand it all but when that which is perfect is come, they would be able to know and understand clearly as though "face to face." This describes the transition period at the beginning of the Dispensation of Grace in which there were sign gifts in operation. The reason it happened that way is as a sign to Israel and a means of divine revelation for the believers. However, this was done away with when the full revelation came.

The kingdom on earth in the Ages To Come also has an introductory period. That kingdom will be introduced by the Great Tribulation. The Kingdom begins in the heavenly places when the Body of Christ is removed from the earth and carries on there during the 70th week of Daniel then proceeds down to the earth and the actual establishing of the kingdom of heaven on earth as prophesied.

The Dispensation of the Fullness of Times is introduced by the Millennium. Have you ever thought about the fact that the first chapter of Luke says that Jesus Christ is going to reign for ever and ever? Scripture says, "Of his kingdom there shall be no end." Does the 1,000 years come to an end? Sure it does. Of His kingdom, there will not be an end so it won't last just a 1,000 years. The 1,000 years is just the beginning. After the one-thousand years, the Great White Throne Judgment takes place where all of the lost and the damned of the ages are thrown out of the kingdom and put down into hell. Only the redeemed go on into the new heaven and the new earth.

Paul talks about the Ages To Come in Ephesians 2:7. That is plural – ages. The Dispensation of the Fullness of Times is one of those ages to come; then comes Eternity.

Those are the five dispensations and the five introductory periods for each.

The basic characteristic* of TIME PAST is a distinction that God has made between the Circumcision and the Uncircumcision. *Please note that I am saying, "the basic characteristic." It is not the only characteristic of Time Past.

Right Division Bible Timeline

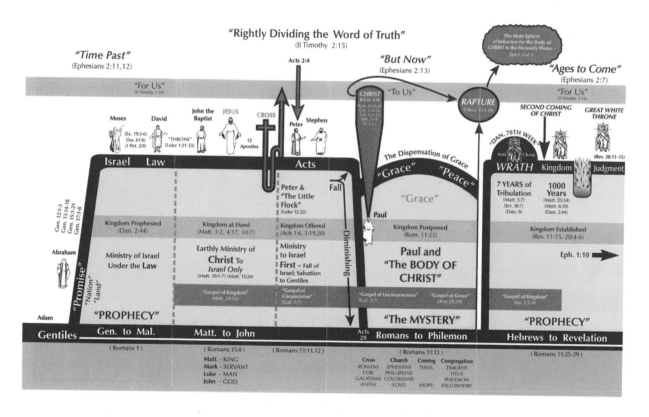

Paul's Prayers

Paul had a lot to say about prayer. Paul often talked about his prayers for the churches he had begun in the BEGINNING of his letter (see Rom. 1:8-10; Eph. 1:15-23; 3:14-19: Phil. 1:3, 4: Col. 1:9-14). Then he shared and taught the doctrine that he received from the Lord Jesus Christ in His ministry from heaven.

For Paul, the power of the gospel and doctrine working in believers began with prayer.

The nation of Israel often prayed for physical things such as the kingdom on earth, rain, crops, food, and healing. But Paul primarily prayed about spiritual, not physical things for the believers.

"For this cause we also . . . DO NOT CEASE to pray for you, and to desire that ye might be filled with the KNOWLEDGE of HIS WILL in ALL WISDOM and SPIRITUAL UNDERSTANDING; That ye might WALK WORTHY of the LORD unto ALL PLEASING, being FRUITFUL in EVERY GOOD WORK, and INCREASING in the KNOWLEDGE of GOD; STRENGTHENED with ALL MIGHT, according to HIS GLORIOUS POWER, unto ALL PATIENCE and LONGSUFFERING with JOYFULNESS" (Col. 1:9-11).

"Cease not to give thanks for you, making mention of you in my prayers; That the God of our Lord Jesus Christ, the Father of glory, may give unto you the spirit of WISDOM and revelation in the knowledge of him: The eyes of your understanding being enlightened; that ye may know what is the hope of his calling, and what the riches of the glory of his inheritance in the saints, And what *is* the exceeding greatness of his power to us-ward who believe, according to the working of his mighty power . . ." (Eph. 1:16-19).

150

About the Author

Marianne Manley teaching Romans

A few years after being saved in 1990, Marianne Manley began teaching in the AWANA (Approved Workmen Are Not Ashamed) program. She has always been interested to know what God says in His word. While she homeschooled her children for 18 years she learned about the value of the King James Version from the ABEKA Book curriculum. Having switched to the King James Bible for about seven years she became convinced that it was the perfect word of God in 2014.

In 2015, Nathan Cody first introduced her to Pauline truth. By watching Les Feldick on Youtube she learned the basics of "rightly dividing the word of truth" (2 Timothy 2:15). Then proceeded to learn more from Richard Jordan and his Grace School of the Bible. Excited about this truth she began teaching an adult class in her home. Realizing she needed help, she also began hosting Berean Bible Ministries in her home and attending that local church in San Juan Capistrano.

To edify the body of Christ she wrote God's Secret in 2017. This book on Romans is a result of a class she taught in 2018.

Other Books by Marianne Manley

Available on Amazon.com

God's Secret A Primer with Pictures for How to Rightly Divide the Word of Truth (also available in Spanish, *El Secreto de Dios*).

First Corinthians: A Commentary

Could God Have a 7,000 Year Plan for Mankind?

AD 34 The Year Jesus Died for All (same content as Could God, in 9x6 size)

Treasure Hunt is the name of the book that she is currently working on.

As a retired Nurse Midwife, Marianne Manley has **also written:**

Birth Stories and Midwife Notes: In God We Trust

Born at Home, Praise the Lord!

Handbook for Christian Natural Childbirth

Christian Childbirth

A Mother's Loving Instruction to Her Daughter

The author may be contacted by e-mail at mariannemanley@sbcglobal.net

Follow her on Facebook at facebook.com/marianne.manley.7

God's Secret Facebook Page at facebook.com/GodsSecretAPrimerwithPictures

Find her on Youtube at https://bit.ly/2R8IUj0 and https://bit.ly/2qIDCPA

This Youtube channel has all of her teachings on Romans and will soon have all the teachings through Paul's letters (Romans to Philemon).

www.Acts9GraceBibleChurch.com

www.Christianmidwife.com